D0780477

Preface

George Herbert died at Bemerton Rectory in Wiltshire more than 340 years ago—no short time in what we call modern history. Why then, after all these years, should we set forth a new biography of this man variously described as priest, poet, scholar, musician, and saint? Will the beautiful life written by Izaak Walton not serve readers today?

In my view, Herbert assuredly merits any amount of attention we now give him. Reputations of all the metaphysical poets rose and fell after the seventeenth century, but our own century has restored Herbert and his fellows to something like their rightful place in literary history. A fuller recognition of their poetic merit is evident in the title of an anthology that includes devotional and secular poets of the period: Barbara Lewalski and Andrew Sabol's *Major Poets of the Earlier Seventeenth Century* (1973). Although the reputation of all these poets has been enhanced, Herbert in particular has emerged as a major devotional poet—some would say *the* major English devotional poet. To understand the circumstances under which he wrote, then, we should have as full and accurate an account of his life as can be developed from the information available. This information has never before been fully considered.

Walton's life of Herbert, although it has been made to serve for more than three centuries, is neither accurate nor dependable. Unfortunately, virtually every treatment of Herbert's life since 1670 has relied almost wholly on Walton's, often paraphrasing or even incorporating without acknowledgment portions of this essay in hagiography, this biography forced by its author to become propaganda for the good old days and the practices of the Church of England before the Civil War. It has also handed on a stereotype of Herbert neither accurate nor becoming. Only in our own century has this typical account of Herbert's life been modified somewhat, in two concise discussions, the first by F. E. Hutchinson in his edition of *The Works of George Herbert* (1941), the other by Joseph H. Summers in *George Herbert: His Religion and Art* (1954).

The purpose of the biography here presented is not to vilify Walton for his failure to understand a nature much more complex than his own, not even for his reluctance to verify carefully material that might contradict his preconceived impressions. It is, rather, to examine all the documents and records that in any way relate to a life of Herbert. If from time to time this effort results in contradictions of statements by Walton, the reader will have at hand the information enabling him to make his own judgments. Walton did not intend to be deceptive, only to set forth what was to him a consecutive, reasonable, and correlated account of a period of some thirty years (with concentration on two or three times within this general range). His approach to Herbert is rooted in contrasts (like his sinner-to-saint treatment of Donne), proceeding from Herbert the man of the fine courtly and academic world to Herbert the simple country parson; inevitably it fails to analyze perceptively a man whose mind was much richer and more diverse. Too often Walton glosses over what he does not know and paraphrases poems to make them serve as biography. (John Butt and David Novarr have served readers well by analyzing Walton's shortcomings.)

Walton left Herbert rather thick-swaddled and sheltered from the inquiry of all but the most skeptical of biographers. True, occasionally even Grosart exclaimed impatiently at some excess of Walton's; but of all the earlier biographers I have read, only J. J. Daniell methodically sought out the sources and documents that had always existed and had always before his time been ignored.

In undertaking this new life of Herbert I have inevitably contracted numerous debts of gratitude as I hunted out my materials. I have therefore to thank many persons, offices, and institutions for help given me since I began this study. Without the cooperation and advice so generously provided, I could not possibly have brought together the information I needed or have given a proper explanation of its significance. Where the interpretation falls short, the fault is my own.

I should like first of all to thank the following persons who have helped me with particular problems or have granted me access to specific materials mentioned in later notes: Professor Matthew W. Black, of the University of Pennsylvania; Mrs. Margaret Bottrall, of Hughes Hall, Cambridge; the late Mrs. Catherine Drinker Bowen, of Haverford, Pennsylvania; the Earl of Bradford; Professor Roy Carroll, of Appalachian State University; Mrs. E. J. Danvers, of Great Missenden, Buckinghamshire; Professor Joseph S. Dunlap, of Butler University, who has generously allowed me to consult and quote from his translations of Herbert's Latin and Greek poems; Dame Helen Gardner, of Lady Margaret Hall, Oxford; Professor Ruth Hughey, of the Ohio State University; Professor Virginia Everett Leland, of Bowling Green State University; Professor Louis L. Martz, of Yale University; Mrs. Alan L. Maycock, of Cambridge; J. R. More-Molyneux, Esq., of Loseley Park, Guildford, Surrey; the late Reverend L. F. Ostler, vicar of Great Gidding, Huntingdonshire; the Duke of Portland; the late Earl of Powis and the present Earl; Professor Katharine E. Reichert, M.D., of the University of Massachusetts; Professor Wolfgang Rindler, of Southern Methodist University; and Professor G. M. Story, of the University of New Brunswick.

Special thanks are due to those who have patiently answered my inquiries about Herbert's handwriting, whether or not we have come to the same conclusions: P. J. Croft, Esq., of Sotheby's, London; Dr. Giles Dawson, of the Folger Shakespeare Library; and Mr. Irby Todd, of the Metropolitan Police Department, Washington, D.C., who generously helped me and sent along my inquiries to his teacher, Mr. Alwyn Cole, of Silver Spring, Maryland.

I am indebted to the following libraries in this country: the Boston Public Library, the New York Public Library, the Duke University Library, the Folger Shakespeare Library, the Houghton Library at Harvard University (for the resources of the George Herbert Palmer collection), the Henry E. Huntington Library, the University of North Carolina Library at Chapel Hill, the Princeton University Library, the University of Virginia Library, and the Yale University Library.

The officers of various libraries and collections in Great Britain have been generous in granting me access to materials related to Herbert, his family, and his contemporaries: the Eton College Library; the Westminster School Library; the Winchester College Library; the Master and Fellows of Clare College, Cambridge; the Master and Fellows of Magdalene College, Cambridge (especially Professor J. A. W. Bennett, the Keeper of the Old Library, and his predecessor, the late Mr. Alan L. Maycock); the Master and Fellows of St. John's College, Cambridge; the Master and Fellows of Trinity College, Cambridge; Miss Heather E. Peek, Keeper of the University Archives, Cambridge; the University Library, Cambridge; the University of Edinburgh Library; the Feoffees of Chetham's Hospital and Library, Manchester; the Bodleian Library, Oxford (particularly Miss D. M. Barratt and Miss Margaret C. Crum, of the Department of Western Manuscripts); the New College Library, Oxford; the Queen's College Library, Oxford; and the National Library of Wales, Aberystwyth.

Among the many persons who have generously shared their knowledge of places and circumstances related to Herbert's life I must thank particularly the Reverend R. J. Colby, vicar of Chirbury; Dr. J. D. K. Lloyd, of Garthmyl, Montgomery, Powys; the Reverend C. Michael Semper, former rector of Montgomery; Miss Olga Newman, librarian, Salop County Library; Mr. P. H. Nightingale, lay assistant to the Bishop of Salisbury; the late Hugh deS. Shortt, Esq., curator of the Salisbury and South Wiltshire Museum (and his successor, Mr. P. R. Saunders); the Very Reverend Fenton Morley, Dean of Salisbury Cathedral; the Reverend Canon Harold Wilson, former principal of Salisbury and Wells Theological College; Miss Pamela Stewart, assistant diocesan archivist, Salisbury Diocesan Record Office; Mr. E. A. Maidment, of Salisbury (who introduced me to *The Festival Book of Salisbury*); Mr. Richard Sandell, librarian, Wiltshire Historical and Archaeological Society, Devizes; the Reverend Ronald Crowther and the Reverend M. H. B. Williams, former rectors of Bemerton; Mrs. P. M. Williams; Mrs. Ruby Eagling, former sacristan of the parish of Bemerton; Major Peter Sturgis and Mr. Jules Sturgis, of Dauntesey; and the Reverend Canon A. T. Johnson, vicar of Warminster, and his churchwardens.

Archivists at several county record offices have helped me to locate essential material. I must thank particularly Miss Enid Dance and Miss G. M. A. Beck, of the Guildford Muniment Room; Peter Walne, Esq., of Hertford, Hertfordshire; Dr. Mary E. Finch, deputy archivist, Lincolnshire Archives Office (and the Dean and Chapter of Lincoln Cathedral, as well); Miss Mary C. Hill, county archivist, Shrewsbury, Salop; and Mr. Brian C. Redwood, county archivist, Chester, Cheshire.

My debts to institutions and persons in London are numerous: to the Trustees of what many of us still think of as the British Museum, though we try to learn the name British Library; the Courtauld Institute; the Lambeth Palace Library; the National Portrait Gallery (particularly Mr. John Kerslake); the National Register of Archives (particularly Miss Felicity Ranger); the Public Record Office (particularly a long succession of patient officers in charge of the Round Room, as well as those who helped me locate the originals of some letters calendared in the *State Papers, Venetian*); Somerset House (particularly Miss Alice Stanley for her help with wills of the Herbert family that were formerly kept there); the University of London Library; the Trustees of Dr. Williams's Library, Gordon Square, London (particularly the Reverend Kenneth Twinn, the librarian); and the Worshipful Company of Goldsmiths (and their librarian, Miss Susan Hare).

I come last to thank my own institution and my own colleagues at the University of North Carolina at Greensboro: the Faculty Research Council for grants that helped greatly in the earlier stages of this study; the university administration for a leave of absence in the spring of 1973 that enabled me to return to England for concentrated research; Professor James Atkinson, of the Department of Romance Languages; Professor Frank Melton, of the Department of History; the late Professor Meta H. Miller, of the Department of Romance Languages; my colleagues in the Department of English; and the staff of Jackson Library (especially the staff of the Reference

Department and those responsible for interlibrary loans: Mrs. Elizabeth Jerome Holder, Mrs. Nancy C. Fogarty, Mrs. Marcia Kingsley, Mrs. Emilie Mills, and Mr. Thomas Minor).

This life of Herbert could not have been written without the help of these and many other persons who have generously and repeatedly taken time to help me at all stages of my work, and I gladly and gratefully acknowledge my indebtedness to them. Not the least of the joys of working with a person like George Herbert is that shared with others who know and love the man and his works.

Except for passages from manuscripts cited in the footnotes, all quotations from Herbert's poems, letters, and prose works are taken from the Oxford English Texts edition of *The Works of George Herbert* (1941), edited by F. E. Hutchinson, used here by permission of the Oxford University Press. Canon Hutchinson's commentary places every subsequent student of Herbert in his debt.

I wish to thank also the Southeastern Renaissance Conference, Scholars' Facsimiles & Reprints, and the University of Chicago Press for permission to draw on work of mine that they have published: "The Williams Manuscript and *The Temple*" (*Renaissance Papers, 1971;* the Southeastern Renaissance Conference); *The Williams Manuscript of George Herbert's Poems* (1977; Scholars' Facsimiles & Reprints); and "George Herbert, Deacon" (*Modern Philology,* LXXII [February 1975], 272–276; University of Chicago Press. © 1975 by The University of Chicago. All rights reserved.).

Transcripts/Translations of Crown-copyright records in the Public Record Office appear by permission of the Controller of H.M. Stationery Office.

AMY M. CHARLES

Greensboro, North Carolina

Contents

Illustrations

Abbreviations

B	Tanner MS. 307, Bodleian Library, Oxford.
B.L.	British Library, London.
Blackstone	Bernard Blackstone, ed., *The Ferrar Papers* (Cambridge: University Press, 1938).
Bodl.	Bodleian Library, Oxford.
Coll. Mont.	*Collections Historical and Archaeological Relating to Montgomeryshire and Its Borders*, I——.
CSPD	*Calendar of State Papers, Domestic.*
CSPV	*Calendar of State Papers, Venetian.*
DNB	*Dictionary of National Biography.*
F.P.	Ferrar Papers, Magdalene College, Cambridge.
GH	George Herbert.
Lee	Edward Herbert, *Autobiography,* ed. Sidney Lee (2d ed.; London: Routledge, 1906).
Life	Edward Herbert, *The Life of Edward Lord Herbert of Cherbury Written by Himself,* ed. Horace Walpole (first public ed.; London: Printed for J. Dodsley, 1770).
L.M.	Loseley MSS., Guildford Muniment Room.
N.L.W.	National Library of Wales, Aberystwyth.
Prayer Book	*Book of Common Prayer.*
P.R.O.	Public Record Office, London.
Rossi	Mario Rossi, *La vita, le opere, i tempi di Edoardo Herbert di Chirbury* (3 vols.; Florence: G. C. Sansoni, 1947).
S.P.	State Papers, Public Record Office, London.
W	Jones MS. B 62, Dr. Williams's Library, London.
Walton	Izaak Walton, "The Life of Mr. George Herbert," in *The Lives of John Donne, Sir Henry Wotton, Richard Hooker, George Herbert, and Robert Sanderson,* with an Introduction by George Saintsbury (London: Oxford University Press, 1927).

Works — *The Works of George Herbert,* ed. F. E. Hutchinson (Oxford: Clarendon Press, 1941).

Special abbreviations used in quotations from manuscript letters and other documents have been expanded in square brackets.

Chronology

1593	3 April	Born at Montgomery.
	20 May	Sir Edward Herbert buried at Montgomery.
1596	15 October	Richard Herbert buried at Montgomery Church.
1597–1599		Magdalene Herbert and Herbert children with Lady Newport at Eyton-upon-Severn.
1599	14 February	Lady Newport's will probated.
1599–1601		Magdalene Herbert in Oxford.
1601	February?	Magdalene Herbert moves family to London.
	11 April	Magdalene Herbert's household at Charing Cross established.
	4 July	Lancelot Andrewes becomes dean of Westminster Abbey.
1604–1605		Probably a day student at Westminster School.
1605	29 June	Elected scholar at Westminster School.
1609	26 February	Magdalene Herbert married to Sir John Danvers.
	5 May	Named King's scholar for Trinity College, Cambridge.
	18 December	Matriculates from Trinity College as pensioner.
1610	1 January	Sends two sonnets to Lady Danvers; mentions "my late Ague."
1613	17 February	Bachelor of Arts.
1614	3 October	Minor fellow, Trinity College.
1616	15 March	Major fellow, Trinity College; Master of Arts.
1617	?	William Herbert dies (probably this year).
	?	Charles Herbert dies.
	2 October	Sublector quartae classis, Trinity College.
1618	1 January	Letter to Buckingham for the university.

	18 March	Letter to Sir John Danvers ("setting foot into Divinity").
	10 or 11 June	Praelector in rhetoric, Cambridge University.
	26 December	Letter to Sir Robert Harley from Charing Cross.
1619	August or September	Journeys to Lincolnshire to visit Frances Herbert Browne.
	After 29 September	Delivers oration in Latin for Cambridge University.
	21 October	Appointed deputy for Sir Francis Nethersole, university orator.
	Late in year	Visits Lancelot Andrewes?
1620	21 January	Named university orator.
1622	16 February	Joseph Mead mentions grave illness of GH.
	29 May	Letter to Lady Danvers during her illness.
	15 December	Sir Edward Herbert dedicates *De veritate* to GH and William Boswell.
1623	12 March	Delivers farewell to James I at Cambridge.
	14 August	Margaret Herbert Vaughan buried in Montgomery Church.
	5 October	Prince Charles and Buckingham return from Spain.
	8 October	Delivers oration during Prince Charles's visit to Cambridge.
	November	Named to Parliament for Montgomery borough.
1624	16 February	Lodovic Stuart, Duke of Richmond and Lennox, dies; opening of Parliament delayed.
	19 February–29 May	Parliament sits; charter of the Virginia Company revoked.
	11 June	Grace of the Cambridge Senate allowing GH a six-month leave.
	?	In Kent?
	3 November	Dispensation by the Archbishop of Canterbury permitting Bishop Williams to ordain GH deacon.
	6 December	Named comportioner at Llandinam, Montgomery.
	11 December	Leave from the oratorship expires.
1625	2 March	James, Marquis of Hamilton, dies.
	27 March	James I dies.
	?	In Kent?

	7 May	Herbert Thorndike delivers funeral oration for James I at Cambridge.
	12 May–12 August	Parliament sits at Oxford.
	21 December	GH and Donne at the Danvers home in Chelsea.
1626	9 April	Bacon dies.
	April or later	At Woodford during illness of his brother Sir Henry.
	4 June	Nicholas Ferrar ordained deacon by Laud at Westminster Abbey.
	5 July	Installed by proxy as canon of Lincoln Cathedral and prebendary of Leighton Ecclesia.
	13 July	Delivers oration at York House for Buckingham's installation as chancellor of Cambridge University.
	After mid-July	Installed at Leighton Bromswold; probably visits Little Gidding.
	25 September	Lancelot Andrewes dies.
1627	6 May	Letter to Robert Creighton from Chelsea.
	8 June	Lady Danvers buried at Chelsea.
	1 July	Donne delivers memorial sermon at Chelsea for Lady Danvers.
	7 July	*Memoriae Matris Sacrum* entered in the Stationers' Register with Donne's sermon.
	21 July	Crown grant of Ribbesford, Worcestershire, to GH, Sir Edward Herbert, and Thomas Lawley (sold later that year to Sir Henry Herbert).
1628	29 January	Robert Creighton named university orator at Cambridge.
	10 July	Sir John Danvers married to Elizabeth Dauntesey.
1628–1629		Living with the Earl of Danby at Dauntesey House?
1629	23 February	Allegation for GH's marriage filed in Salisbury.
	26 February	Bond for GH's marriage filed in Salisbury.
	5 March	Married to Jane Danvers at Edington Priory; residence at Baynton House.
	24 May	Responsible for the preaching of a sermon at Lincoln Cathedral.

1630	10 April	William Herbert, third Earl of Pembroke, dies.
	16 April	Presented by the Crown to the living of Fugglestone-with-Bemerton.
	26 April	Instituted rector of Bemerton by Bishop Davenant; induction at St. Andrew's Church, Bemerton.
	16 May	At Lincoln Cathedral to preach there in person for the last time (thereby missing Trinity Sunday ordination at Salisbury)?
	19 September	Ordained priest at Salisbury Cathedral.
	October	Arthur Woodnoth visits at Bemerton.
1632	15 August	Dorothy Vaughan buried at Bemerton.
	29 September	Ferrar's translation of Valdesso and GH's letter and notes sent to Ferrar.
1633	January or February	GH's poems carried to Ferrar by Edmund Duncon.
	24 February	Sings to the lute.
	25 February	Dictates will to Nathanael Bostocke.
	1 March	Dies in Bemerton Rectory.
	3 March	Buried in St. Andrew's Church, Bemerton.
	12 March	Will proved by Arthur Woodnoth.

A Life of George Herbert

CHAPTER 1

Montgomery, Shropshire, and Oxford (1593–1601)

The Herbert Family

George Herbert, Barnabas Oley tells us, *"was extracted out of a Generous,* Noble, *and Ancient Family."*[1] The name of the Herbert family first emerged near the Welsh border shortly before 1460, when it was assumed as a family surname in the English style, apparently by the sons of Sir William ap Thomas of Ragland Castle (d. 1466).[2] Both the elder son, William Herbert, first Earl of Pembroke, and Sir Richard Herbert of Colebrook (or Coldbrook) were beheaded in 1469 after their capture by Lancastrian rebels at the battle of Edgecote.[3] The Earl of Pembroke was buried at Tintern Abbey, his younger brother (for whose life he had pleaded) at Abergavenny.[4]

Both Herbert lines descended from the sons of Sir William ap Thomas were later united by the marriage of Edward Herbert (George Herbert's elder brother, who became the first Lord Herbert of Chirbury) and Mary Herbert, daughter and heir of Sir William Herbert of St. Julians.[5] Through the marriage of Herbert's parents, Magdalene Newport and Richard Herbert, the Herberts were joined with the princely Welsh line

[1] *Herbert's Remains* (London: Printed for Timothy Garthwait, 1652), sig. b 6, unnumbered.

[2] *Coll. Mont.*, III, 341.

[3] W. J. Smith, ed., *Herbert Correspondence* (Cardiff: University of Wales Press, 1963), pp. 3–6; "Pedigree of the Herbert Families," facing p. 412.

[4] *Life,* p. 9. (This edition has been used throughout save when the Lee notes are of special importance.) See also Lee, pp. 9n and 167–171.

[5] *Life,* p. 10.

of Powys, since Mrs. Herbert's father, Sir Richard Newport, was a descendant of Wenwynwyn, prince of upper Powys.[6]

Both the grandfather and the father of George Herbert's immediate family were men who took an extensive part in the life of Montgomeryshire during the time when Wales was emerging into a broader life with England. Throughout the course of a long life Sir Edward Herbert, born in 1513 or 1514, was a powerful figure in Montgomery and along the border, where he held extensive lands. As early as 1546 he served as *ringild,* or collector of the King's rents of assize, for Montgomery.[7] Like his father before him, he held the title of Constable of Montgomery Castle, and in 1553 obtained the lordship of Chirbury. He was also *Custos Rotulorum.* Three times between 1553 and 1588 he served as sheriff and as Member of Parliament for the county. He was also courtier, Squire of the Body to Queen Elizabeth, and noted soldier.[8] At the advanced age of seventy-five he put forth a tremendous effort to be returned as knight of the shire for Montgomery (after not having sat in Parliament since 1571), defeating his brother-in-law Arthur Price of Newtown, who at the time of the election brought to Montgomery numerous supporters. It was no ready victory; but whether by great numbers, influence upon the sheriff, or control of food and lodging for the visitors from Newtown during a lengthy electoral session, Herbert was once more returned as knight of the shire.[9] To the end of his life he remained active in public affairs in Montgomery.[10]

Sir Edward Herbert, says his grandson and namesake, made his fortune with his sword, particularly at St. Quentin in

[6] *Burke's Landed Gentry,* I, 605, as quoted in *Coll. Mont.,* VI, 409. See also the MS. volume "The Descent of the Herberts," I 5, p. 67, Stone Passage, Lacquer Bookcase, Powis Castle.

[7] *Coll. Mont.,* IV, 258.

[8] Smith, *Herbert Correspondence,* p. 5.

[9] J. E. Neale, *The Elizabethan House of Commons* (New Haven: Yale University Press, 1950), pp. 82, 99–110.

[10] For a more extended record of Sir Edward Herbert's public offices see *Coll. Mont.,* III, 131, 133, 134, 137, 145, 147, 149, 150, 152, 156, 157, 160, 303, 307, 310, 319, 329, 341–368; IV, 249, 254, 258. He served as sheriff, justice of the peace, magistrate for the county, member of the grand jury, and steward of the lordship of Montgomery.

France, but also in battles against various rebels during the reigns of Edward VI and Mary.[11] Nearer home he attempted to keep the peace along the Welsh border:

My grandfather was noted to be a great enemy to the outlaws and thieves of his time, who robbed in great numbers in the mountains in Montgomeryshire, for the suppressing of whom he went often both day and night to the places where they were, concerning which thô many particulars have been told me, I shall mention one only. Some outlaws being lodged in an alehouse upon the hills of Llandinam, my grandfather and a few servants coming to apprehend them, the principal outlaw shot an arrow against my grandfather which stuck in the pummel of his saddle, whereupon my grandfather coming up to him with his sword in his hand, and taking him prisoner, he showed him the said arrow, bidding him look what he had done, whereof the outlaw was no farther sensible than to say he was sorry that he left his better bow at home, which he conceiv'd would have carryed his shot to his body, but the outlaw being brought to justice, suffer'd for it.[12]

The Herberts' efforts at peace-keeping sometimes led to the most unpeaceful affrays. Richard Herbert had his own difficulties with other bands of ruffians. It is entirely possible that one such encounter at Llanerfyl contributed, years later, to his early death:

. . . my father, whom I remember to have been . . . of a great courage whereof he gave proof, when he was so barbarously assaulted by many men in the church yard at Lanervil, at what time he would have apprehended a man who denyed to appear to justice; and for defending himself against them all, by the help only of one John ap Howell Corbet, he chaced his adversaries untill a villain coming behind him did over the shoulders of others wound him on the head behind with a forest bill untill he fell down, thô recovering himself again, notwithstanding his skull was cutt through to the Pia Mater of the brain, he saw his adversaries fly away, and after walked home to his house at Llyssyn, where after he was cured, he offered a single combat to the chief of the family.[13]

Like his father, Richard Herbert held a number of local and county offices, adding the influence of his station and char-

[11] *Life*, p. 4. [12] Ibid., p. 5. [13] Ibid., pp. 3–4.

acter to the developing sense of order and responsibility in this part of Wales. Without question, the father's longevity limited the possibility of broader service for the son before 1593, when old Sir Edward died; and Richard Herbert himself died (probably in his forties, perhaps younger) only three and a half years later. He served in at least one, perhaps in two, sessions of Parliament: on 31 October 1584 he was elected to the Parliament of 1585/86; and at least one later record names him as having been elected in April 1580 to serve late in the Parliament of 1572 (dissolved on 9 April 1583).[14]

Among a variety of local offices, Richard Herbert served as sheriff of Montgomery in 1576 and 1584 and as magistrate for the county or for the borough numerous times.[15] In 1592 and 1593 he and his father served simultaneously. This Richard Herbert is variously identified as of "Llyssen," Montgomery Castle (1584), Walcote, and Gray's Inn.[16] Edward Herbert, writing nearly half a century after his father's death, remembered the respect that even Richard Herbert's enemies bore him: "As for his integrity in his places of Deputy Lieutenant of the county, Justice of the Peace, and Custos Rotulorum which he as my grandfather before him held, it is so memorable to this day that it was sayd his enemies appeal'd to him for justice, which they also found on all occasions. His learning was not vulgar, as understanding well the Latin Tongue, and being well versed in history."[17]

In the absence of any record of Richard Herbert's birth, we may only attempt to set limits based on his father's age and on the date of his own marriage. Sir Edward Herbert's first son was probably not born before the 1530's or long after 1560. When his father died in 1593 Richard Herbert was probably already close to mid-life.

[14] *Coll. Mont.*, II, 312; W. R. Williams, *Parliamentary History of Wales from the Earliest Times to the Present Day* (Brecknock: Privately printed by Edwin Davies and Bell, 1895), p. 147.

[15] *Coll. Mont.*, II, 194; III, 310, 314, 319, 322, 330; IV, 249, 251, 254, 258, 259, 267, 268, 269, 270, 273, 281, 282, 286; VI, 409–430. See also Lee, p. 3n.

[16] Richard Herbert was admitted to Gray's Inn from Barnard's Inn, one of the inns of Chancery, in 1579. See Joseph Foster, *The Register of Admissions to Gray's Inn, 1521–1589* (London: Privately printed by the Hansard Publishing Union, 1889), p. 54.

[17] *Life*, p. 4.

The marriage of Richard Herbert to Magdalene Newport took place at Lady Newport's family home at Eyton-upon-Severn, Shropshire, most likely during the spring or early summer of 1581, with Ranulph Sharp (or Shawe), the vicar of St. Andrew's, Wroxeter, performing the ceremony.[18] Richard Herbert would have been somewhat older than his bride, who was probably twenty-one at most. His son Edward remembered him "to have been black haired and bearded, as all my ancestors of his side are said to have been, of a manly or somewhat stern look, but withall very handsome and well compact in his limbs."[19] His bride was a woman of remarkable beauty, if we may judge from the portrait at Weston Park.[20] During the years of this marriage—about fifteen in all—Richard Herbert became the father of ten children; the last born seven months after his death.

The first child, who was to become the first Lord Herbert of Chirbury, was born at his mother's home at Eyton (as several of the others may have been) and, because of his delicate health, spent most of the years of his childhood there under the care of his grandmother, who was also his godmother.[21] Although Edward Herbert could not always recall exactly in what year he had been born nor how old he was, it is probably safe to assume that the year was 1582 rather than 1583 (the year usually given for his birth), and the date 3 March.[22] No baptismal record is known; but since his sister Elizabeth was baptized at Montgomery on 10 November 1583, it is patently impossible that he could also have been born in 1583. It is likely then that

[18] Ibid., p. 26. The parish registers for the period are not extant, but the names of the vicars are listed in the parish history.

[19] Ibid., p. 3.

[20] See my "Mrs. Herbert's *Kitchin Booke*," *English Literary Renaissance,* IV (Winter 1974), 164–173. The only known portrait of Mrs. Herbert is reproduced in color in that article, and in black and white here on p. 37.

[21] P.R.O. PROB 11/93, fol. 16.

[22] At the time Edward Herbert wrote his *Life* in the 1640's he was in his sixties, sick and half blind. Sometimes he is very exact about dates and circumstances, sometimes approximate, sometimes discursive. When he gives a precise date, it is usually accurate. But for his own birth he tells the place and the hour ("between the hours of twelve and one of the clock in the morning"), utterly forgetting to add day, month, and year. He also recalls that at the time of his grandfather's death in 1593 he was eight years old—a good three years off the mark. See the *Life,* p. 2.

his parents had married in the spring or early summer of 1581 and that he was born the following year.

The other Herbert children were Margaret (born about 1585–1586), Richard (born about 1587–1588), William (baptized at Montgomery on 12 March 1589/90), Charles (born about 1592), George (born on 3 April 1593), Henry (baptized at Montgomery on 7 July 1594), Frances (born about 1595), and Thomas (baptized at Montgomery on 15 May 1597).[23] In an age when many families lost some or even all their children in infancy and childhood, Magdalene Herbert brought all ten of these children to adulthood.

Izaak Walton, the first biographer to set forth the details of George Herbert's birth, gives 3 April 1593 as the date and Montgomery Castle as the place. Although there is no corroboration of the date and no known record of Herbert's baptism, there appears no reason not to accept this date.[24] Walton's life of Herbert was first published in 1670, three years before the death of Herbert's last surviving brother, Henry, to whom Walton undoubtedly had access through Sir Henry's daughter Magdalene (who married Charles Morley, son of Bishop Morley of Worcester and later Bishop of Winchester, whom Walton had served as a steward or factor).

But the probable accuracy of Walton's date for Herbert's birth does not require acceptance of his statement of the place of birth as Montgomery Castle. It is altogether likely that Walton assumed that, since the castle had been the residence of Herbert's brother Edward, it had also been the residence of their father. Edward Herbert, however, had to make extensive repairs and (eventually) additions to the castle when he went to live in it in the first decade of the seventeenth century; records of the earlier time suggest that, rather than living in the castle, Herbert's father and his grandfather had finally lived instead at Black Hall.[25] (A possible site of this house, in the valley from

[23] The baptismal dates here are taken from the Montgomery Parish Registers.

[24] Walton, p. 260.

[25] Richard Herbert had also lived at Llyssyn. It is possible that some of his children were baptized there or at Eyton; but the parish registers have not survived.

which the promontory of the castle rises, is marked even today by the existence of the Black Hall cottages.)

Edward Herbert writes of his grandfather and his grandfather's house: "He delighted also much in hospitality, as having a very long table twice covered every meal with the best meats that could be gotten, and a very great family. It was an ordinary saying in the countrey at that time, when they saw any fowl rise, 'Fly where thou wilt thou wilt light at Black-hall,' which was a low building, but of great capacity, my grandfather erected in his age; his father and himself in former times having lived in Montgomery castle."[26]

Black Hall, then, rather than Montgomery Castle, is probably the home to which Richard Herbert brought his bride, and the place where George Herbert was born.[27] Information found by J. D. K. Lloyd makes it almost certain that neither George Herbert nor any other Herbert of his generation was born in the castle itself, which must have been uninhabitable and uninhabited during the years of Richard and Magdalene Herbert's marriage.[28]

Like his brothers and sisters, George Herbert was born and spent his earliest years in the border country of Montgomery and Shropshire, where his immediate forebears had expended their efforts to keep the peace and establish order. Once he left this region, it is unlikely that he returned to it for extended periods of time; but the early years in his father's house of Black Hall and his grandmother's at Eyton-upon-Severn undoubtedly developed the sense of family and place that formed part of the continuing stability of his view of life.

The Death of Richard Herbert

Whatever young Herbert learned of his family's performance in "the way that takes the town" did not come to him at

[26] *Life*, p. 5.

[27] It is of some interest that Mrs. Herbert is identified in the portrait at Weston Park as "Richard Herbert of Black Halls wife, being Daughter of Lord Newport of High Ercall." The inscription, inaccurate in its latter part, probably is not contemporary with the portrait.

[28] "Where Was George Herbert Born?" *Archaeologia Cambrensis*, CXIX (1970), 139–143.

first hand from his immediate forebears. About six weeks after Herbert's birth his grandfather died and was buried, on 20 May 1593, in an unmarked grave in the church of St. Nicholas at Montgomery.[29] The child could scarcely have known his father or retained many memories of him, because Richard Herbert died when George was only three and a half years old. Edward Herbert's account of his father's death conveys a sense of the anxiety in the household during the weeks of Richard Herbert's illness: "I had not been many months in the University, but news was brought me of my father's death, his sickness being a Lethargy, Caros, or Coma Vigilans, which continued long upon him; he seemed at last to die without much pain 'thô in his senses. Upon opinion given by Physicians that his disease was mortal, my mother thought fit to send for me home."[30] Yet even Edward, the eldest of the children, was only fourteen when his father died; and probably most of the young Herberts knew more of their father through reputation and oft-repeated tales than through their own experience and memory.

When Richard Herbert died, his wife was but two months pregnant with their last child, Thomas. With winter at hand,

[29] Montgomery Parish Registers.

[30] *Life,* p. 25. My friend Katharine E. Reichert, M.D., of the University of Massachusetts, has referred me to the definitions of coma in Robley Dunglison's *Dictionary of Medical Science* (5th ed.; Philadelphia: Lea and Blanchard, 1845), from which I quote: "A profound state of sleep from which it is extremely difficult to rouse the individual. It is a symptom, which occurs in many diseases. Two varieties are distinguished. 1. The Coma vigil, Coma agrypnodes, Pervergilium, Vigiliae nimiae, Typhonia, Veternus, Agrypnocoma, Carus lethargus vigil, Typhomania . . . which is accompanied with delirium. The patient has his eyes closed, but opens them when called; and closes them again immediately. This state is accompanied with extreme restlessness. 2. Coma Somnolentum, C. Comatodes;—in which the patient speaks when roused, but remains silent and immovable in the intervals. Coma is a deeper sleep than sopor, but less so than lethargy and carus." If Edward Herbert had not been many months at Oxford, as he says, and had been sent there by his parents when he was twelve (*Life,* p. 24), Richard Herbert might be thought to have died in 1594, when his son Edward was actually twelve. Had he done so, however, it would be rather awkward to account for the existence of Frances and Thomas, the youngest children, or to refute the evidence of the date of his death recorded in the parish registers. Once again, Edward Herbert recalled his own age inaccurately. Probably he had gone up to Oxford in the spring or summer of 1596, when he was fourteen. The date of his matriculation from University College was 10 May 1596, as H. W. Garrod points out in "Donne and Mrs. Herbert," *Review of English Studies,* XXI (1945), 170.

the children's care and education to be supervised, the affairs of her husband's estate to be put in order, and the recollection of her own mother's experience of widowhood in mind, Magdalene Herbert probably began at once to undertake the steps toward settling her husband's estate.

Her husband, she said, had died intestate.[31] Wills of the period were often drawn only in prospect of imminent death (as we may see later in the wills of Margaret and Dorothy Vaughan—and indeed, of George Herbert himself). Under the circumstances, it is surprising that as many testators managed as did to express their wishes about the disposal of their estates before further sickness or death prevented them. Richard Herbert evidently expected to follow the habit of many of his family and other contemporaries and to make his will only *in extremis.* Given the particular illness he suffered, probably there were intermittent periods of consciousness when he may have attempted to draw up his testament.

The impression conveyed by his eldest son is that Richard Herbert was unable to execute a valid will, not that he made no attempt at all to write one: "my father having made either no Will or such an imperfect one, that it was not proved."[32] The wording strongly suggests that Richard Herbert had left some sort of will that was not accepted for probate; he was therefore, for practical purposes, intestate.

Yet, from his wife's account, we know one of the provisions he intended, apparently set down in some preliminary form: annuities of forty pounds each for his younger sons (then five) and dowries for his three daughters. Later Edward Herbert, as heir, agreed to pay the dowries his father intended but declined to allot the full forty pounds each to his brothers (including Thomas, the posthumous child), even though his mother offered to match the amount he paid.[33]

Probably when efforts to probate Richard Herbert's will proved unavailing, Mrs. Herbert applied instead for an administration award, which was finally granted to her and her

[31] L.M. 2014/103. I am glad to thank J. R. More-Molyneux for permission to examine this and all other Loseley manuscripts at the Guildford Muniment Room and at Loseley House.

[32] *Life,* p. 52. [33] L.M. 2014/103; L.M. 349/7.

son Edward on 3 May 1597.[34] In the meantime she bought out from the Court of Wards and Liveries her own marriage license (for a fine of forty pounds) and her dower rights to lands in Montgomery, Shropshire, and Merioneth, probably as a means of assuring her own rents and other income.[35]

Another step that had to be taken without delay was to secure the wardship of Edward Herbert, before anyone else tried to acquire it, wardships at the time being more a matter of profit for the Crown and the guardians than of protection of the rights of the ward. Immediate action was required to sue out Edward Herbert's wardship through the Court of Wards and Liveries.

Although Edward Herbert's summation of the process is succinct ("My mother thought fit to send for me home, and presently after my father's death to desire her brother Sir Francis Newport to hast to London to obtain my wardship for his and her use joyntly, which he obtained"),[36] suing out a wardship was by no means a simple process. It was a complex series of steps that involved visits to various offices and officials (the Lord Treasurer, the Attorney of the Wards, an appointed commission, the county feodary, the Clerk of the Petty Bag, and at times the Common Pleas and Chancery) and the preparation of various schedules and exhibits.[37] Clearly the best way, if their plans were not to miscarry, was to seek experienced help; and the records of the Court of Wards and Liveries show that Newport worked through Sir George More of Loseley Park, Keeper of the Tower and (in time to come) the unwilling father-in-law of John Donne. More is listed as the "Clerke," with Newport himself the "Comyttie," the person to whose charge the ward was committed.[38]

Some rather fulsome remarks in several letters that Edward Herbert wrote to More in 1602 and 1603 have unfortunately led to the erroneous assumption that More, rather than New-

[34] P.R.O. PROB 6/5, fol. 206: "Mense Maii 1597/ Richardus Herbert/ Tertio die emanuit com̄issio Magdalene Herberte Relicte et Edwardo Herbert filio/ Richardi Herbert nuper de Montgomerie in com Montgomerie dest:/ Johannis Smith notari."

[35] P.R.O. WARDS 9/158, fols. 198ᵛ–199. [36] *Life,* p. 25.

[37] B.L. Harl. MS. 1938, fols. 29–30, "Instructions to begge a Ward."

[38] P.R.O. WARDS 9/348.

port, was Herbert's guardian. Not knowing whether the four extant letters[39] are the only ones Herbert wrote to More during this period or whether they represent but part of a larger series clouds the picture: Herbert lays on the flattery artfully and enjoys his young man's exercises of wit; but there is nothing to indicate whether these are occasional or habitual indulgences, nor whether Herbert had any particular motive in such flattery when his wardship was drawing to a close and More would be called upon to take part in decisions about some of the expenditures of the wardship.

The first of these four letters is dated from Eyton on 17 August 1602, the other three from Montgomery Castle the following year, on 28 August, 12 October, and 4 December. Three of the four superscriptions include the word *father:* "To the right wor^th^ and his honorable friend Sr George More Knight, his beloued father"; "To my much honored father Sr George More at Loseley in Surrey"; and "To my most honored father Sr George More knight at Loseley." The first letter also salutes More as "Woorthy father." Kempe, accepting these exaggerated compliments at face value (despite Edward Herbert's explicit statement that his mother "thought fit to desire her brother Sir Francis Newport to hast to London to obtain my wardship for his and her use joyntly, which he obtained"),[40] then went on to ascribe Mrs. Herbert's memorandum—"The case betwene my sonne and me is this . . ."[41]—to Sir George More and thereby to becloud the issue still further for subsequent students who have not had the opportunity to examine the original document.[42]

Removal to Eyton

With the arrangements for the wardship safely in hand, Mrs. Herbert prepared to leave Montgomery and to remove to her mother's home at Eyton, probably not long after the birth and

[39] L.M. 2014/99–102; in Alfred John Kempe, ed., *The Loseley Manuscripts* . . . (London: John Murray, 1835), pp. 347–359.
[40] *Life,* p. 25.
[41] L.M. 2014/103; discussed more fully in Chapter 2, below.
[42] See especially the discussion of Edward Herbert's wardship in Joel Hurstfield, *The Queen's Wards: Wardship and Marriage under Elizabeth I* (Cambridge, Mass.: Harvard University Press, 1958).

baptism of Thomas Herbert in May 1597. Edward had returned to Oxford, but most of the other children must still have been with their mother, Elizabeth and Margaret (aged thirteen and eleven or twelve) to be educated at home and the next oldest boys, Richard and William, likely to be sent off shortly to live with one schoolmaster or another as part of the process of being "brought up in learning"—to borrow their brother Edward's phrase.

For the family the most important events of their sojourn at Eyton were undoubtedly Edward's marriage and their grandmother's death, both of which contributed to the decision to remove to Oxford in 1599. On 28 February 1598 Edward Herbert was married at Eyton to Mary Herbert, daughter and heir of Sir William Herbert of St. Julians (or Gillians), who had stipulated that his daughter might marry only one whose surname was Herbert; else his lands in Monmouthshire and Ireland would descend to another part of the Herbert line.[43] From what Mrs. Herbert later wrote about this match, it is clear that she was attempting to provide for her son's future; and though he mentions that he was but fifteen at the time of his marriage, be became sixteen three days later. But in 1598 the last day of February was Shrove Tuesday, and the wedding had therefore to be performed before the beginning of Lent.[44] In all likelihood the bride remained at Eyton until the time when the rest of her husband's family proceeded to Oxford, probably early in 1599.

Margaret Bromley Newport died within a year of her grandson's wedding. Unlike many of her contemporaries, she had written her will almost seven years earlier, taking particular notice of her godsons and "nephews" (as grandchildren were often referred to at the time), Edward Herbert and Richard Newport.[45]

Lady Newport's death marked the end of another period in the lives of her daughter and her daughter's children. Before she departed for Oxford, however, Magdalene Herbert made one splendid gesture to the past, to the years in Montgomery,

[43] *Life*, pp. 25–26.

[44] It is interesting that when Mrs. Herbert herself married a second time, it was likewise just before the beginning of Lent, in 1609.

[45] P.R.O. PROB 11/93, fol. 16. The date of probate is 14 February 1599.

and to her dead husband, by erecting a canopied tomb in his memory in the Lymore Chapel of the church of St. Nicholas at Montgomery. At Wroxeter her grandparents and her parents had been commemorated in two table tombs of great beauty, the earlier of them perhaps by Richard Parker of Burton-on-Trent, known as "the alabaster man."[46] The more elaborate tomb at Montgomery includes not only the recumbent figures of man and wife and representations of eight of their ten children, but a figure of a cadaver placed where the wife expected to be buried, a rather grim *memento mori* intended ultimately to be superseded when Magdalene herself came to be buried there. But her marriage to Sir John Danvers in 1609 brought about instead her burial at St. Luke's. Chelsea; but the beautiful effigy of the lady at Montgomery remains to mark her original expectation.[47]

Richard Herbert is not quite lost sight of in the inscription; nor are Mrs. Herbert's ancestors ignored: "Heare Lieth the Body of Richard Herbert Esquire Whose Monument was Made at the Cost of Magdalene his Wife Daughter to Sr Richard Newport of Highe Arcall in the County of Salop Knighte (deceased) & of Dame Margaret his Wife Daughter & Sole Heire to Sr Thomas Bromley Late Lord Chiefe Justice of England & one of the Executors of the Late Kinge of Most Famous Memorie Kinge Henry the Eighte AN̄O DOM̄ 1600."[48]

That the dates of Mrs. Herbert's own life and death do not appear is not surprising; even on the Bromley and Newport tombs at Wroxeter the dates of the widows were never added. Perhaps she was wise, in all, to see that what mattered to her was set forth in the original inscription.

Removal to Oxford

Again at a fork in the road after her mother's death, Magdalene Herbert decided this time to proceed still further into England and to move her household to Oxford for the remainder of Edward's time there. Probably she and her daughters and most of her sons made this journey early in 1599. Edward Her-

[46] John Salmon, *The Church and Parish of Wroxeter, Shropshire,* p. 7.

[47] In *A Guide to Montgomery* (5th ed.; Montgomery: Montgomery Corporation, 1972), p. 26, J. D. K. Lloyd, well known as Montgomeryshire historian, suggests that this tomb was probably built by Walter Hancock of Much Wenlock.

[48] This effigy is the only likeness of Richard Herbert now known.

bert puts it: "Not long after my marriage"—though for him periods of time are always approximate—"I went again to Oxford together with my wife and mother who took a house and lived for some certain time there."[49]

There is, unfortunately, no other record of Mrs. Herbert's residence in Oxford except that first set forth by Izaak Walton a good seventy years later; the earlier part of the account (one of his most earnest and unsupported passages) has led to confusion about just when it was that the friendship between Magdalene Herbert and John Donne began: "For these reasons she indeared [Edward] to her own company: and continued with him in *Oxford* four years: in which time, her *great* and *harmless wit,* her *chearful gravity,* and her *obliging behaviour,* gain'd her an acquaintance and friendship with most of any eminent worth or learning, that were at that time in or near that University; and particularly, with Mr. *John Donne,* who then came accidentally to that place, in this time of her being there: it was that *John Donne* who was after *Doctor Donne,* and Dean of *Saint Pauls London:* and he at his leaving Oxford, writ and left there in a verse a Character of the Beauties of her body, and mind."[50]

Despite other inaccuracies in this passage, Walton is unlikely to have invented Donne's chance visit to Oxford. As secretary to Sir Thomas Egerton, Donne may well have stopped in Oxford to see Francis Wolley, Egerton's stepson, an undergraduate about Edward Herbert's age.[51] If Francis Wolley provided the occasion for Donne's visit, he may also have introduced the visitor to Mrs. Herbert. Since Wolley took his degree and left Oxford in December 1599, the meeting probably took place earlier that year, but there is no evidence of the further development of the friendship until 1607.[52]

The education of Edward Herbert's younger brothers by

[49] *Life,* p. 26. [50] Walton, p. 264.

[51] He is probably the Mr. "Woley" mentioned in the *Kitchin Booke.* See Chapter 2, below.

[52] Most recent studies incline toward an earlier date for "The Autumnall" than Edmund Gosse's 1625—or even that of 1607 suggested by the letters of Donne to Mrs. Herbert that Walton published. See Rossi, I, 39–40; Helen Gardner, "Lady Bedford and Mrs. Herbert," in her ed. of *The Elegies and The Songs and Sonnets* (Oxford: Clarendon Press, 1965), pp. 248–258, especially pp. 252–254; and R. C. Bald, *John Donne: A Life* (Oxford: Clarendon Press, 1970), pp. 118–119.

various tutors and schoolmasters continued during the stay in Oxford, as we may deduce from the records of books purchased for them in the months after they had left the university city. Young George Herbert had undoubtedly been introduced to the elements of learning long before his family moved once again, early in 1601, this time to London.

CHAPTER 2

Charing Cross, Westminster, and Chelsea (1601–1609)

Mrs. Herbert's Household at Charing Cross

In April 1601 Magdalene Herbert established at Charing Cross the first permanent home her family had known since her husband's death and her removal from Montgomery. It is likely that she had arrived from Oxford some weeks earlier and had lived in lodgings while she found a suitable house and had it made ready. Edward Herbert sets the time of his arrival in London as shortly before the Essex rebellion in February.[1]

In contrast with Mrs. Herbert's establishment of a temporary residence in Oxford for two years, of which we know very little, her removal to Charing Cross early in 1601 and establishment of a home that would be maintained through 1618 and probably later are carefully recorded by her steward, John Gorse. Through Gorse's account in the *Kitchin Booke* that begins on 11 April 1601, we know who made up the household, who sat down to meals, how well they ate and were entertained, and what some of the incidental expenses of the household were.[2]

Money to pay for food and a variety of incidental expenses was given to Gorse at least once a week and sometimes oftener, usually in amounts of two or four pounds. Sometimes Mrs. Herbert paid out this money; but just as often Edward Whittingham acted as her agent. On at least one occasion Gorse received the household money as part of a larger sum ("being p^{te} of the x^{li} wch I had of her").[3] When Mrs. Herbert and the greater part of the household had departed to the country for

[1] Lee, p. 43n.

[2] The *Kitchin Booke,* which the late Earl of Powis kindly permitted me to examine, is at Powis Castle. See the description and facsimile in my "Mrs. Herbert's *Kitchin Booke,*" *English Literary Renaissance,* IV (Winter 1974), 164–173.

[3] *Kitchin Booke,* fol. 2^{v}.

I. Magdalene Newport Herbert. From the portrait at Weston Park, possibly by Sir William Segar. Reprinted from *English Literary Renaissance*, IV (Winter 1974), 165, with permission; © *English Literary Renaissance.* Reproduced by kind permission of the Earl of Bradford T.D.

the summer, Gorse had £ 3 15*s*. on hand undisbursed. During the rest of the time he kept the *Kitchin Booke* he received five payments (a total of forty pounds) from one John Laiton, the first on 8 July, the last on 21 August.

On the evening of Saturday, 11 April, when the members of the household had settled into their new home, they marked the occasion with a "Drincking," with twenty-eight persons on hand, and refreshments of veal, lamb, and eggs. On the following day, Easter Sunday, twenty-nine persons sat down to both dinner and supper. The guests on these two days, however, were not wholly the same ones; as a matter of fact, guests who returned for successive meals are far outnumbered, in the steward's book, by those present for a single meal. The custom attests a wide and varied acquaintance at the time of Mrs. Herbert's first coming to London.

Mrs. Herbert's "ordinary Howshold" included twenty-six persons in all. She herself wrote their names on the title page of the household account book Gorse had begun:

A Kitchin Booke Contayninge the expences of my howse
in London begining vpon Satterdaie the xi of Aprell 1601
With the names and nomber of my howshoulde

Gentlewomen
Magdalin Harbertt.
Mary Herbertt.
Eliza: Herbertt.
Margarett. Herbertt.
Frauncis Herbertt.
Eliza: Detten.

Gentlemen
Edward Herbertt.
Ric: Newport.
Ric: Herbertt.
George Herbertt.
Henry Herbertt.
Thomas Herbertt.

Nurses & Chambermayds
Jone Vaughan, nurss.
Katherine Higgins.
Jane Manneringe.
Frauncis Doughtie.

Servingmen
Edw: Whittingham.
Humphrey Jones.
Henry Heath.
Thomas Manneringe.
William Norbury.
Fra: Warnner.
John Gorse.
Ric: Barnett.
William Morris.
Edw. Heyward.

Eight of the ten Herbert children, then, were at home when this household was first established, along with Edward's wife Mary; William and Charles, still in the country at the time, did not join the others until 29 April. During May and June Mrs. Herbert apparently had all ten of her children at hand, from Edward, now nineteen, to Thomas, who became four in May. Richard Newport was her nephew, and Elizabeth Detten probably the daughter of friends or relatives in Shropshire or Montgomery.[4]

The Herbert children must have been a lively, stubborn, and high-spirited lot, if we may judge from George Herbert's reference (in "Affliction" [II]) to his "sudden" soul and from Edward's comment that George "was not exempt from passion and choler, being infirmities to which all our race is subject"[5]—to say nothing of evidence of Edward's own high spirits and quickness to welcome the occasion for a duel, or the sort of pride that later would lead Thomas in a "sullain humour" to retire from the sea "to a private and melancholy life, being much discontented to find others preferred to him."[6]

But a dwelling to accommodate a household the size of Mrs. Herbert's would have been a large one, and apparently it had grounds extensive enough for the keeping of pigs and poultry (both of which should be housed at some distance from the dining table), for a spring garden[7]—and probably for the children to exercise outdoors and work off some of their high spirits. Richard, at least, practiced archery at this time; Gorse records the purchase of "a Bowe and Sixe Arrowes" for him on 29 June.[8] On 5 July "Mr. Williams of the Queenes Stable" came to supper, perhaps in connection with riding lessons for some of the children.[9] Certainly Richard and William, the brothers who eventually went off to fight on the Continent, must have shared Edward's enthusiasm for fencing and for riding the great horse (the horse used in battle, not hunting; Edward Herbert did not approve of hunting on horseback). But if Edward's nearly disastrous experience in learning to swim is any indication, Mrs. Herbert's command on that occasion ("my mother upon her blessing charged me never to learn Swimming, telling me further, that she had heard of more drowned

[4] Charles, p. 169n. [5] *Life*, pp. 12–13. [6] Ibid., p. 15.
[7] *Kitchin Booke*, fol. 32. [8] Ibid., fol. 54^{v}. [9] Ibid., fol. 58^{v}.

than saved by it")[10] probably kept the younger children away from the water—at least so far as she knew.

From the testimony of both Edward Herbert and John Donne, it appears that Mrs. Herbert in many ways followed her mother's habits and practices, particularly in her hospitality, her almsgiving, and her care for the poor. In addition, Margaret Bromley Newport, writes her grandson (perhaps thinking that his own mother should have emulated her), after her daughters were married, "deliver'd up her estate and care of housekeeping to her eldest son Francis, when now she had for many years kept hospitality with that plenty and order as exceeded all either of her country or time, for besides abundance of provision and other good cheer for guests, which her son Sir Francis Newport continued, she used ever after dinner to distribute with her own hands to the poor, who resorted to her in great numbers, alms in money, to every one of them more or less, as she thought they needed it."[11] In his memorial sermon for her daughter Magdalene in 1627, Donne speaks of "that body that was eyes to the blinde, and hands, and feet to the lame, whilst it liv'd" and stresses her acts of charity:

> For, for our families, as we are *Gods Stewards;* For those without, we are his Almoners. . . . as shee receiv'd her *daily bread* from God, so, daily, she distributed, and imparted it, to others. In which office, though she never turn'd her face from those, who in a strict inquisition, might be call'd idle, and vagrant Beggers, yet shee ever look't first, upon them, who *labour'd,* and whose *labours* could not overcome the *difficulties,* nor bring in the *necessities* of this life; and to the sweat of their browes, shee contributed, even her *wine,* and her *oyle,* and any-thing that was, and any thing that might be, if it were not, prepar'd for her own table.[12]

Although he admired his grandmother's hospitality and generosity of spirit, Edward Herbert was critical of his mother's similar style of living, complaining that she "took house and kept a greater family than became either my mother's widow's Estate, or such young beginners as we were."[13] Some impres-

[10] *Life,* p. 10. [11] Ibid., p. 11.

[12] John Donne, *A Sermon in Commemoration of the Lady Danvers,* in *The Sermons of John Donne,* ed. George R. Potter and Evelyn M. Simpson (Berkeley: University of California Press, 1956), VIII, 89.

[13] *Life,* p. 13.

sion of the extent of Mrs. Herbert's hospitality may be gathered from the *Kitchin Booke* in which John Gorse records the names of the great variety of guests who joined the Herberts at dinner and at supper during several months in 1601.

Seldom were the Herberts without guests at meals—actually, only nine times during the period before Mrs. Herbert went to the country for the summer. Even on the occasions when the mistress was a guest at someone else's table, guests were (usually) being fed at her own. During the first thirteen weeks Gorse kept his book, at least ninety-five different visitors ate at Mrs. Herbert's table, and about twenty of their servants ate with the household servants. Some of those who came most often were linked to the Herberts by ties of blood or of origin—the Lawleys of Spoonhill, Shropshire (sons of Mrs. Herbert's sister Elizabeth); Robert Harley, husband of her niece Mary; and Lady Bromley, probably her cousin or her aunt. There were also Welsh visitors with such names as Davies, Lloyd, Morgan, ap Ollyver, and Price.

Thomas Lawley, Harley, and one Edward Cooke were clearly the most frequent guests at meals. Lawley ate forty-one meals at Mrs. Herbert's table between 9 May and 29 June; Harley took at least some meals there during twelve of the thirteen weeks the family were in residence; but the otherwise unidentified Edward Cooke who ate ninety meals with the family during the period covered by the *Kitchin Booke* was far and away the most faithful of the lot.[14]

Gorse's accounts offer several clues to the location of Mrs. Herbert's house through the mention of several taverns nearby. At two of these he made purchases, probably on short notice or at odd times when regular household supplies were unexpectedly depleted. Butter, which this household used generously, was the item Gorse had to send out for on three occasions, twice to the Swan and once to the George.[15] On another occasion he paid twelve shillings to a porter to carry a trunk and a hamper "to the Maydenhead."[16] The amount is three or four times what he ordinarily paid to porters who carried meat and other purchases from the markets; and even

[14] Charles, pp. 170–171. [15] *Kitchin Booke,* fols. 20ᵛ, 22, 35.
[16] Ibid., fol. 60ᵛ.

the greater weight of this load probably does not account for the greater cost. The Swan and the George, therefore, were probably closer to Mrs. Herbert's house.

Whatever the location of the house at Charing Cross, it was obviously near a church. Not only did Mrs. Herbert see to it that prayers were conducted morning and evening in her home, but, Donne tells us, she herself went to church for the daily offices: "From this I testifie her *holy cheerfulnesse,* and *Religious alacrity,* (one of the best *evidences* of a *good conscience*) that as shee came to this place, *God's house of Prayer,* duly not onely every *Sabbath* . . . but even in those *weeke-dayes.*"[17] From his knowledge of the household at Chelsea he adds a lively picture of Mrs. Herbert urging her brood along to church and a quiet one of the Sunday evening psalm-singing: "And, as she ever hastned her *family,* and her *company* hither, with that cheerful provocation, *For God's sake let's go, For God's sake let's be there at the Confession;* So her selfe, with her whole family, (as a *Church* in that elect *Ladie's* house, to whom *Iohn* writ his second *Epistle*) did, every Sabbath. shut up the day, at night, with a generall, with a cheerful *singing of Psalms;* This *Act of cheerfulnesse,* was still the last Act of that family, united in it selfe, and with *God.*"[18]

Nor was psalm-singing the only music heard in that household, we may be sure. Both Edward and George were accomplished lutenists, and George played the viol as well. Probably other members of the family sang and played these and other instruments.

Entertainment for guests varied. Ordinarily they and the family must have provided their own diversion, probably musical; but from time to time Gorse mentions the visits of various musicians and dancers who came to provide entertainment. On Saturday, 20 June, Mrs. Herbert sent Jane Mannering to Gorse for two shillings "to gyve Musicians."[19] A wind-instrument maker was on hand (surely to provide instruments for some of the household) for supper during one of Dr. John Bull's visits.[20] Morris dancers came to the house on 7 June;[21] and "a Blynde harper and his boys" appeared at supper on Thursday,

[17] Donne, p. 86. [18] Ibid. [19] *Kitchin Booke,* fol. 49.
[20] Ibid., fol. 22^{v}. [21] Ibid., fol. 40^{v}.

30 April, the harper himself returning at supper the following Saturday.[22] Rather surprisingly, Gorse mentions card-playing as another diversion of the household: on one occasion Mrs. Herbert had been playing cards and losing money and had to send to Gorse for funds to pay off her debt.[23]

During the months for which John Gorse kept the *Kitchin Booke* in 1601, several famous musicians visited the Herbert house—John Bull for suppers in April and May (at the first of which a swan pie was cut), William Byrd for three meals between 14 and 25 June.[24] Both men were doctors of music and members of the Chapel Royal. Will Heather (or Heyther), a lay vicar of Westminster Abbey, who would later become a member of the Chapel Royal and at this time shared a house with the historian William Camden, was on hand for six meals between 16 May and 5 July;[25] and on Tuesday, 7 July, the day of the general dispersal of the household for the summer, Richard and George Herbert went to spend the rest of the summer in his house, apparently nearby at Westminster. From Gorse's records of the purchase of a grammar and a Cordelius for George, it is clear that this young Herbert would also be working away at his Latin.[26] Surely at Heather's house he must have encountered Ben Jonson's master, William Camden; and it is to be hoped that the older scholar took much joy in the progress of the younger one.

During the course of the summer Gorse looked after the needs of both sets of brothers living away from home. For Richard, who seems to have been hard on his clothes, he bought a girdle and a dozen points on 21 July and a "Payer of worsted Stocking[es]" and "a Payer of Shewes" on 6 August, and had another pair of shoes mended the following week.[27] The quire of paper bought on 21 July may have served both Richard and George, but it was George who needed a "Penner" that same day and paper for "a Coppie and Phrase booke" on 17 August.[28]

[22] Ibid., fols. 15^{v}, 17^{v}. [23] Ibid., fol. 27.
[24] Ibid., fols. 5^{v}, 22^{v}, 45, 45^{v}, 51^{v}. [25] Ibid., fols. 26^{v}, 43, 45^{v}, 51, 58^{v}.
[26] Ibid., fol. 65^{v}. [27] Ibid., fols. 62^{v}, 63, 67^{v}. [28] Ibid., fols. 62^{v}, 69^{v}.

Education of the Herbert Children

Although Edward Herbert, as the eldest and apparently favorite son (if we may judge by the superscription of his mother's letter of 12 May 1615),[29] benefited extensively from his mother's protection of his interests, her care for his education, her maintaining a household suitable for him and his bride at Oxford and later in London, it is evident that Magdalene Herbert took particular care of her other children, considering the needs and abilities of each one. No two of the Herbert sons followed the same pattern in education, but probably all the children received their first instruction from their mother. Edward, a sickly child, recorded that his family "did not think fit to teach me so much as my Alphabet until I was seven years old,"[30] but he was later taught not only his letters, but his grammar and his earliest books by a schoolmaster in his grandmother's house at Eyton. The handwriting of the five sons of whose handwriting we have samples shows similarities in the basic formation of letters that suggest similarities in early instruction; and it is likely that Mrs. Herbert, who took great care with her own hand, was the first teacher of penmanship for most of her children.

From the *Kitchin Booke* we may gather that the children's instruction continued throughout the year, whether they were in school, were sent to live with various tutors, or were spending some interval at home with the rest of the family. Gorse records ten occasions on which tutors or schoolmasters came to the house at Charing Cross. A Mr. Ireland (probably the Mr. Ireland of Croydon with whom William and Charles would spend the summer) came once only, on 15 April.[31] Thereafter, a Mr. Phillips appeared at irregular intervals, more often than not bringing another schoolmaster with him. (It is possible, of course, that Ireland was the second, unnamed schoolmaster who appeared, since the two boys who would be his charges that summer arrived from the country on 29 April.)[32]

Gorse's careful record of the purchase of various school

[29] Magdalene, Lady Danvers, to Sir Edward Herbert, 12 May 1615, P.R.O. 30/53/10.

[30] *Life,* p. 23.

[31] *Kitchin Booke,* fol. 6.

[32] Ibid., fols. 8^{v}, 10, 10^{v}, 23, 32^{v}, 41^{v}, 42.

books and supplies for the children also attests that they continued their studies throughout the year. Repeatedly he bought quires of paper to make copybooks and phrase books for them, "Pynn dust," "a Penner for Mr George," copies of Cato Senior for Charles and of Cordelius for both George and Charles.[33]

Although Edward Herbert says that all his brothers were "brought up in learning"[34] (meaning probably that they had attended good grammar schools, at the least), the records now existing provide information about only four of the Herbert sons: Edward at University College, Oxford; William at Queen's College, Oxford; Charles at Winchester and at New College, Oxford; and George at Westminster School and at Trinity College, Cambridge. It is likely that Lancelot Andrewes played some part in Charles's going to Winchester and in George's going to Westminster. There is no record known of grammar school for Henry or for Thomas; but Henry must obviously have studied French before he was sent to Paris to study at the Abbey of St. Martin-des-Champs. (It is entirely probable that he and George both used Randle Cotgrave's *Dictionarie of the French and English Tongues* [1611] in their study of French, even likely that its use of proverbs as illustrations contributed to the continuing interest these brothers shared in "outlandish" [i.e., foreign] proverbs.) But the Herberts were apparently facile in learning other languages, and at this time modern languages were usually studied outside the schools. Even so, there is no doubt that Henry was "brought up in learning," like the rest. Among his papers at the National Library of Wales is a series of Latin poems on the virtues.[35]

Information about the education of the posthumous seventh son, Thomas, is pitifully thin. From the time of his baptism at Montgomery on 15 May 1597[36] until his naval service in 1616 under Captain Benjamin Joseph of the *Globe,* there are only two scattered bits of information about him, neither closely related to his education. Edward Herbert wrote rather obliquely to his guardian, Sir George More, on 4 December 1603 to thank him for his favor to "my little brother"[37]—apparently meaning that More had helped young Thomas to become a

[33] Ibid., fols. 60v–67v. [34] *Life,* p. 13. [35] N.L.W. MS. 5300 B.
[36] Montgomery Parish Registers. [37] L.M. 2014/102.

page to Sir Edward Cecil in Germany. The next specific piece of information about Thomas is that he was (like Edward) at the siege of Juliers in 1610.[38] We may therefore infer that he was of the household and under the supervision of Sir Edward Cecil. Thereafter he became a sea captain of some note, but left off seafaring when he felt himself undervalued, and apparently turned to writing satiric and scurrilous verse.[39] From the writings attributed to him in the *DNB* (some of the attributions require close re-examination), it would appear that this youngest brother, Thomas, had also been "brought up in learning."

The information about the education of the three Herbert daughters is naturally less, because their education would have taken place at home. Certainly they were brought up to read and to write at least as well as other young women of their station and time; they knew something of the life of London, encountered the broadening influences of a great variety of visitors to their mother's house, and respected learning. Since Mrs. Herbert herself obviously knew something of law, theology, and estate management, it is likely that her daughters were also brought up with some knowledge of these concerns that played a part in most seventeenth-century lives. From the interest that Elizabeth took in providing books for George's study[40] and from the sole surviving letter of Frances[41] we have some evidence that Mrs. Herbert had seen to it that her daughters developed the ability to share some of the interests of their brothers and their husbands.

Beyond this, all is assumption; but we shall not go far astray if we suppose that the woman to whom Donne addressed the *La Corona* sonnets took a deep interest also in the religious development of her children. The writings of Edward, George, and Henry all attest a deep and lasting concern with religion

[38] *Life,* p. 13.

[39] For a time in the 1630's Thomas worked as a deputy for his brother Henry in the Office of the Revels. See Edward Arber, *A Transcript of the Registers of the Company of Stationers of London, 1554–1640* (London, 1877), IV, 350, 355, 356.

[40] Letter V, *Works,* pp. 376–377.

[41] Frances, Lady Browne, to Sir Henry Herbert, 28 June 1647, B.L. Add. MS. 37157.

that must have been fostered in all the Herbert children from their childhood.[42]

Family Affairs, 1603–1606

After the *Kitchin Booke* the next dated references to the affairs of the Herbert family are the two documents among the Loseley manuscripts referring to Edward Herbert's wardship, the first of them a memorandum drawn up by Mrs. Herbert about 1603, when Edward Herbert came of age,[43] the second an arbitration award (dated 4 June 1604 and indented on 14 June 1604) that apparently took the first document into account, signed by Sir George More, Herbert Croft, and John Morice.[44] Sir Francis Newport may have been the committee of Edward Herbert's guardianship (i.e., the one to whom the responsibility was delegated; the word is accented on the first syllable); but it is clear that Mrs. Herbert was the one who actually managed Edward's affairs during the years of his minority. On behalf of the estate she paid off her husband's debts, adding £400 of her own money; procured Edward's wardship at a cost of some £800; and, at a cost of nearly £1000 more, arranged for his marriage ("worth not much lesse that 30000 li"). She borrowed £1800 from her brother Sir Francis Newport and paid 500 marks in interest on it. Then, adds Mrs. Herbert, Edward's "wives estate (contrary to our expectancy) beinge intangled with great debts, and vpon these extreme forfectures as the brech of one might have bye the ov[er]throwe of her whole estate, and neyther of them able neyther in yers or abilityes to vndertake the paymt of them, wth many griefs of minde and hazard of mine estate (if his wief had died before issue betwene them) I vndertooke the paymt of them, repayinge myself as I

[42] Henry Herbert composed two series of prose devotions, "The Broken Heart" (Bodl. MS. Don. f. 26) and "Henry Herbert his golden harpe; or Heavenly Hymne &c." (Bodl. MS. Don. f. 27; also Huntington Library [San Marino, Calif.]. MS. 85). Rebecca Warner includes as an appendix to *Epistolary Curiosities: Series the First* (Bath: Richard Cruttwell, 1818), pp. 191–193, "Prayers and Meditations in Old Age" by Henry Herbert.

[43] Magdalene Herbert, "The case betwene my sonne and me is this . . .," L.M. 2014/103.

[44] L.M. 349/7.

could wth the receipt[es] of her land[es], wch notwthstanding they came in by pieces, in comparison of the greate summes wch I expended for the debts yet all layd together equalled not my disbursem^{ts} by much, how much I have payd more then I received I cannot justly say because we differ vpon the accompt." Her concern, of course, was not only for her own estate, but for the interests of her younger children.

Finally, says Mrs. Herbert, whereas the Court of Wards would have allowed Edward a mere £10 yearly to maintain himself and his wife, "I have yerlye spent vpon him in his education and in maytenance of his famelye, and that increase of port wch his so great advancem^{t} in marriage necessarily brought with it, 500† for these 7 yeres wherby I have not only bredd him in such sort as he now is, but also [pre]vented his runninge in debt whiles he was vnder age, wch would have ben heavye vpon him, this in 7 yeares besides the interest of it Account[es] by vnto 3500†."

This summation of Mrs. Herbert's concludes with her "demande[s]" that her son first confirm the assignment made to her brother; that he give his brothers and sisters the amounts she asks (£1000 to each of the girls, the sons to receive the annuities of £40 that their father intended, and Thomas, born posthumously, to be included with the other five younger sons). At the same time she proposes to remit the £330 "due for arrerage since his fathers death." In all, she refers to "your consideracons what you think me worthy of." The plural pronoun "you" suggests that her memorandum, nominally addressed to Sir George More, was intended to be examined by others as well, probably the committee of three who later drew up the arbitration award.

This arbitration award guaranteed that the younger brothers would have a basic maintenance—nothing munificent, but a kind of competency. Even if it had been paid on time in the succeeding years, it would not have been lavish; and often, especially when Edward Herbert was out of the country, his bailiffs in their country stubbornness did not meet the terms of the agreement, and the brothers were kept waiting, despite the best efforts of Sir John and Lady Danvers. Particularly for the brothers who were university students—William, Charles, and

George—these delays must have been wearisome and embarrassing.

Other events of general interest and importance were of course taking place in England as the Herberts lived out their individual and collective lives, some touching them closely, others passing by virtually unnoted. Lancelot Andrewes, who was installed at Westminster Abbey as dean in July 1601, undoubtedly became as close a friend of the Herberts as his predecessor Gabriel Goodman had been; and Andrewes would appear to have been the most likely sponsor for George Herbert when he entered Westminster School as a day student in 1605 (the year usually assumed). Andrewes and Herbert remained firm friends until Andrewes' death in 1626.

The funeral of Queen Elizabeth, James's coming to London (Edward Herbert having gone to meet him on the way, at Stamford), Mrs. Herbert's memorandum described above, and yet another visitation of the plague followed fast one upon another in 1603. In 1603 also Charles Herbert entered Winchester School; the register there notes the election on 29 July of Charles "Harbert," of Montgomery, aged ten. In the following year the Hampton Court Conference occupied public notice even as the Herberts adjusted to the arbitration award settling matters about Edward's wardship, including the validation of the dowries of £1000 each for the sisters and of annuities of £30 for the younger brothers. In 1604 or 1605 the eldest daughter, Elizabeth, married Henry Johnes of Albemarles, probably not at Montgomery, but possibly at Wroxeter. Early in 1605, probably on 30 March (though the warrant itself bears no date) Edward and Richard Herbert were beneficiaries of a royal grant:

Sr Ed. Herbert — The Office of Cheif fforester of Snowden forest.
Office — The Constableship of Conway Castle & Stewardship
of his ma[jesties] land[es] [par]cell of the Monastery of
Bardsey in the County of Carnarvan with the
vsuall fees & proffit[es] to the same belonginge xiiis. iiiid.
graunted vnto Sir Edward Herbert and Richard
Herbert for terme of their lives Vppon surren-

> der of l[ettres] patente y[t] the same office hereto-
> fore graunted vnto Roberte Berrye & Thomas
> Goodman for terme of their lives; subscribed
> by the Erle of Nottingham[45]

In 1605 Edward Herbert also served as sheriff for Montgomeryshire.[46]

George Herbert, though he was attending Westminster School, probably still lived at home at the time of the Gunpowder Plot in November 1605, as did his brother Edward, then Member of Parliament for Merioneth. Edward, forewarned (like Glendower) in a dream, happily elected not to go to Parliament on the fatal day: "In the third yeare of King James the Gunpowder Treason hapening Myselfe who was chosen Kt of the Shire for Merionethshire as having resigned my pretence in Montgomeryshire to S[r] William Herbert at his entreaty did then Lodg in my Mothers house neare Charing Crosse. The night before this horrible Conspiracy was to bee acted I was two severall tymes warned in my sleepe not to goe to the Parliament that day which though I tooke but for dreaming fell out to be an Admonition."[47] It must have been a memorable time for all, not least for the Westminster scholars, with the shock of treason and the thrill of danger emanating from buildings within very sight of their peaceful school grounds.

No other event of great moment is recorded of the Herberts until nearly a year later, on 3 November 1606, when Margaret Herbert was married to John Vaughan of Llwydiarth at the church of St. Nicholas, Montgomery.[48]

George Herbert at Westminster School

In the meantime George Herbert, like his brother Edward before him, probably carried on his studies with several tutors or schoolmasters until he entered Westminster School as a day student.[49] The Elizabethan statutes of 1560 decreed that there

[45] S.P. 78/63, fol. 303. [46] *Coll. Mont.*, V (1872), 479.

[47] Quoted from Draft A of Edward Herbert, *Autobiography,* in R. I. Aaron, "The 'Autobiography' of Lord Herbert of Cherbury," *Modern Language Review,* XXXVI (1941), 193–194.

[48] Montgomery Parish Registers.

[49] The Elizabethan statutes of 1560 are quoted in Arthur F. Leach, *Educational Charters and Documents, 598 to 1909* (Cambridge: University Press, 1901),

be forty grammar scholars and ten singing boys or choristers.[50] They also required that, to enter the school, a boy be seven years old, know the eight parts of speech, and be able "to write at least moderately well." Furthermore, he must have been a day student for a whole year before he could be elected scholar; and he might not have "an inheritance of more than £10 [a year]."[51] The elections took place on 29 June, St. Peter and St. Paul's Day,[52] with Lancelot Andrewes, as dean, serving as one of the electors. Herbert's training in Latin probably enabled him to place easily in the fourth of the seven forms at Westminster.

The curriculum of the Renaissance grammar school has often been described. The major emphasis was on grammar, logic, and rhetoric, taught largely through translation and retranslation of Latin texts. At Westminster, however, special emphasis was given also to two subjects of particular importance to Herbert, the study of Greek and the practice of music. Westminster departed specifically from the Eton curriculum in requiring the study of Greek as early as the fourth form.[53] And whatever other music they may have heard from the abbey during the rest of the week, the grammar scholars were to be taught for an hour on Wednesday afternoon and again on Friday afternoon by the choristers' master.[54] Surely the music at the abbey and in the school played a large part in developing Herbert's interest in liturgical music and in his concept of "Church-musick" as his path to the door of heaven.

One of Herbert's schoolmates at Westminster was a London lad named John Hacket, seven months his senior, who would later share many of Herbert's years at Trinity, become chaplain to Bishop Williams and later himself Bishop of Lichfield and Coventry. Because of Hacket we learn much about both Westminster and Trinity in his time and Herbert's.

The Westminster records of admissions for this period have not survived. The only information about the date of Herbert's

---

pp. 496–524. The standard account of the school is that by John Sargeaunt, *Annals of Westminster School* (London: Methuen, 1898). A more recent and very readable account is that of Lawrence E. Tanner, *Westminster School: A History* (London: Country Life, 1934).

[50] Leach, p. 497. [51] Ibid., p. 501. [52] Ibid., p. 499.

[53] Sargeaunt, pp. 36–50; Tanner, pp. 6–7. [54] Leach, p. 513.

entry into the school (which does not make clear whether he was then a day student or a scholar) is Walton's statement that Herbert was tutored at home, "where he continued, till about the age of twelve years; and being at that time well instructed in the Rules of Grammar, he was not long after commended to the care of Dr. *Neale,* who was then Dean of *Westminster;* and by him to the care of Mr. *Ireland,* who was then chief master of that school."[55] Richard Neile, who succeeded Andrewes as Dean of Westminster Abbey after Andrewes' election as Bishop of Chichester on 31 October 1605, was in fact installed on the day of the Gunpowder Plot.[56] Herbert could not have been "commended" to him before that time—that is, late in 1605. Herbert's year as a day student probably began, then, in the latter half of 1604, before his twelfth birthday rather than after, but assuredly while Andrewes was still dean.

Hacket is generally supposed to have entered Westminster earlier than Herbert because of the seven-month difference in their ages; but all later records show them as contemporaries. Hacket apparently remained a day student. The time of their admission at Westminster is of importance in evaluating Hacket's statements about Andrewes as dean and sometime schoolmaster, as these remarks are set forth by his biographer, Thomas Plume.[57]

We may assume that Herbert, like Hacket, acquired habits of "rising betimes, and constant study."[58] Although Herbert did not, like Hacket, remain a day student, it is probable that Herbert (though not "sufficiently tasqued when he went home" at night during his first year) was similarly "never permitted to know what idleness or vanity was by his own leisure or experience."[59]

Both boys were honored in due time by being elected Westminster scholars for Trinity College. Plume states unequivocally that Hacket first came to the notice of Lancelot Andrewes when he was dean and occasionally taught the boys in the ab-

[55] Walton, p. 262. [56] Sargeaunt, p. 62.

[57] Thomas Plume, ed., *A Century of Sermons . . . Preached by . . . John Hacket* (London: Printed by Andrew Clark for Robert Scott, 1675), pp. i–liv.

[58] Ibid., p. iv. [59] Ibid.

sence of their master, Richard Ireland; and Herbert during his year as day student must have shared this experience.

Ten or eleven years after Hacket, Herbert, and their Westminster classmate Walsingham Shirley had proceeded to Trinity College, the St. John's fellow they had known as proctor was named Dean of Westminster. The record that Hacket has left of John Williams' inquiries about how Lancelot Andrewes had fulfilled the duties of the deanship provides considerable detail about the influence of Andrewes on the scholars at Westminister:

His Predecessors . . . were Men of good Report. . . . Dr. *Andrews* for advancing Learning in the School. . . . He [Williams] had heard much what Pains Dr. *Andrews* did take both day and night to train up the Youth bred in the public School, chiefly the *Alumni* of the College so called. For more certain Information, he called me from *Cambridge* in the *May* before he was Installed, to the House of his dear Cousin Mr. *Elwis Winn* in *Chancery-Lane,* a Clerk of the Petty-Bag, a Man of the most general and gracious Acquaintance with all the great Ones of the Land that ever I knew. There he moved his Questions to me about the Discipline of Dr. *Andrews.* I told him how strict that excellent Man was, to charge our Masters, that they should give us Lessons out of none but the most Classical Authors; that he did often supply the Place both of Head School-master and Usher for the space of an whole week together, and gave us not an hour of Loitering-time from morning to night. How he caused Exercises in Prose and Verse to be brought to him, to examine our Style and Proficiency. That he never walk'd to *Cheswick* for his Recreation, without a brace of this young Fry; and in that way-faring Leisure, had a singular dexterity to fill those narrow Vessels with a Funnel. And, which was the greatest burden of his Toil, sometimes thrice in a week, sometimes oftner, he sent for the uppermost Scholars to his Lodgings at night, and kept them with him from eight till eleven, unfolding to them the best Rudiments of the *Greek* Tongue, and the Elements of the *Hebrew* Grammar, and all this he did to Boys without any compulsion of Correction; nay, I never heard him utter so much as a word of Austerity among us. Alas! this is but an Ivy-Leaf crept into the Laurel of his Immortal Garland. This is that *Andrews,* the Ointment of whose Name is *sweeter then all Spices, Cant.* 4. 10. This is that celebrated Bishop of *Winton,* whose Learning King *James* admired above all his Chaplains; and that King, being of most excellent Parts himself, could the better discover what was Eminent in another. Indeed he was the most Apostolical and Primitive-like Divine, in my Opinion, that wore a Rochet in his Age; of a most venerable Gravity, and yet most sweet in all Commerce; the most Devout that ever I saw, when he appeared before God; of such a Growth in all kind of Learning, that very able Clerks were of a low Stature to him. . . . I am transported even as in a Rapture to make this Digression: For who could come near the Shrine of such a Saint, and not offer up a few Grains of Glory upon it? Or how durst I omit it? For he was the first that planted me in my tender Studies, and water'd them continually with his Bounty. The Occasion that brings in this, was the new Dean's addition to his Pattern, that looking into such a Mirror, he might keep up the Learning of that happy Plantation, that it might never hear [bear?] worse, then as Mr. *Camden* testifies for it, *Felix eruditorum in Ecclesiam & Rempublicam proventus.* Eliz. p. 61. Fol.[60]

Hacket's biographer, Thomas Plume, concludes his account of Hacket's days at Westminster with an anecdote that also mentions Herbert:

To tell how well he passed the Circuit of that School I need say no more but what his *Master Ireland* said, at parting, to *him* and *George Herbert,* who went from thence to *Trinity Colledge* in *Cambridge* by election together, That he expected to have credit by *them two* at the *University,* or would never hope for it afterwards by any while he lived: and added withal, that he need give them no counsel to follow their Books, but rather to study moderately, and use exercise; their parts being so good, that if they were careful not to impair their health with too much study, they would not fail to arrive to the top of learning in any *Art* or *Science.*[61]

Their master judged well; both Hacket and Herbert continued to earn high academic honors at Cambridge.

Family Affairs, 1607–1608

While Herbert was studying at Westminster, the rest of the family were pursuing their own ways. Edward Herbert was making Montgomery Castle once more fit for residence, repairing and building; Elizabeth and Margaret were also living in

[60] John Hacket, *Scrinia Reserata: A Memorial Offer'd to the Great Deservings of John Williams, D.D.* . . . (In the Savoy: Printed by Edw. Jones for Samuel Lowndes, 1693), I, 44–45.
[61] Plume, p. v.

Wales, growing into their lives in their new homes. On 1 July 1608 William matriculated at Oxford from Queen's College.[62] Charles was at Winchester after 1603,[63] although he seems to have spent some time with Sir George More at Loseley Park as well. As a matter of fact, a letter largely about Charles suggests some of the difficulties Mrs. Herbert was undergoing.[64]

In bringing up her large family without a father's care and supervision, Mrs. Herbert at times inevitably suffered over one or another of her children, all of whom undoubtedly had wills of their own. In a letter to Sir George More dated 14 March 1607 (probably Old Style) she alludes to her concern for her son Charles, then a young man about sixteen, probably just at the point of proceeding from Winchester to New College, Oxford: "My sonn Charles hath so long been troublesom vnto you, as that I may iustly feare, you are nearer being weary of him, then ridd of him, yet so far am I from desire of doeing you further trouble as that I shal beseech you not to suffer your self to receiue any wrong from him, whosoeuer [whatsoeuer?] he and I doe loose by it." Whatever anxieties the adolescent Charles had been causing his mother, however, she appears to have been even more concerned over unspecified difficulties with Edward that had brought her considerable distress: "Since Wednesday Ned Herbert is rod hom towards his wife, he hath put me in no less, but another feare, since the ending of that you know of, which makes me know the miseries of this lyfe, and to place my contentment in that, I hope and looke for, and in nothing I haue or inioy." The inferences are all too shadowy for us to hazard any guess about what gave rise to these remarks, but there is no question that Mrs. Herbert loved much and suffered much because of her eldest and perhaps favorite son. It is most unlikely that her taking a second husband after more than twelve years of widowhood much improved the relationship with Edward; but apparently this

[62] The original records at Queen's have not survived. This date is taken from J. Foster, *Alumni Oxoniensis . . . 1500–1714* (Oxford: Parker, 1891–2).

[63] Rossi (I, 48) suggests that William was also a student at Winchester. His name does not appear in the Winchester records.

[64] Unbound Correspondence: Sir George More, 1600–1632, L.M. Warden Sewell's record at New College gives 4 June 1611 as the date of Charles Herbert's matriculation.

second husband earned the respect and affection of several of the younger Herberts, including George.

Mrs. Herbert's Marriage to Sir John Danvers

Although Mrs. Herbert had moved her family about from time to time, the earlier shifts, of venue only, brought nothing like the changes that resulted from her marriage to Sir John Danvers in 1609. As much as twentieth-century readers may have been told that marriages in this earlier day were more often based on alliances of fortune and estate than on personal considerations or preferences, it is difficult for our century to contemplate some of the strangely balanced marriages proposed for Queen Elizabeth or the actual marriage between Mrs. Herbert, a widow in her forties, mother of ten children, and a much younger man who appears to have been one of the ornaments of his age, so handsome that on the Continent "People would runne after him in the Street to behold [admire] him."[65] He came of a fine Wiltshire family, allied through his mother with the Stradlings; and his elder brother Henry was the Earl of Danby. He became active in the Virginia Company (surely in part for profit, but certainly also for the advancement of religion, one of the interests this otherwise oddly assorted couple shared).

How Magdalene Herbert met Sir John Danvers is now impossible to say; there are no obvious links of origin or of close friends. Danvers may have come to the Herbert household as a friend of Edward Herbert or of Richard Newport, even of John Donne. It is not beyond possibility that the couple met through the Herberts of Wilton House, the young Earls of Pembroke and of Montgomery.

The wedding took place late in the winter of George Herbert's last year at Westminster School. John Chamberlain, writing to Sir Dudley Carleton on 3 March 1609, mentions this wedding among other recent ones: "Young Davers is likewise

[65] Bodl. Aubrey MS. 2, fol. 53. Most parts of this manuscript are in final form, ready for the printer, but there are occasional gaps in factual information, or alternative (and undecided) wordings are suggested. In the passages quoted I have placed Aubrey's alternative or additional wordings in parentheses, rather than in square brackets, to emphasize that these are his own alternatives and in no way emendations of mine.

wedged to the widow Herbert (mother to Sir Edward) of more then twise his age."[66]

This young stepfather, more of an age to be an elder brother, would prove a good friend to George Herbert for the remainder of that young man's life. It is likely that Herbert had only vague memories of his own father; but from the letters he later wrote Danvers from Cambridge, it is clear that he liked and trusted his stepfather. It is only one of the troubles and disillusionments that Herbert's early death averted, that he did not live to see his stepfather one of the regicides.

Nor is evidence lacking of the amity between Sir John and the other Herbert children. Elizabeth Herbert Johnes lived as a member of his household about fourteen years. Margaret Herbert Vaughan, who died in August 1623, left him one of her best horses ("Item I gyve and bequeathe to Sr John Danvers knight my best Coult").[67] On 26 December 1628 Henry received from his stepfather Lady Danvers' copy of the *Works* of James I (now at the Houghton Library, Harvard University). Frances Herbert and her husband Sir John Browne named Danvers as godfather for their eldest son, and Danvers later arranged for the boy to study at Little Gidding.[68]

But Edward Herbert was something else again. A stepson of sixteen, like George Herbert, is quite a different matter from a stepson of twenty-six or twenty-seven; and Danvers was indisputably of the same generation as Edward Herbert, possibly a year or two older, but just as possibly a year or two younger. Although Danvers' letters amply show his concern for his eldest stepson and something of his later handling of Edward's business affairs, there is no surviving record of Edward's attitude toward Danvers; and Edward's omission of all mention of Danvers in his autobiography has generally been taken to indicate resentment toward him.

The portion of Edward Herbert's *Life* dealing with the time of his mother's second marriage is taken up with the details of his efforts to persuade his wife to make a settlement upon their son and, failing that, to give himself leave to travel abroad. He

[66] John Chamberlain, *The Letters* . . . , ed. Norman E. McClure (Philadelphia: American Philosophical Society, 1939), I, 288; S.P., Jas. I, XLIV, 6.

[67] P.R.O. PROB 11/142, fol. 79.

[68] Blackstone, p. 4.

was perhaps either too much absorbed in his own affairs or too resentful of the possibility that his mother's estate would come under control of a young man who was, like himself, admired for his appearance and bearing but none too much assured of his future direction. Indeed, the terms in which he mingles financial with familial concern in attempting to persuade his wife may well have resulted from a realization that followed his mother's remarriage.

I demanded then whether she was willing to do so much for them as I wou'd; whereupon she replying demanded what I meant by that, I told her that for my part I was but young for a man, and she not old for a woman, that our Lives were in the hands of God, that if he pleased to call either of us away, that party which remained might marry again, and have Children by some other, to which our Estates might be disposed; for preventing whereof I thought fit to motion to her, that if she wou'd assure upon the son any quantity of Lands from 300 *l.* a year to 1000 *l.* I wou'd do the like; but my wife not approving hereof, answered in these express words, that she wou'd not draw the Cradle upon her head.[69]

Edward Herbert's earlier reluctance to provide annuities for his brothers in the full amount intended by his father and his undoubtedly critical attitude toward his mother's household expenses at Charing Cross (already referred to in part) emphasize his concern over her outlay in a way not at all becoming to him:

When I had attained the age betwixt 18 or 19 years, my mother together with my self and wife removed up to London, where we took house and kept a greater family, than became either my mother's widow's Estate, or such young beginners as we were, especially since six brothers and three sisters were to be provided for. . . . My mother 'thô she had all my father's Leases and Goods which were of great value, yet she desired me to undertake that burthen of providing for my brothers and sisters, which to gratify my mother as well as those so near me, I was voluntarily content to provide thus far as to give my six brothers thirty pounds a piece yearly during their lives, and my three sisters 1000 *l.* a piece, which Portions married them to those I have above-mentioned.[70]

In contrast, he was lavish in his praise of his grandmother, who remained a widow. And though he omitted all mention of

[69] *Life,* p. 56. [70] Ibid., p. 52.

Danvers, Danvers was to serve him well in several matters of business during his Continental travels.

Danvers and Edward Herbert

The four letters sent by Sir John Danvers to his eldest stepson between 26 November 1614 and 24 June 1615 are ample record of the pains Danvers took in looking after Herbert's business affairs while Herbert was working his way north from Italy into the Low Countries and France.[71] (Herbert's journeyings of 1614–1615 took him to Heidelberg, Turin, Lyons, Amsterdam, Paris, and the Hague, among other places.) A letter written later, during Herbert's first ambassadorship at Paris, urges his help in procuring vinedressers and handlers of silk worms and emphasizes the aims of the Virginia Company.[72] In all these letters it appears that the men are on the most amicable terms.

In the first letter Danvers tells of receiving money from one of Herbert's bailiffs and expecting more of another, receiving rents, paying bonds and advancing money of his own to pay an obligation of Herbert's, and says that the brothers' annuities have not been paid on time (a perennial ailment). Later he arranged matters of credit with Philip Burlimachi and forwarded letters of credit to Herbert at Lyons, at Amsterdam, and at Paris. The letter to Florence (2 March 1615) was sent in care of William Herbert; the letter of 24 June refers to "the abbay of St Martin in Paris where your brother is"—probably Henry, who developed his skill in the French tongue and later served as a kind of secretary during Edward's first ambassadorship.

The tone of all of Danvers' letters is serious, sometimes even earnest; it is obvious that he is doing his best to look after his stepson's interests. The salutation of all four letters is "S^r^"; the complimentary closes vary from assurance of ready service to such warmer greetings as "Now wth my harty well wishes for your happines I will rest yours"[73] and "I hope . . . that I shall ever be worthy of your true love."[74]

Several comments of Lady Danvers in her letter to Edward

[71] P.R.O. 30/53/7, 26 November 1614; P.R.O. 30/53/10, 2 March 1615; P.R.O. 30/53/10, 8 April 1615; N.L.W. MS. 314A, 24 June 1615.

[72] P.R.O. 30/53/3, 27 July 1620. [73] 8 April 1615. [74] 24 June 1615.

Herbert of 12 May 1615 suggest that he had been feeling neglected during his travels, despite the best efforts of Sir John and Lady Danvers. She, for her part, endeavored to reassure him of her concern and of her husband's love for him:

> My deare sonne: it is straunge to me to here you to complayne of want of care of you in your absence when my thoughts are seldom remoued from you which must assuredly set me workinge of any thinge may doe you good. And for writinge, the one of us yf not both neuer let messinger passe without letters. Your aboad is so short in any one place and we so vnhappy in giuinge you contentment as our letters come not to your hande, which we are sorry for. And to tell you further of Sr John Dau̅e̅rs Loue which I dare sweare is to no man more. He is and hath beene so careful to keep you from lake of money now you are abroad as your Baylifs faylinge payment as they continually doe and pay no man. He goeth to your Marchaunt to offer him self and all the power he can make to supply you as your occasions may require. Mistake him not but beleeue me there was neuer a tenderer hart or a louinger minde in any man then is in him towards you who haue power to Com̅aund him and all that is his. . . . Let [your deare Children] my Deare sonn draw you home and affoorde them your care and me your comfort that desire more to see you then I desire any thinge ells in the world. And now I end with my dayly prayers for your health and safe retorne to
>
> Your euer Lovinge mother
> Magd: Dau̅e̅rs[75]

The address reads, "To my best beloued sonn Sr Edward Herbert Knight."

Herbert apparently did not heed even this loving plea, but seems to have remained abroad through 1616 or early 1617.[76] Even without further letters from Sir John and Lady Danvers, we may assume that they continued to look after Edward Herbert's business affairs, to fret over his wayward bailiffs, and to send letters to him at every opportunity. Edward's neglecting to mention Sir John as his stepfather, then, says far more of his being caught up in himself and his own interests than it does of Danvers' kindliness and friendliness, of what the seventeenth century would have called his obsequiousness, his readiness to serve. When we consider his brothers' and sisters' relationship with Danvers, Edward does not come off well, but rather as if

[75] P.R.O. 30/53/10. [76] Lee, pp. 95–97.

he were the one out of step. Whatever may be said of the "prickliness" of Welsh heritage (which Edward Herbert called "choler"), it is rather amusing to reflect that only the diplomat among them seems to have had difficulty in accepting a stepfather to whom most of the others showed friendship and loyalty far more than perfunctory.

The Danvers Home at Chelsea

At the time of the Herbert-Danvers marriage probably only Frances and Henry were still living with their mother at Charing Cross. The house that Magdalene Herbert's children had known as their most permanent home continued to be a home for Sir John and Lady Danvers; but beyond this residence close to the heart of governmental and mercantile activity, from 1609 on they probably spent most summers at Sir John's home in Chelsea, a house assuredly noted for its architecture, gardens, and hospitality.

Among his other interests, Danvers became engrossed in laying out gardens after the Italian style—and did so with enthusiasm at several houses during his lifetime. His interest must certainly have been whetted by his travels. "He had well travelled France & Italie," with Thomas Bond, and it was in those places that people ran after him in the street.[77] From John Aubrey's description of the garden at Chelsea we occasionally have a glimpse of the house as well.

The Danvers house in Chelsea faced south, toward the river. Aubrey is probably wrong in locating it "in the very place where was the House of Sr Thomas More Ld Chancellor of England";[78] but the remainder of this passage provides the information that the principal bedchamber was "on the west side: out of the Hall."

The entry was through a gateway flanked by "two spacious, elegant Pyramides [of brick covered with finishing mortar, but pointed with freestone: about twenty foure foot high.] which stood on the spires of the Gate." (Aubrey goes on to say that in Sir Thomas More's time there had been a gatehouse, from whose height More and his dog were accustomed to enjoy the prospect of the river and to contemplate, and adds a rather

[77] Bodl. Aubrey MS. 2, fol. 53. [78] Ibid., fol. 55.

alarming tale about the intrusion of a dangerous Tom of Bedlam.)[79] Aubrey sketches the pyramids and praises their construction: "The Pyramides are the most beautifull, and taking of any that ever I saw: for there is a criticall proportion in them, that is neither too high or too low. . . . These Pyramids, since Sr John Danvers death haue been mended & are sett awry: before they were most exact & clear."[80]

Windows opened north and south from the hall of this "elegant and ingeniose" house:

As you sitt at Dinner in the Hall, you are entertaind with two delightfull Vista's: one southward over the Thames & to Surrey: the other northward into that curious Garden. . . .

You did not enter directly out of the Hall into the Garden: there was a low semicircircular wall to hinder the im̄ediate pleasures and *totall* view primo introitus. But first you turned on the right or left hand,[81] downe a paire of staires of ten steppes which landed you in a kind of Boscage (Wildernesse) of Lilac's, Syringa's &c. (Sweet Briar &c. Holly—Juniper): and about 4 or 5 Apple trees and peare trees. In the west end of this Boscage was the figure of the Gardiners wife in freestone coloured: at the east end of the Gardiner's the like: both accoutred according to their *Callings*.[82] The east and west ends of this little darke, shadie Boscage delivered you into the stately great gravelled Walkes of the garden, East & West: where you were first entertained with two most stately pieces of sculpture of Freestone, scilicet #

The length of this Garden is . . .

The breadth of it is . . .

The breadth of the two great gravelled walkes, w[ch] runne south and north, is four yards over.

At the four corners of the Garden: sc. about the Ovall, are 4 low Pavilions of Brick leaded flatt: some are firre trees, and Pine-trees: Shumacks; and the quarters all filled with some rare plant or other.

#On the east side of the Hall is a neat little Chapell or Oratorie, finely painted: next by it a Drawing-roome, whose Floor is chec-

[79] Ibid., fol. 55[v]. The brackets here are Aubrey's. [80] Ibid., fol. 55.

[81] Aubrey includes a sketch of an architectural barrier "opposite to y[e] stairway to hinder y[e] entrance to y[e] Garden."

[82] See *The Note-Book and Account Book of Nicholas Stone,* ed. Walter Lewis Spiers, Walpole Society (Oxford: University Press, 1919), VII, 50. Spiers mentions also that John Schoerman, a craftsman from the Low Countries whom Stone employed, "executed for Sir John Danvers of Chelsea, two sitting figures of shepherds and a group of Hercules and Antaeus, for which he received respectively £6 and £16."

quered, like a Chess-board, wth Box and Eugh pannels of about six inches square. At the East and West ends of the House (or Yard) are two, high fastigiated Turrets: the Fans whereof are the Crest of Danvers, sc. a golden Wyvern volant. The Fan turns a spindle which hath a cantred-wheele that turned the Index (or sagitta)—externally at the 4 severall sides, to point to y[e] point of y[e] Compass the wind blowes.

I have spoken of the excellency of the two great Figures on the Pedestalls; and of their Passions, attested by that great Master in Painting Seignoro Vario. I come now to those Figures at the four entrances of the Ovall-green: where M[r] Stone hath not only out-done himselfe, in the symmetrie, proper accoutrements, &c.: sc. Tar-box, scrip Sheep-crooke, Dog, sheep-marke sc. D and baskets of Flowers: but, likewise, in his expressing Love-passions in the very freestone: where you read rustick beauty mixt with antique innocent simplicitie: there you may behold the faithful Shepherd, and the faithfull shepherdesse: who haue the honestest innocent countenances that can be imagined which yet remain (1691) after seventy years.

. . . . .

Now if Zeuxis and Aristides obtaind such praise in painting in colours the inward affections and qualities of the mind: sure he deserues more praise that does performe the same in sculpture.

As for the Sphinxes at the south entrance of this Ovall, they are as well humoured in their kinds. . . .

Between the two great gravelld Walks is an Ovall Bowling-green. The length of the longest Diameter three Chaines (inclusive). The shorter diameter or breadth, two Chaines ½.

To this Ovall Bowling-green are four Avenues sc: East, west, north, & South: at each of which, are two figures opposite, exquisitly cutt in Freestone by M[r] George Stone.

On the West side a Shepherd & Shepherdesse opposite sitting. . . .

On the East side a shepherd & sheperdesse. . . .

On the North side a shepherd & sheperdesse. . . .

On the South side two Sphinxes.

The Ovall gravell-walke is two yards, over.

In each Quadrant about the Ovall thirty Cypresses, at about four foot distance.

The Banke of the Ovall, is one foot high.

2 Chaines South below the Ovall green.

2 Chaines North from the Ovall green.

Now, as at Lavington the ground lay uneven, & irregular: The skill was, there, to reduce it into some regularity & evenesse. è contra here, the ground lay plain (flatt, and the businesse was to make elevations &

depressions. So at the north part of the garden here the earth is excavated in the shape of a Wedge . . . foot deep: where at the bottom (which is as deep as ye Thames) is a round Well or Basin . . . foot diameter curbed with freestone: over this flatt-square (where the Well is) is a high arch of 25–30 foot up over (above) which is a fine Banquetting roome: the windowes whereof are painted glasse: over this roome are flatt Leads from whence you enjoy the prospect of ye Garden &c. This building is of Brick and is a gracefull Tower to your view of the Garden: Now, as you goe (descend, downe) from this gay Paradise into the darksome, deep Vault (Grotto) where the Well is, it affects one with a kind of Religious horrour. Round about the Well, are fine potts of choice Plants. Of the earth that was digged up for the making of this deep-walke & Grotto, was made the Terrace, that reaches West & east, above it: from where you might overlook the Garden. At each end of this Terrace is a neat House to sitt and retire; covered with Cornish slatt, as in the margent.[83]

This gracious, almost idyllic setting was the home in which George Herbert spent the last of his school holidays before matriculating at Cambridge. He must have returned to it and to the house at Charing Cross from time to time during the ensuing years. Aubrey tells us that Sir Francis Bacon was a frequent visitor,[84] and it is clear from John Donne's letters that he was another familiar visitor in the Danvers household.[85] Some estimate of the degree of friendship Donne felt for this household may be drawn from remarks in a letter addressed to his brother-in-law, Sir Nicholas Carey, on 21 June 1625: "I go to a family, to which I owe much, and therefore must intreat you to be my surety for one debt to them which ys, some tyme, this Summer, to bestow a Bucke upon me."[86] In his will Donne bequeathed to Danvers "what Picture he shall accept of those that remayne vnbequeathed."[87] His memorial sermon on Lady Danvers is a monument that needs no comment.

Between Easter and Trinity terms and between Trinity and Michaelmas terms George Herbert must have come home nu-

[83] Bodl. Aubrey MS. 2, fols. 55–57. Words in parentheses are added or alternate terms of Aubrey.

[84] John Aubrey, *Brief Lives,* ed. Oliver Lawson Dick (Ann Arbor: University of Michigan Press, 1957), p. 9.

[85] R. C. Bald, *John Donne: A Life* (Oxford: Clarendon Press, 1970), pp. 373, 463, 471, 472–476.

[86] Ibid., p. 472.

[87] Ibid., p. 567.

merous times to stay with this family and to watch the Thames flowing by to the south and to walk in the gardens to the north of the house. The only specific information we have, however, comes in a brief sentence in a letter from Donne, who took refuge in Chelsea during the plague in 1625: "Mr *George Herbert* is here."[88] But that visit would occur many years in the future, after the major part of Herbert's life at Cambridge.

[88] Quoted ibid., p. 276.

CHAPTER 3

Cambridge (1609–1623)

Herbert at Trinity College

Herbert's admission at Trinity College, Cambridge, on 5 May 1609 determined the course of his life for many years to come. In accordance with the Elizabethan statutes he and two other boys from Westminster School, John Hacket and Walsingham Shirley, had been named the Westminster scholars at Trinity in the preceding year, at the same time Henry King was chosen one of the Westminster scholars named to Christ Church, Oxford.[1] The names of Hacket, Herbert, and Shirley appear in

[1] W. W. Rouse Ball and J. A. Venn, eds., *Admissions to Trinity College, Cambridge* (London: Macmillan, 1916), I, 3–4; Trinity College Admissions and Admonitions, 1560–1759, fol. 249. There is now no record of Herbert's matriculation, because subscriptions at the time of matriculation were not required before 1613. (I am indebted for this and all subsequent information from the University Archives to Miss H. E. Peek, Keeper of the Archives.) Baker's Cambridge Collections, a manuscript transcribed from an earlier one, says, however, that "Geo: Harbert" matriculated at "Conv. 2" on 18 December 1609, under Dr. Duport as Vice-Chancellor (B.L. Harl. MS. 7041, fol. 121^{v}). Clearly both Hacket and Herbert began their residence in Cambridge during the autumn of 1609, when their names first appear in records of Trinity College as receiving two bursar's payments of 3*s.* 4*d.* each; and from that time on they received their stipends regularly, so far as we can tell from extant records (Trinity College Senior Bursars' Accounts, Book D, 1601–1621, containing records for 1601, 1602, 1604, 1606, 1608, 1609, 1610, 1612, 1614, 1615, 1616, 1618, 1621.) The quarterly stipend of 3*s.* 4*d.* each continued through 1614. In 1615 their quarterly stipends as "discipuli" were increased to 10*s.*, and this was the amount until the latter part of 1616/17. Despite some misplacement of accounts in this book, it appears that in the last two quarters of that year Hacket received £1 6*s.* 8*d.* and Herbert £1 11*s.* 8*d.* After the account resumes in 1618, each received a quarterly stipend of one mark (13*s.* 4*d.*), along with the other fellows, and annual payments of £2 13*s.* 4*d.* each as lectors domestic. Again in 1621 both received stipends of one mark as fellows, as well as the single payment ("liberat") of 33*s.* 4*d.* made to each of the masters and fellows.

the Trinity College Admissions Book as "admissi et iurati" on 5 May, and probably all three took up residence at Cambridge before the Michaelmas term.

The master at the time of Herbert's admission was Thomas Nevile, the great builder ("a splendid, courteous, and bountiful Gentleman," Hacket called him),[2] who died in the spring of 1615 and was succeeded by John Richardson, the Regius professor of divinity.[3]

Among the fellows Herbert would have known was Francis Nethersole, who preceded him as orator.[4] Other fellows at Trinity included Henry Fairfax, Giles Fletcher, and Francis Kynaston.[5] Charles Chauncy, the future president of Harvard College, entered Trinity the spring after Herbert began residence.[6] The two men who later acted as his deputy orators entered several years later, Herbert Thorndike matriculating in 1613, Robert Creighton as elected scholar from Westminster in 1614.[7] One other Westminster student who entered during Herbert's time later made an important contribution by publishing Herbert's *Musae Responsoriae* in 1662: James Duport, who matriculated in 1622.[8]

Of the Regius professors at Trinity in Herbert's day we should note especially John Richardson (professor of divinity from 1607 to 1617), Samuel Collins (professor of divinity from 1617 to 1651), Robert Metcalfe (professor of Hebrew from 1608 to 1645), Andrew Downes (professor of Greek from 1585 to 1625), and Robert Creighton (professor of Greek from 1625 to 1639).[9] Donne's friend Samuel Brooke was a chaplain at Trinity during the earlier part of Herbert's time there.[10]

We may infer from Herbert's Cambridge letters that he found the university life congenial to his interests and studies. Hacket must have spoken frequently about the college in the

[2] John Hacket, *Scrinia Reserata: A Memorial Offer'd to the Great Deservings of John Williams, D.D.* . . . (In the Savoy: Printed by Edw. Jones for Samuel Lowndes, 1693), I, 24.

[3] Ball and Venn, I, 63–64.

[4] Ibid., II, 221.

[5] Ibid., II, 216, 211, 217.

[6] Ibid., II, 246; *Works*, p. xxv.

[7] Ball and Venn, II, 262, 264.

[8] Ibid., II, 296.

[9] Ibid., I, 16–17, 62–64; II, 264, 270, 327.

[10] R. C. Bald, *John Donne: A Life* (Oxford: Clarendon Press, 1970), p. 308; Ball and Venn, I, 49.

hearing of his biographer Plume, because Plume comments on how often Hacket gave "great thanks to *God* that *he* was not bred among rude and barbarous people, but among civil and learned *Athenians;* that he was not disposed to some *Monkish Society,* or ignorant Cloyster, but to the *Greece* of *Greece* it self, the *most learned* and *Royal Society* of *Trinity Colledge,* which in that and all other Ages since the Foundation equalled any other *Colledge* in *Europe* for plenty of incomparable *Divines, Philosophers,* and *Orators.*"[11] Among those Hacket mentioned particularly were "his learned Tutor, Dr. *Simson,* that wrote the *Church History,* Dr. *Cumber* a great Critick, Dr. *Richardson Regius Professor,* Dr. *Nevil* a very splendid and sumptuous Governor; the great Hebrician and Chronologer Mr. *Lively,* one of the *Translators* of the *Bible,* the famous and most memorable Dr. *Whitgift,* sometime Master, afterwards Archbishop of *Canterbury.*" It was, said Hacket, "almost impossible for any man to continue ignorant under the advantage of so great Examples, and influence of such incomparable Instructors."[12]

Several men at neighboring colleges probably came to know Herbert during his years at Trinity, especially Nicholas Ferrar, at Clare Hall, and John Williams (who served a year as junior proctor), at St. John's.[13] Barnabas Oley, who entered Clare in 1617, probably knew at least who the young lecturer was. Simonds D'Ewes, also at St. John's after 1618, writes of having attended "Mr. Harbert's public rhetoric lectures in the University."[14] A little farther to the south, at Peterhouse, was another student who would be much influenced by *The Temple* and write in imitation of it: Ralph Knevet of Norfolk, who matriculated in 1616.

There were others, of course, whose ties with the university

[11] Thomas Plume, ed., *A Century of Sermons . . . Preached by . . . John Hacket* (London: Printed by Andrew Clark for Robert Scott, 1675), pp. v–vi.

[12] Ibid., p. vi. A detailed account of student life and studies at Cambridge a decade or so later is given in Harris F. Fletcher, *The Intellectual Development of John Milton,* vol. II (Urbana: University of Illinois Press, 1961).

[13] Hacket, I, 18; Plume, p. vii.

[14] Simonds D'Ewes, *The Autobiography and Correspondence . . .,* ed. J. O. Halliwell (London: Richard Bentley, 1845), I, 106, 121. See also I, 108, where he tells of attendance at Commencement and at various lectures and academic exercises.

brought them to Cambridge from time to time. Herbert may have met Sir Francis Bacon in London; or their acquaintance may have begun when Bacon feasted the entire university during the Christmas of 1613.[15] Bacon also served as Member of Parliament for Cambridge in 1614; and some years later it would become Herbert's duty to write him officially on behalf of the university.

James's court was often nearby at Royston or at Newmarket, but members of the royal family also appeared rather frequently in Cambridge itself. Early in 1613, at the time of the marriage of the Princess Elizabeth to the Elector of the Palatinate, King James and other members of the court were at Newmarket several times, Prince Charles and the Prince Palatine in Cambridge, and the King in Cambridge early in March.[16] Another famous royal visit to Cambridge took place in March 1615, when St. John's presented *Emilia,* a Latin comedy by a Mr. Cecill, on 7 March; Clare presented a five-hour performance of George Ruggle's *Ignoramus* on 8 March; and Trinity presented *Albamazar* by a Mr. Tomkis on 9 March and the pastoral *Melanthe* by a Mr. Brookes on 10 March. On 13 March the King departed from Cambridge, but King's College, not to be outdone by the others, presented Phineas Fletcher's *Sicelides* that evening all the same.[17] Bishop Andrewes had attended the King during this visit, and shortly afterward John Donne was given the honorary doctor's degree James had wanted, though not because of the inclination of the university.

James obviously enjoyed visiting Cambridge and sharing in the academic exercises and entertainments there, and it would be surprising if he had not made the acquaintance of George Herbert before 1620, when Herbert wrote his letter and graceful epigram upon the gift of a copy of James's Latin works,

[15] G. Goodman, *The Court of King James the First,* ed. J. S. Brewer (1839), I, 282.

[16] John Chamberlain, *The Letters . . .,* ed. Norman E. McClure (Philadelphia: American Philosophical Society, 1939), I, 419, 430, 434; Hacket (I, 22), gives further details of this visit.

[17] F. G. Fleay, *A Chronicle History of the London Stage, 1559–1642* (London: Reeves & Tanner, 1890), p. 259. The occasion of this visit is commemorated at Trinity in the west face of the Great Gate.

probably on 20 May 1620: "Why, O stranger, dost thou remind us of the Vatican and Bodleian? A single book is a library to us."[18]

That Herbert was acquainted with the master and fellows of Trinity and with many of the others already mentioned must be assumed, because the surviving records do not mention such matters as his friendships and associations. One fact it would be useful to know is who his tutor was. Each student at Trinity, from the time of the foundation, had apparently been assigned to a specific tutor. Unfortunately, systematic records were not kept before 1635,[19] and there is therefore no college record showing which of the fellows undertook the tutelage of George Herbert. A good possibility, however, is Henry Fairfax, who was a minor fellow when Herbert matriculated, and was sworn major fellow in the succeeding spring, on 23 March 1609/10.[20] Such a relationship would account for the otherwise unverified but continuing legend of their intimate friendship, the sole recorded basis for which appears to be an anonymous statement quoted by a nineteenth-century editor of the Fairfax papers.[21]

In the absence of specific knowledge of the identity of Herbert's tutor or of his course of readings, probably we shall do best to assume that he followed much the same sort of program that Milton was to find at Christ's in the third decade of the

[18] Walton, pp. 270–271; *Works,* pp. xxix, 604; trans. Alexander B. Grosart, ed., *The Complete Works,* Fuller Worthies' Library (printed for private circulation, 1874), III, 451.

[19] Ball and Venn, I, 18–19. Plume recorded (p. vi) that Hacket's tutor was a "Dr. *Simson,* that wrote the *Church History.*"

[20] Trinity College Admissions and Admonitions, 1560–1759.

[21] *The Fairfax Correspondence,* ed. George W. Johnson (2 vols.; London: Richard Bentley, 1848). See *Works,* p. xxvi, and Joseph H. Summers, *George Herbert: His Religion and Art* (London: Chatto and Windus, 1954), pp. 33, 208. Johnson quotes the passage I refer to in I, 64–65: "Mr. Henry Fairfax . . . was Fellow of the College at the same time that Mr. George Herbert, of the same college, was Orator of the University, with whom he was familiarly acquainted: their dispositions were much alike, and both very exemplary for learning and piety." Ball and Venn note (II, 216) that Fairfax became Master of Arts in 1616. By the time John Scott drew up his Cambridge records ("Tables"), dated 10 April 1619, Fairfax was no longer listed among the fellows of Trinity; or so it would appear from the transcript of the "Tables" made by Thomas Hull in "The Foundation of the University of Cambridge," a manuscript volume in my possession.

century.[22] Both as student and as fellow, Herbert would follow the tradition of the time. The foundation had already been well laid in his school; and Herbert continued to achieve academic distinction at Cambridge as he had already done at Westminster. His studies emphasized what we now call humane letters—the humanities and the liberal arts—but he obviously had some knowledge of the science of his time as well.

Academic Achievement

During the years since 1601, when Gorse recorded the only specific references to his schoolbooks, Herbert had advanced commendably in his studies. His election at Westminster in 1608 to one of the three scholarships at Trinity is one evidence of his attainment. His academic career at Cambridge is certainly another. Although the assessment here must be based only on such external facts as his proceeding to degrees and his ranking in the *Ordo Senioritatis,* it is clear that he earned his reputation as a scholar. In the year he proceeded Bachelor of Arts, 1612/13, there were 193 bachelors in all. In the *Ordo Senioritatis,* which ranks the first twenty, Herbert stands second and Hacket sixth among those named; their Westminster classmate Walsingham Shirley stands eighteenth.[23] Three years later, when Herbert and Hacket proceeded Master of Arts, Herbert ranked ninth and Hacket eleventh.[24]

It is not surprising to find both men becoming sublectors at Trinity in due time. (The system of lectures within the college operated through a head lecturer [Lector Primarius], assisted by four sublectors, elected for one-year terms, in Greek, Latin, mathematics, and Greek grammar.) But they first were sworn

[22] The best treatment of the curriculum of the day is found in the second volume of Fletcher's *Intellectual Development of John Milton.* Herbert's education at Westminster and at Trinity is the subject of Donald A. Lawniczak's "George Herbert and His Classmates at Cambridge, 1609–1628" (Ph.D. dissertation, Kent State University, 1967).

[23] After this ranking the other bachelors are grouped by colleges. The *Ordo Senioritatis* was originally an order of academic precedence; see John Venn, Introduction to *Grace Book* Δ (Cambridge: University Press, 1910), especially pp. viii–x; and J. R. Tanner, ed., *The Historical Register of the University of Cambridge . . . to the Year 1910* (Cambridge: University Press, 1917), p. 396, as well as Grace Book E, 1590–1620, p. 181, Cambridge University Archives.

[24] Grace Book E, p. 240.

minor fellows (3 October 1614) and then major fellows (15 March 1615/16). On 2 October 1617 Herbert wrote in the college records, "Georgius Herbert sublector quartae classis iuratus," and on the following line Hacket wrote, "Johannes Hacket praelector tertiae classis iuratus."[25]

No other record of Herbert's academic achievement or of his responsibilities within the college is now known. Although one of the Senior Bursar's Accounts in Book D (1616) begins "Liber Herbert," it is unlikely that Herbert ever held the office; the senior bursar at the time was probably William Whewell, Francis Martin, or Thomas Whalley.

Letters from Cambridge

Beyond the record of these external facts of Herbert's progress, however, the years at Cambridge are important for what his Cambridge letters reflect of his attitudes, interests, and development. Nowhere else do we have such immediate evidence of what the young Herbert was like. Of his nineteen extant English letters, ten were written from Cambridge between 1610 and 1622, and an eleventh when he was in London during Christmas of 1618. (All the later extant letters were written from Bemerton.)

The first and the last Cambridge letters were written to his mother. In the first, of which Walton transcribed only a fragment, we catch a glimpse of the young student and poet, taking himself very seriously, scorning secular poetry, dedicating his verses to God: "For my own part, my meaning (*dear Mother*) is in these Sonnets, to declare my resolution to be, that my poor Abilities in *Poetry,* shall be all, and ever consecrated to Gods glory."[26] In contrast, in the letter of 29 May 1622 we find the mature, sober scholar, full of words of Christian consolation for his mother in her illness. During the intervening years he had developed not only in secular and in sacred knowledge, but simply through various experiences—of ill health, of afflictions temporal and spiritual, of the knowledge of God on which he bases so many of his comfortable words. It is a letter that shows some of Herbert's habits as a rhetorician, especially in its

[25] Trinity College Admissions and Admonitions, 1560–1759.
[26] *Works,* p. 363.

dividing and partitioning of his topic (as we see later in his contrast between inclining and restraining grace, in the letter to Arthur Woodnoth),[27] its juxtaposition of "earthly Troubles" and "heavenly Joyes," of "Earthly preferment, and . . . Heavenly," its enumeration of the types of affliction.

In this letter Herbert was obviously working very hard not only to comfort his mother, but to raise her spirits. He is honest and open in recognizing that her death may ensue, and he does not dodge the issue. One of his most revealing statements emerges in this candid acknowledgment: "For my self, *dear Mother,* I alwaies fear'd sickness more then death, because sickness hath made me unable to perform those Offices for which I came into the world, and must yet be kept in it."[28] (Herbert himself had been gravely ill in February of 1622.) Throughout the letter he anticipates her discouragement in sickness and refuses to let her succumb to it, insisting that she be of good cheer, casting all her care on the Lord, rejoicing even in the face of affliction.

Despite the care for his mother's welfare apparent throughout the letter, Herbert is almost formal in his courtesy to her, beginning with an unadorned "Madam" and closing with "Your obedient Son." In the course of the letter he calls her *"Madam"* or *"Dear Madam,"* only once *"dear Mother."* This habit of courteous restraint runs through all the Cambridge letters; "Sir" or "Brother" is the salutation in all the others save the one to his sister Elizabeth, which begins "Most dear Sister." Only in one of the letters to Nicholas Ferrar is there a salutation to match this in warmth: "My exceeding Dear Brother."[29] But respect, love, and concern for friends and family are present in all his letters.

That any of Herbert's letters have survived is really most surprising. Edward Herbert's correspondence as ambassador and numerous papers of Henry Herbert have been preserved by their descendants; but George Herbert had no descendants, and his papers are supposed to have been burned at Highnam House during the Civil War. That any remained, therefore, even at Walton's time of writing, is remarkable; and the other Herbert letters transcribed and published by Rebecca Warner in *Epistolary Curiosities* in 1818 exemplify what is probably true

[27] Ibid., p. 381. [28] Ibid., p. 373. [29] Ibid., p. 378.

of all these letters, that each was preserved because its recipient cherished it. Dozens of other letters have perished without trace; each of these nineteen recommended itself to its recipient's care for a special reason.

The six letters Herbert wrote to Sir John Danvers are a case in point. The young man who had become Herbert's stepfather early in 1609 had obviously become his good friend as well, and at times his champion: this much is clear from the letters Herbert wrote him from Cambridge. In point of fact, Danvers was the only father that Herbert ever knew, and these letters attest the extent of Herbert's trust (as surely as does his will, of which he made Danvers overseer). In them he expresses himself variously, but with as great candor as he ever used to any other human being.

Because Danvers was not related to him by blood, Herbert could speak more directly to him than he might perhaps have spoken to his family (ordinarily called "friends"). There was sufficient distance that he might without offense write freely; but there is an air of dignity and respect even when Herbert is urging that his annuity be doubled or explaining the attractions of the oratorship.

The first, undated letter to Danvers is a graceful note of thanks for the recent gift of a horse. No doubt both Danvers and his young stepsons had been trained in horsemanship from their earliest years,[30] and the gift of a fine horse was both a natural choice (in an age when good horsemanship was requisite) and a generous response to Herbert's request. Henry Johnes, husband of Herbert's sister Elizabeth, wrote Sir Henry Herbert on 27 February 1633/34 offering such a gift for young William Herbert, then nearing his eighth birthday: "I would desire to knowe how my cozen, William Herbert, your sonne, is. If he be ready for the riding of a horse, I will provide him with a Welch nagg, that shal be as mettlesome as himselfe."[31] The horse that George Herbert received from Danvers was

[30] Note the references to riding the great horse in *The Country Parson* (*Works*, p. 277) and in *Life*, pp. 45, 47.

[31] Rebecca Warner, ed., *Epistolary Curiosities: Series the First* (Bath: Richard Cruttwell, 1818), p. 19.

"every way fit for me"[32]—suited to the *manage* Herbert had been taught.

Canon Hutchinson assigns a date of 1617/18 to this letter on the basis that the seond letter, which mentions riding to Newmarket, bears the date 1617/18. But Herbert could have ridden to Newmarket whether or not he kept a horse of his own: in the seventeenth century, all land travel was on foot or by horse; and Hobson, after all, was close by. Perhaps a better basis for dating this letter would be that it is the only one of the six that stresses Herbert's obedience to his stepfather: "And therefore let it be sufficient for me, that the same heart, which you have won long since, is still true to you, and hath nothing else to answer your infinite kindnesses, but a constancy of obedience" and the complimentary close "Your most obedient Servant." (Only in the second letter to his mother do we elsewhere find this adjective: "Your most obedient Son.") In the later letters to Danvers, Herbert was "faithfullest," "humblest," "extreme," and "readiest"—but not again "obedient." And though he is courteous in all the letters, in the other five it is more the tone of one adult writing to another, even when Herbert is asking Danvers to speak in his behalf. The matter of the date of Letter II cannot be settled now; but probably an earlier date is more likely than that of 1617/18, when Herbert was a lecturer at Trinity and had begun his study of divinity.

The dating of Letter V is also problematical, and the date of 1618 assigned to it probably too late. That Henry Herbert was in Paris in 1618 is not adequate reason: Henry Herbert had been in Paris at least as early as 1615, perhaps 1614, and his presence there in 1618 in itself establishes nothing about the date of Letter V. Better evidence for a later date exists in the presence of Elizabeth Herbert Johnes in the Danvers household and in Herbert's remark "after I have enter'd into a Benefice."[33] If the brother mentioned in the second postscript is Edward, the date may be late 1616 or early 1617, when Edward returned from an extended tour of the Continent.

In content, the letter to his kinsman Harley, written at the behest of Danvers, is like many of the newsletters of the day—a

[32] *Works*, p. 364.

[33] See note 41 below about the dating of *W*.

miscellany as varied and chatty as those of John Chamberlain or Joseph Mead. Aside from showing something of Herbert's English syntax when he wrote in haste, it is of interest for two reasons, the place from which it was written and the address (not transcribed in the Hutchinson edition). That it was written from Charing Cross on Boxing Day, 1618, makes clear that Lady Danvers did not give up residence at Charing Cross when she remarried, but that she and her husband continued to use both this house and Sir John's, probably seasonally except when (as in 1625) the house at Chelsea served for an extended period as a welcome haven from the plague.

This letter and the one to Arthur Woodnoth are both hastily written in Herbert's italic hand. The address of this letter, however, is written in a very different hand, a round secretary hand very much like that of the English poems in *W*, reading

To my Noble ffreind
Sr Robert Harley Knight
of the Bath at
Brompton Casle

Herbert's signature has been covered by some inept repairs to the letter, but can be read by translumination.[34] If the English poems in *W* are indeed in the hand of a copyist—an idea set forth by Grosart a century ago and thereafter accepted without question—it is interesting that Herbert took his copyist along home for Christmas.

The letters to his sister and his brother are among our most important evidence of Herbert's relations with his family. Elizabeth, nearly ten years his senior, whom he describes in other letters as "my dear sick Sister,"[35] had apparently taken a special interest in Herbert's studies, and his concern for her suggests a strong bond of affection between them. Her illness, which probably lasted even longer than the fourteen years Edward Herbert mentions and required her being in London for better medical attendance,[36] separated her from her husband and her daughters in Wales, although her son, young Henry Johnes,

[34] B.L. Loan MS. 29/202, fol. 119. I am glad to thank the Duke of Portland for permission to examine the original and to have copies made for study.

[35] *Works*, pp. 367, 371. [36] *Life*, p. 15.

was apparently with her in London for a time.[37] Herbert's concern for both her good opinion and her health is not merely perfunctory.

It is the letter to Henry Herbert, however, that merits the closest attention. George and Henry, born only fifteen months apart,[38] were particularly close, probably having shared tutors when they were at home, and continuing to share the glory and the burden of being younger brothers of Edward. The rueful postscript of this letter speaks volumes: "My brother is somewhat of the same temper, and perhaps a little more mild, but you will hardly perceive it." We do not know what the issue was, nor do we need to.

The date of this letter is uncertain, but is a matter of some importance, because the date given by Mrs. Warner and accepted by Canon Hutchinson is somebody's conjecture (perhaps that of a descendant of Sir Henry's), particularly bothersome because George's own tone of elder brother is rather overdone if we assume that a young man of twenty-five was sending all this excellent advice to a young man of twenty-four. If the chief reason for accepting Mrs. Warner's date of 1618 (which she apparently copied from the cover of the letter, not from the end of the letter itself, Herbert's usual place for the date) is that Henry Herbert was in Paris at that time, it is not sufficient, because as we have already noted, Henry Herbert is known to have been in Paris in 1615 and perhaps even earlier.[39]

Because of the postscript, this letter must be dated at a time when Edward Herbert was in England. Since he had left England early in 1614 and did not return until late 1616 or early 1617,[40] the times are limited more specifically. The letter itself is of some help. It is neither the sort of letter to send to a man who has already lived in a foreign country for several years (certainly if the writer himself has never visited the country), nor the sort of brotherly advice one sends to an adult. Expressions like "whereof I would not have you ignorant" and "mark

[37] *Works,* p. 371. See also her husband's letter in Warner, pp. 17–19.

[38] Walton is the source for the date of George Herbert's birth. The date of Henry Herbert's baptism, in the Montgomery Parish Registers, is 7 July 1594.

[39] See note 51 below. [40] Rossi, I, 212, 257, 259.

what I say," as they are used here, would probably not go down well with a man who had attained his majority and lived for several years in the French capital. The letter has much more the sound of one that would have been sent during Henry's early residence in Paris: "You live in a brave nation. . . . Bee covetous, then, of all good which you see in Frenchmen. . . . Let there be no kind of excellence which you seek not . . . have a good conceit of your wit . . . write you freely to mee in your letters." In the spring of 1614, Henry would have been nineteen; he had not been at a university (whereas George, at twenty-one, was a Bachelor of Arts already well on his way to a minor fellowship at Trinity) and had probably never before been so far from home and family. It is altogether likely that about the time this letter was written, Herbert was also composing parts of "The Church-porch."[41] It may even be that "some of those observations I have framed to myself in conversation" that Henry was to receive "by peeces" took form as stanzas of "The Church-porch."

English Verse Written at Cambridge

George Herbert was not generally known for his English poems until after his death and the subsequent publication of *The Temple* at Cambridge in 1633. From the accounts of both Walton and John Ferrar it appears that not even so close a friend as Nicholas Ferrar was aware of the existence of Herbert's English poems until Edmund Duncon was commissioned to carry them to Ferrar shortly before Herbert's death.

In the absence of any manuscript evidence of the circulation of Herbert's English poems during his lifetime, there is no ground for assuming that Bacon had read any of Herbert's English poems or that it was the English poems that led to his dedicating the translation of *Certaine Psalmes* (1625) to Herbert. Bacon's acknowledgment of Herbert's part in translating *The Advancement of Learning* into Latin refers to Herbert's fitness in "Diuinitie, and Poesie," no more; the compliment could apply to English verse or to Latin verse, published or unpublished.[42]

[41] *Works,* p. 482, where Hutchinson points to parallels between this letter and the reference in *W* to "ffrench sluttery."

[42] Ibid., p. xl.

Copies of Herbert's English poems in commonplace books at the Cambridge University Library, the Bodleian, the British Library, and the University of Edinburgh Library are all derived from printed versions. Aside from small groups of amateur musicians (particularly in Salisbury) to whom he had perhaps sung some of his English lyrics, then, Herbert was not known as a writer of English verse until the publication of *The Temple,* which must have occurred before Michaelmas of 1633.

A century after this publication the later, fuller manuscript of *The Temple* (what we now call *B*, the probable source of the edition of 1633) was deposited with other Tanner manuscripts in the Bodleian Library. Nearly a century and a half later still, the Reverend Alexander B. Grosart called attention to an earlier, shorter manuscript that had passed through the Mapletoft family (related by marriage to the Ferrars) and was ultimately deposited in Dr. Williams's Library, Gordon Square, London. (This earlier manuscript is identified as *W*.)

Both manuscripts are succinctly described by Canon Hutchinson in his excellent edition of Herbert. For the purpose of the general student, the important differences are these: *W* includes 77 poems (plus "The Dedication" and "L'Envoy"), *B*, 163 (plus these); *B* is clearly the later of the two, includes revised versions of many *W* poems, and is much more subtle in its arrangement and order. *B* was copied at Little Gidding during a short period of time from whatever original Herbert sent to Ferrar, whereas *W* had been developed over a longer period and the poems copied in according to a detailed plan that was neither chronological nor consecutive. Herbert worked intimately with *W* over a period of some years; but though he prepared the original of *B*, he never saw or handled the manuscript itself. *W* was for some years the main body of his poetry, English and Latin; *B* represents, save for the position of one poem, the final order of *The Temple.*

Grosart's rather ready assumption that the earlier manuscript was copied by an "amanuensis" is all assertion and no demonstration: Grosart did not even know Herbert's signature when he saw it, and actually reproduced a supposed autograph that the rankest amateur would have rejected; yet dislodging Grosart's assumption is a lengthy and tedious work that only those dedicated to meticulous detail will be willing to undertake or to read about. Nonetheless, I think there is good reason to suppose that Herbert himself was the copyist, using the secretary hand that he and the other Herbert sons seem to have been taught by their mother.

Whoever the copyist was, he worked with great care. Although he was an amateur scribe at best, he painstakingly fitted every line in to its allotted space; his spellings are simpler than those of the Little Gidding copyists and generally closer to what we see of Herbert's own practice in the two holograph letters in English; he has generally caught his own mistakes (whereas the Collett sisters, the probable copyists of *B*, sometimes failed to catch theirs, and dropped one irretrievable line). He worked over a period of time, as we may see in the changes in style of such letters as *c, r, e, C, p,* and *P* in the running heads and in the titles of poems; and in the middle section, "The Church," he apparently laid out the work with special care to accommodate his plan of order, working from front and back and completing his copying in the middle of the section. If Herbert was not the actual copyist, he must have worked with him far more closely than one normally does with a copyist instructed to begin at the beginning, continue to the end, and bring back the completed work.

There is little external evidence for dating Herbert's English poems, and the remarkable skill shown in many of the *W* poems limits the possibilities of establishing chronology on stylistic grounds alone. Only the New Year's sonnets of 1610 have been specifically dated; and these were assuredly not Herbert's first efforts in English verse.

Virtually nothing in *W* refers directly to contemporary events; and any attempt to assign dates to these poems therefore involves the risky exercise of considering biographical data and psychological likelihood in order to evaluate earlier assumptions about the time of their composition. George Herbert Palmer's effort to establish a chronological order for all the poems in his edition of 1905 operated more from the impressions of a lifelong and devoted student of Herbert than from evidence; moreover, it did great violence to Herbert's concept of order and of joy in the triumphant conclusion. Professor

Palmer assumed that all poems not included in the earlier manuscript were written after this volume had been compiled; that all the *W* poems were written before Herbert went to Bemerton, merely because they do not mention the priesthood; and that the focus of the *W* poems was Herbert's decision to be ordained priest.

This approach to chronology assumes a lapse of nearly twenty years between the sonnets of 1610 and the completion of the volume that supposedly records Herbert's conviction of vocation, as though a man who had written no poetry in the meantime could possibly have composed the skillful poems in *W* or developed its careful order and progression of thought. A period of concentrated writing of English verse is not likely to follow prolonged neglect of English verse. It is far more likely that most of Herbert's English poems were written before he went to Bemerton than that the major part of his composition of poetry was postponed until the busiest period of his life, amid circumstances different from all those under which he had spent his first thirty-five years. Professor Helen White noted also the time Herbert would have needed for reflection and contemplation: "Moreover, marked changes in one's way of living are not usually conducive to that high degree of concentration of the involuntary faculties of the mind that seem to be necessary for poetry, and very recent experience does not always come through to expression with the same immediacy of emotional effect as more removed feeling and imagining."[43] Surely the question asked in 1610—"Why are not *Sonnets* made of thee?"—did not wait until nearly 1630 to be taken up again, with variations, in "Who sayes that fictions onely and false hair / Become a verse?" The procrastination Herbert acknowledged was more probably a matter of submitting his will and accepting his vocation than of following his declared intention of writing devotional verse.

W, rather than being the work of a man in his thirties who had been in deacon's orders several years, is the book of a layman, probably of a much younger layman. The author of the poems in this manuscript is still seeking employment (and

[43] Helen C. White, *The Metaphysical Poets* (New York: Macmillan, 1936), p. 171.

writes two poems on the subject); the deacon would already have taken at least one important step toward finding it.[44]

The first and the third sections of *W* ("The Church-porch" and "The Church Militant," as in the later versions) are long poems of types Herbert did not again undertake. These, along with the didactic "Charmes and Knots" and at least a dozen of the sonnets, are perhaps the earliest of Herbert's extant English verses. Canon Hutchinson's judgment that "The Church Militant" is an early poem[45] seems to me entirely reasonable: its affinities with Donne's *Second Anniversarie* (1612), the tone of its references to Spain, and its sanguine prophecy of the spread of religion to America all suggest an early date. The difficulties and the declining fortunes of the Virginia Company between 1618 and 1624, when its charter was revoked, would scarcely have encouraged any steady hope on the part of Herbert's stepfather and his associates, to whom the colony represented in significant measure an effort to spread religion. The appointment of Sir Edward Herbert as ambassador to France in the spring of 1619 marks another probable terminus for composition of both long poems in that uncomplimentary strictures on the French by the ambassador's brother would not have improved relations already difficult enough to maintain.

A date at least as early as 1614 is possible for the composition of "The Church-porch." A reader first encountering this didactic poem that has tried the memories of generations of English schoolboys may well wonder to whom it was addressed. The usual answer is "a young man much like Herbert." The poem, in the same six-line stanzas as "The Dedication" offering Herbert's poetic first fruits to God, masks its didactic tone somewhat through the use of witty epigrams, many of them in the wry, astringent spirit of the *Outlandish Proverbs.* Still, the admo-

[44] Herbert may even have found, somewhat earlier than is usually supposed, what he considered suitable employment. As Canon Hutchinson has pointed out, Herbert "constantly denounces idleness" as "The great and nationall sin" (*Works,* p. 562). The word Herbert uses to describe his obligations as orator is *employment;* in the letter of May 1622 to his mother he writes: "I wish earnestly that I were again with you: and, would quickly make good my wish but that my employment does fix me here, it being now but a month to our *Commencement*" (*Works,* p. 372).

[45] *Works,* p. 476.

nitions sound more like Laertes than Polonius, even when (as Canon Hutchinson has noted)[46] the poem echoes the advice Herbert (in Letter IV) sent to his brother Henry in Paris.

For several reasons it is likely that the poem *was* addressed to Henry Herbert, the brother with whom George shared many of his interests and sympathies.[47] From the tone of the postscript to Letter IV (noted above), we may assume that they submitted with what grace they could to their lot as younger brothers of Sir Edward. (Henry's wry comment to an old friend, many years later—"His Lordship deals like an Elder brother, & the Lord forgive him"[48]—could only have been born of experience and forbearance.)

The accents of elder brother in "The Church-porch" are made more palatable in stanza after stanza in which wit echoes the delight the two younger brothers took in proverbs (an interest already mentioned that may well have been fostered by their appreciation of the French and English proverbs used for illustration in Cotgrave's *Dictionarie* of 1611, a volume they would almost inevitably have used in developing their share of the family skill in languages). Their interest continued well into their adult years, as we can see in the "outlandish" proverb George cites in Letter XII (in speaking of their joint concern for the daughters of their sister Margaret) and others used in poems, and in the more than seventy proverbs Henry copied at Ribbesford in 1637.[49]

The parallels between the reference to "ffrench sluttery" and the admonitions in Letter IV[50] support the suggestion that "The Church-porch" was written for Henry Herbert at the time of his earliest encounter with life in France. The date 1618 assigned to the letter (discussed earlier) must certainly be set aside: records published only in 1961 establish Henry's presence in Paris as early as 1615, when he had not yet reached his majority and his brother's advice would have been more palatable than it might have been three years later. Several entries in the Declared Accounts of the Treasurer of the

[46] Ibid., pp. 480, 482.

[47] Thomas, the posthumous son, is not likely to have been the brother addressed, because he had been abroad even before the siege of Juliers in 1610.

[48] Sir Henry Herbert to Richard Griffith, 12 June 1634, P.R.O. 30/53/7.

[49] N.L.W. MS. 5301 E, 6 August 1637. [50] *Works*, p. 482.

Chamber mention sums paid Henry for official duties;[51] and Henry is probably the brother referred to in the letter to Sir Edward from Danvers on 24 June 1615. Other letters had been directed to Edward at "the abbay of St. Martin in Paris where your brother is"[52] (probably the Abbey of St. Martin-des-Champs, generally known as a center of humane letters and culture, where Henry may have been sent to improve his fluency in French). Henry's imprisonment at Boulogne later that year brought forth a protest from James himself.[53]

There is good reason, then, for supposing that the first long poem in *W* was intended for Henry Herbert when he first went to France, although 1615 is the earliest date for which we now have evidence of his presence there. Letter IV, discussed earlier, makes possible an earlier conjectural date for Henry's being in Paris; and though the composition of the poem probably extended over a period of time, it is true that the remarks on "ffrench sluttery" occur late in the poem, on folio 11. (The poem ends on folio 13^{v}.) If the date of the letter falls early in 1614, then the poem may have been under way as early as 1613.[54]

Chronology is not the principle of order in *W*, any more than it is in the final version of *The Temple*. Any specific year cited for the composition of any of the poems in *W* therefore refers to only one time during which Herbert was writing one or more of these poems. "Affliction" (I), one of his most autobio-

[51] "Dramatic Records in the Declared Accounts of the Treasurer of the Chamber, 1558–1642," *Malone Society Collections*, VI (1961), 133.

[52] Sir John Danvers to Sir Edward Herbert, 24 June 1615, N.L.W. MS. 314a.

[53] James I to Louis XIII, 25 August 1615, P.R.O. 78/63. See also Sir Ralph Winwood's letter of 8 September 1615 in B.L. Stowe MS. 175, fol. 343.

[54] Hutchinson has remarked (*Works*, p. 477) the similarity of Herbert's "dressing, mistressing, and complement" ("The Church-porch," l. 80) and Donne's "dressing, Mistressing and complement" (in "To Mr. Tilman after he had taken orders," *The Divine Poems*, ed. Helen Gardner [Oxford: Clarendon Press, 1952], pp. 32–33, 101). The question of whether Donne borrowed from Herbert or Herbert borrowed from Donne cannot now be settled conclusively, and the line therefore cannot be used in the dating of Herbert's poem. Donne, whom Herbert had known for some years, was in Cambridge early in 1615 and might well have seen some of Herbert's poems at that time. The title of Donne's poem says only when it was sent to Tilman, not that it was written for him or when it was composed. Herbert used two of these terms again in *The Country Parson* (*Works*, p. 277).

graphical poems, may have been composed about 1617: a close examination shows a remarkable number of parallels with Herbert's state and experience during the years 1616 to 1618. Were it not found in this earlier collection, it might easily be assumed to derive from experience much later in his life; indeed, Walton's paraphrase of "my friends die" has generally led to an assumption that the poem must have been written during the mid-twenties (though before Herbert became a canon of Lincoln Cathedral in July 1626).

The word "friends" at that time might be used as it is generally used today (and as Herbert used it sometimes), to refer to persons not of one's family; but it might also refer to one's kinsmen only or to a combination of kinsmen and others.[55] If Herbert here used the word as his elder brother Edward did, "my friends" meant approximately what "my folks" means in the American Middle West today—"my family" or "my relatives." Edward Herbert, writing of his sickliness in childhood, comments: "I remember this defluxion at my ears above-mentioned continued in that violence, that my friends did not think it fit to teach me so much as my alphabet until I was seven years old." In several collections of contemporary letters "friends" refers to kinsmen, as in a letter of Henry Johnes, a Carmarthenshire sheriff (probably written before 1584), urging his son's suit with a kinswoman of Sir Edward Stradling, Mistress Barbara Gamage (or Gamadge). The young man has spoken to his prospective father-in-law, "hathe obtaind his goodwill to repaire unto the gentlewoman and her frendes to talke therein; and consideringe yor interests and my la: in her to be suche (beinge yor neare kinswoman)."[56] Again, Mrs. Herbert uses "ffriendes" to refer to family in a document written about 1603.[57] Herbert himself uses it three times in such a sense in the letter to his stepfather dated 18 March 1617/18.[58]

The "friends" who died in 1617, shortly after Herbert's partial recovery of health, included at least one of his older brothers, and probably two. Magdalene Herbert Danvers *had* been

[55] *Oxford English Dictionary.* For Edward Herbert's use, see the *Life,* p. 23.

[56] John Montgomery Traherne, ed., *Stradling Correspondence* (London: Longman, Orme, Brown, Green, and Longmans, 1840), p. 164.

[57] L.M. 2014/103.

[58] *Works,* pp. 364–365.

singularly fortunate in bringing her family of ten to adulthood in that era. The first death among the younger generation was that of Margaret Herbert's husband, John Vaughan, before 16 June 1615.[59] Then Charles Herbert, fellow of New College, Oxford, the brother next elder than George, died in 1617. William Herbert died in the Low Countries, probably late in 1616 or early in 1617.[60] The loss of two brothers in their mid-twenties, one an able and courageous soldier, the other a promising scholar and something of a poet, would be enough to overwhelm a stronger young man certain of his abilities and assured about his career; George Herbert might well protest that he had recovered his health only to lose his life. The protest, rising from experience of human frailty, bereavement, and defenselessness, summarizes and assesses his life up to a certain point—something far more pervasive than disappointment of supposed "Court-hopes."

This interpretation of "friends" to mean Herbert's family is one of the main reasons for urging the year 1617 as a likely date for "Affliction" (I), but other allusions and attitudes in the poem afford strong support. The speaker, caught in academic surroundings not of his choice, repeatedly contrasts his ineffectuality with his natural inclinations and emphasizes a sense of betrayal because his present life affords no feeling of usefulness or satisfaction. The impression of ineffectuality is heightened by figures (taking the town, raising a siege) drawn from a life more active than his palliative but unrewarding servitude. By 1617 five of Herbert's brothers had distinguished themselves in military exploits or otherwise met the demands of active life with physical courage; Herbert, major fellow of Trinity and Master of Arts, now setting foot into the study of divinity, had been restrained by sickness for years, even before he wrote the sonnets of 1610, but particularly during the vacation of

[59] Sir Francis Newport to Sir Edward Herbert, 16 June 1615, P.R.O. 30/53/10.

[60] *Life*, pp. 12, 122. About this time also, Elizabeth Herbert Johnes may have fallen into the lingering sickness that lasted the rest of her life. A letter of Lady Danvers on 12 May 1615 mentions the recent birth of a son to Lady Johnes; and if Letter V, dated 1618 by Walton, belongs rightly to 1615, it may be that her decline began with this confinement (Lady Danvers to Sir Edward Herbert, 12 May 1615, P.R.O. 30/53/10).

1617, when he endured some serious illness,[61] perhaps that mentioned in stanza 5. The lack of employment decried here and in the two poems asking for use of his talents was perhaps partially satisfied by his appointment as sublector quartae classis at Trinity on 2 October 1617.[62]

Although it would be hazardous to venture further in assigning specific dates to other *W* poems, it is not likely that their composition extended over more than a few years. The long poems, the poems more obviously experimenting with visual effect, and most of the sonnets probably represent earlier poetic effort. The arrangement of the poems fits a general concept of spiritual development that, as it grew, brought about revisions in both poems and order, as well as expansion of the entire volume. When he determined the order in *W*, Herbert had settled upon certain points about man's relationship to God but had not yet experienced all the dimensions of that relationship. These circumstances support a date about the time of Herbert's "setting foot into Divinity."[63]

"Setting foot into Divinity"

Any sort of crisis and resolution in Herbert's life reflected in the poems in *W* is more likely to have been the decision to begin the study of divinity than either of the later decisions

[61] *Works*, pp. 364–365. Other parallels may be noted between "Affliction"(I) and this letter.

[62] Trinity College Admissions, 2 October 1617.

[63] *Works*, p. 364. Actually, there were two periods during Herbert's Cambridge years when he might have had the leisure, even during illness, to collect some or all of his English poems in *W*—the time between taking his bachelor's degree in 1613 and being made minor fellow at Trinity on 3 October 1614, and an even longer time between taking the master's degree in 1616 and his appointment as sublector quartae classis at Trinity on 2 October 1617. It is possible that "The Church Militant," for example, was copied into the blank book during one period, before anything else, and other poems added later. The variations in running heads suggest such a process. Evidence of Herbert's absence from hall, probably because of sickness, may be found in the Trinity College Steward's Book, 1580–1632 (which includes 1606, 1610, 1612, 1615, 1619, and 1622 only). Both Hacket and Herbert were given 12*s.* 8*d.* for the fourth quarter of 1610, probably for a period of eleven weeks after Christmas (listed under "Extracões for the Schollers"). No further such listing for Herbert occurs until the book for 1615, which mentions payment of "Extracões for the Schollers" in 1616 seven weeks for Herbert (7*s.*) in the Michaelmas term and one week (8*d.*) in the following term. By this time, however, Herbert was a major fellow of Trinity, not a scholar.

about taking holy orders. The ordination as deacon that had to precede Herbert's installation as canon at Lincoln Cathedral in July 1626 has too often been made to appear a matter of expediency, almost of last resort, after the collapse of hopes of preferment at court. There is good evidence to show that, aside from the possible interruptions of sickness, Herbert proceeded rather steadily in his study of divinity not long after he became Master of Arts and major fellow of Trinity in 1616.

The extant records mention little about Herbert from the Commencement of 1616 until he became sublector at Trinity in October 1617. It is possible that the sickness he refers to in Letter III in March 1618 ("You know I was sick last Vacation, neither am I yet recovered")[64] may have begun as early as the autumn of 1616, when Herbert apparently did not take meals in hall for a period of six weeks nor for one week in the following quarter.[65]

If Letter V, which refers to Henry Herbert's being in Paris, is dated with its predecessor, in 1615, the earliest recorded date of Henry's being there, it becomes clear that George Herbert had early expected not only to study divinity but to enter holy orders ("after I enter'd into a Benefice").[66] At twenty-four, writing to his stepfather, he stated unequivocally his intention of "setting foot into Divinity."[67] Both Letter III and Letter V should be read carefully, not only for the words but for the sense of purpose in their writer. To Danvers he wrote also of "those infinite Volumes of Divinity, which yet every day swell, and grow bigger," many of them published on the Continent, some of which Henry had managed to buy for him in Paris.[68]

The intention of studying divinity is again clearly stated in Letter VIII (6 October 1619), in the second of Herbert's letters to Danvers about Sir Francis Nethersole's support in Herbert's quest for the oratorship at Cambridge. Sir Francis, himself

[64] *Works,* p. 364.

[65] Trinity College Steward's Book, 1580–1632. This account appears to be for 1616, although the official heading reads 1615.

[66] *Works,* p. 367. [67] *Works,* pp. 364–365.

[68] *Works,* p. 365. A fair sampling of such books may be seen in the volumes from the chained library at Chirbury, many of them from the Herbert family, now deposited in the Salop County Library in Shrewsbury. See W. Wilding, "On a Library of Chained Books at Chirbury" (British Archaeological Association, 1883), pp. 394–401.

once public orator, "fears I have not fully resolved of the matter, since this place being civil may divert me too much from Divinity, at which, not without cause, he thinks, I aim; but, I have wrote him back, that this dignity, hath no such earthiness in it, but it may very well be joined with Heaven; or if it had to others, yet to me it should not, for ought I yet know; and therefore I desire him to send me a direct answer in his next letter."[69]

This passage has sometimes been interpreted as an equivocal comment upon a letter that was not itself free of equivocation. Herbert, writing of a man for whom the civil advantage of the oratorship had exceeded the academic, has gracefully avoided impugning Nethersole's actions, at the same time affirming his own impression that this place need not divert the new orator from divinity. If Herbert's reply sounds equivocal, the reason lies at least in part in the tone of Nethersole's remarks. In a letter to Danvers, who for at least eighteen months had been receiving his stepson's pleas for money for books of divinity, the wording "Divinity, at which, not without cause, he thinks, I aim" may be taken almost as a bit of rueful humor. Probably Danvers had already heard more than enough about Herbert's aim toward divinity.

Herbert's intention in his studies, then, is clearly stated at several times; and though the matter of holy orders is seldom mentioned directly, there is no reason that it should have been. The pattern for students like Herbert had been well established: fellows of Trinity who were Masters of Arts were to be ordained deacon after seven years.[70] Herbert would therefore have been expected to take orders as deacon in the spring of 1623.

Professor Novarr suggests that in Herbert's letter to his

[69] *Works*, p. 370.

[70] David Novarr, *The Making of Walton's "Lives"* (Ithaca: Cornell University Press, 1958), p. 517. Edward Herbert's dedication of the manuscript of *De veritate* to George Herbert and to William Boswell (Edward Herbert's secretary) on 15 December 1622, asking them to read it and to expunge anything they might find therein contrary to good morals and the true Catholic faith, again calls into question the view that George Herbert's goals at this time were secular. B.L. Sloane MS. 3957 is a fair copy of this work, with the title and dedication in Edward Herbert's hand. The holograph copy is at St. John's College, Cambridge.

mother, written on 29 May 1622,[71] the choice between taking orders and resigning his fellowship had been on his mind.[72] What course she had urged on her son is unclear from his response; her remark several years later that it was not for his "weak body, and empty purse, to undertake to build Churches"[73] may reflect her attitude that he had not the physical strength to carry out the duties of a deacon as he interpreted them. Nothing in the letter at hand, however, makes clear whether she had spoken of secular or sacred "Earthly preferment." That Herbert severed his long connection with Cambridge soon after her death suggests that she had been instrumental in his continuing so long in an anomalous position.

Latin Verse Written at Cambridge

Most of Herbert's extant Latin verse was written during the later years at Cambridge. The occasional poems in Latin published during his years there include two verses for his contemporary Prince Henry under the title "In Obitum Henrici Principis Walliae," in *Epicedium Cantabrigiense* . . . (1612), and a poem entitled "In obitum Serenissimae Reginae Annae," in *Lacrymae Cantabrigienses* . . . (1619).[74] Toward the end of his residence in Cambridge, however, he wrote three important groups of Latin poems, none of them published during his lifetime.

The *Musae Responsoriae,* the earliest of Herbert's four series of Latin poems, probably were among his first fruits as orator. Although Andrew Melville's verses to which these are a reply had been written as early as 1603/4, on the occasion of the Millenary Petition, they were not published until 1620. It is possible that (as Walton says) some of Melville's verses were brought into Westminster School during Herbert's days there and that he wrote some parts of his rejoinder at that time; but most (if not all) of Herbert's verses in reply were probably

[71] *Works,* pp. 372–374. [72] Novarr, pp. 518–519. [73] Walton, p. 279.

[74] Two unpublished poems to the Elector Palatine, discovered by Leicester Bradner, are mentioned near the close of Chapter 6, below. All of Herbert's Latin verse is considered in some detail by W. Hilton Kelliher in *The Latin Poetry of English Poets,* ed. J. W. Binns (London: Routledge & Kegan Paul, 1974), pp. 26–57.

written between the publication of Melville's *Anti-Tami-Cami-Categoria* in 1620 and his death in 1622. In polemics there is no point in striking after the iron has cooled.

As public orator, Herbert may well have felt called upon to defend from Puritan criticism Cambridge (and Oxford), along with the larger matter of the practices of the Church of England. Although his reply, with its triple dedication to James, Charles, and Lancelot Andrewes, could be construed as an attempt to gain royal or ecclesiastical favor, the work was not intended for the public eye and did not appear in print until many years after Herbert's death.[75]

In the *Musae Responsoriae*, as in much other Anglo-Latin verse, a poet indulges his arts of wit and rhetorical skill in a performance surprising to readers who know Herbert's English verse only. But as Professor Summers has pointed out, it is important to note how in his fourth epigram Herbert limits the topics for discussion: not holy authors, not the nature of God, but sacred rite, the "ceremonies and polity of the Church of England," as Canon Hutchinson puts it.[76] With all Herbert's display of knowledge and skill, one might easily see these verses only as a young man's immoderate indulgence at the expense of an elder; but even here, in the Latin verse so unlike Herbert's English verse, one must also note what he does not say. (To value Herbert's restraint, one need only consider, for contrast, Milton's remarks on Salmasius.) In the last poem but one Herbert expresses commendable respect for his adversary—who was, after all, a learned and highly regarded scholar. Herbert's curbing his tongue in refraining from full-scale attack on the Puritans is probably less a result of Puritan influence at Trinity than of his own natural moderation and ultimate dislike of religious controversy for its own sake.

The greatest significance to Herbert of the rites Melville had attacked is their symbolic importance. As early as the *W* version of "The H. Communion" (later rejected) he had declared his indifference whether or not Communion bread is changed (an attitude Canon Hutchinson sees as "typically Anglican");[77] and

[75] See *Works,* p. 588, for an account of the part played by William Dillingham and James Duport in this publication.

[76] Summers, pp. 55–56; *Works,* pp. 588–589.

[77] *Works,* p. 548.

both there, and in some of these Latin poems, the temptation is to dismiss Herbert's words as equivocal, facile, even glib. Joseph Summers' comment shows perceptive appreciation of Herbert's defense of Anglican practice: "Yet Herbert could afford to be witty about almost any specific rite exactly because of the nature of his belief in the ritual. He valued symbols and order for the sake of the thing symbolized and for the reasonableness of order in an ordered universe. He never defended any specific rite primarily as divinely inspired or essential to salvation, but as 'just' or beautiful or reasonable."[78] His wit preserved his balance and avoided the extremes of his opponents. Although the poems in *Musae Responsoriae* are a far cry from "Church-rents and schismes" and even further from "The British Church," in Herbert's respect for the forms and order of the Anglican use they are closer in spirit than his other Latin poems are to his English ones.

One stage of revision of the English poems in *W* may have taken place about the time Herbert was copying into it the two sets of Latin poems called *Passio discerpta* and *Lucus,* perhaps in preparation of a volume of the poems both English and Latin of Mr. George Herbert. These Latin poems, written in Herbert's italic hand, frequently employ the Greek *e* that he apparently began using during the twenties; and a number of revisions in the English poems are written in the same hand.

Herbert had been accustomed to write Latin verse at least from the time he was in the upper forms at Westminster School, but no clues to the dates of composition appear in most of these poems. *Passio discerpta,* concentrating on Christ's passion and death, may well be a Lenten exercise; if it was indeed written before the poems in *Lucus* (as its position suggests), it may have been composed during Lent of 1622 or 1623. The year 1623 is usually taken as the earliest likely date for *Lucus,* because Numbers XXVI–XXVIII refer to Urban VIII, who became Pope in August 1623.[79] The anagram "Roma" (XXV) may be the one promised in *Musae Responsoriae,* XXX, "De lupe lustri Vaticani."

Lent of 1622 is the most likely time for the composition of

[78] Summers, p. 56. [79] *Works,* p. 591.

Passio discerpta. Herbert was gravely ill during February; on 16 February Joseph Mead, writing from Christ's College, mentioned as "home news" the death of the junior proctor, Mr. Parkinson, then a few lines later remarked, "Our Orator also they say will not escape being at deaths dore."[80] Herbert's illness at this time may be inferred also from the dates of his absence from meals in hall at Trinity for twelve weeks during the quarter beginning in March, for which he was allowed 6*s.* 8*d.* weekly, according to the Steward's Book (although the total of £3 also listed does not agree with these figures). From the wording of Letter XI, written to his mother on 29 May 1622, it is clear that Herbert had not spent this time at Chelsea because of her illness, but rather had remained in Cambridge. This period of absence from meals in hall, the longest one mentioned for Herbert in the extant records at Trinity, might well have been the time for the composition of *Passio discerpta,* and even of some of the poems in *Lucus,* which has less of internal unity.

The tone of some poems in *Passio discerpta* comes closer to that of Crashaw's "Divine Epigrams" (like "On the wounds of our crucified Lord") than to the economy and restraint of most of Herbert's English verse. Some of the details were naturally evoked by the subject. (Milton abandoned his poem "The Passion" after eight stanzas, before he was well embarked on the details of Christ's suffering.) In Herbert's English poems, only in "The Sacrifice" (which after all represents a conventional type) and perhaps in "The Agonie" do we find this kind of extended exploration of Christ's suffering, such lingering on earth and gore.

Lucus, as the name suggests, is a collection of Herbert's Latin epigrams and other verses on a variety of topics, not necessarily recorded in the order of their composition. The style of these poems again is markedly different from all the varied styles of Herbert's English verse, as if he took on elements of Latin style with Latin language. Particularly in the epigrams he is brusque,

[80] B.L. Harl. MS. 389, fol. 116^{v}. Hutchinson (*Works,* p. 582) supposes that this passage refers to Herbert's predecessor, Sir Francis Nethersole; but Mead's next letter, of 23 February, makes the distinction of "once our Orator" in referring to Nethersole.

taunting, truculent, pointedly witty, displaying his learning in a way seldom even suggested in the English verse. Here he rarely strikes the note of quiet assertion, balance, and "grave livelinesse" whose strength often lies in what is left unsaid.

The only other poem in *Lucus* that suggests a date of composition is Number XXXII, "Triumphus Mortis," with ironic comments about war that could well have been written at the time Herbert was preparing the oration he delivered before Prince Charles at Great St. Mary's on the afternoon of 8 October 1623. In it Herbert forsook the usual sort of empty conventional compliment that the orator was expected to offer and directed his remarks instead to Charles's return from Spain as an augury of peace, praising Charles for having sought peace at the danger of his own life. The most remarkable passages in the poem are those urging the benefits of peace by juxtaposing the ways of peace with those of war.[81] Since the tenor of these passages is in keeping with the basic irony of "Triumphus Mortis"[82]—that through war, death becomes the victor over life—it is possible that poem and oration were written within a short time of each other.

Official Posts

During his later years in Cambridge, at the same time he was reading divinity, Herbert held several official posts in the college and in the university that may have satisfied some of his longing for employment.

Herbert's income increased (as we shall see later) as his academic responsibilities increased; even the incomplete extant records show that when Herbert was fellow (and tutor) and sublector at Trinity, and praelector and orator in the university, his penury was somewhat lessened and he could more readily lay out money for books without having to fast as a result. But though he may have had funds more nearly answerable to his expenses, he had less time than ever to do all he

[81] *Works,* pp. 446–448, 601–602.

[82] Another version of this poem, called *Inventa bellica,* was first published by William Pickering. A manuscript of *Inventa bellica* (Mun. A. 3. 48), found in Chetham's Library, Manchester, is described by G. M. Story in "George Herbert's *Inventa Bellica:* A New Manuscript," *Modern Philology,* LIX (May 1962), 270–272.

wanted to do: the refrain in most of his letters is the demands on his time.

Within his college Herbert carried whatever responsibilities his fellowship entailed, almost certainly serving each year as tutor to several of the students.[83] His skill in performing these duties may be inferred from his selection as one of the four lectors domestic in October 1617.[84] The following year he became the praelector in rhetoric in the university, and in 1620 the public orator.

In the absence of any Trinity College lists of tutors and pupils of this period, we may draw some likely parallels about Herbert's work as tutor with that of his friend John Hacket, whose schooling and early career often parallel Herbert's. A series of eleven letters from Hacket to Robert Hobart, "at the seale office in Falcon allie ouer against St Dunstans," records a variety of the concerns a tutor of the time might be expected to show for a pupil. These letters about Hobart's ward and nephew John Hobart were written during a period of two and a half years, beginning on 3 March 1618/19,[85] when young Hobart apparently entered Trinity and almost immediately fell into the serious illness that his tutor was ultimately to attribute to overindulgence of a particular sort: "The first occasion of his sickness is now reuealed by his one confession. He ouercharged his stomach wth a bag pudding eleuen daies since and took a surfet, I would to God He had disclosed that secret sooner."[86]

After John Hobart's removal to recover at the home of another uncle, Edward Hobart of Langley, Norfolk, his tutor, freed of the burden of making arrangements with apothecary

[83] If A. G. Hyde's estimate of 400 students at Trinity at this time is right (*George Herbert and His Times* [New York: Putnam's; London: Methuen, 1906], p. 44), the average number of students for each of the sixty-two fellows would have been 6 or 7. John Scott's "Tables," transcribed in "The Foundation of the University of Cambridge," mention sixty fellows and 360 students in 1619 (fols. 30–31).

[84] Trinity College Admissions and Admonitions.

[85] Bodl. Tanner MSS. 283, fol. 110 (3 March 1618/19); 286, fol. 43 (10 March 1618/19), fol. 49 (12 May 1619), fol. 37 (20 June 1619), fol. 39 (8 September 1619); 74, fol. 227 (29 September 1619); 286, fol. 17 (19 October 1619), fol. 34 (5 July 1620), fol. 23 (19 July 1620); 115, fol. 206 (13 December 1620); 286, fol. 7 (10 October 1621).

[86] Bodl. Tanner MS. 283, fol. 110.

and physician, could turn his attention to the next task of providing for the expected arrival of the sons of one Lord Hobart. In the following letter Hacket gives some assessment of young Hobart's academic talents ("for his first entrance into his studies was so towardly, that I much desire He should build further upon so good a foundation") and encloses a bill for charges (including medicine) for the quarter from Lady Day to Midsummer Day.[87]

In the next letter, written nearly three months later, Hacket mentions that his pupil has taken up the study of music: "for this quarter He hath added some practise in musique, not endangering I assure you his booke care, for it is but one hower in a day, and it is a qualitie wch will bee impressed into him the better in his tender yeares." He continues about the care of his pupil's clothes: "And as yong ones vse to do, He partly outgrowes, and partly weares out his apparel apace, so that wth your leaue I must take order to haue a suit of apparel made him against Michaelmase." Lord Hobart's two sons have not yet come to Cambridge, nor let Hacket know their plans. His words imply some criticism of their delay: "if it had pleased my Lord they need not haue had there names entred into ye Colledg so soone, or had a chamber prouided for them, being there coming is so tardie."[88]

The sixth letter in the series, written on Michaelmas 1619, includes Hacket's most detailed appraisal of young Hobart's performance: "I then let you vnderstand of your nephewes entring into musick, and not onlie other good parts (whereof there is extraordinarie great hopes in him) and no hinderance. Notwithstanding the long impediment of his sickness, He is able to dispute very prettily in Logick, and made tryal of it at the last satterday, and He hath attained to a prettie tast in ye Greeke tonge. But his chiefest commendations is his diligent seruing of God, hauing not been absent once since Midsummer from the chapel and St Maries. He will bee a good example for my Lords sons against they come to Cambridg, and I would faine know the time, for Dr Richardson thinkes I deluded him in procuring a chamber of him for them."[89]

[87] Bodl. Tanner MS. 286, fol. 37.
[88] Ibid., fol. 39.
[89] Bodl. Tanner MS. 74, fol. 227.

In other letters it is clear that the tutor regularly received money to pay toward the expenses of his charge, arranged for him to visit his mother, hired a horse for him in preparation for a journey, and continued to watch over his health. By October 1619 Hacket was able to speak of John Hobart as "my best pupil your cosin."[90] In both July and December of the following year he planned to visit his pupil during the ensuing holidays "to set him forward in his studies, and to keep what is learnt from obliuion."[91]

A tutor at Trinity College in the time of Hacket and Herbert, then, might find himself brought into much greater contact with his pupil's family because of his responsibility for his health and his personal arrangements than is generally true in our day. If Hacket took such interest and performed such tasks, it is not unlikely that Herbert found himself with similar duties, both as a tutor and as a lector domestic.

In 1618 Herbert received his first appointment to a university post: he was named one of the four "Barnaby lecturers" chosen on St. Barnabas' Day (11 June) or its eve. Four of these lectureships had been established by Sir Robert Rede, in mathematics, philosophy, rhetoric, and logic. Herbert's particular responsibility was to lecture in English on classical authors—"for the special benefit of first-year students," says Hutchinson.[92]

Two contemporary records refer to Herbert as a university lecturer—a student's comment by young Simonds D'Ewes and a colleague's remark by John Hacket, both of them favorable. D'Ewes, an avid student at St. John's who would hurry to Great St. Mary's to listen for a full day to the disputations and orations at Commencement,[93] writes of two lecturers who impressed him especially: "Nor was my increase in knowledge small, which I attained by the ear as well as by the eye, by being present at the public commencements, at Mr. Downes his public Greek lectures, and Mr. Harbert's public rhetoric lectures in the University."[94]

[90] Bodl. Tanner MS. 286, fol. 17.
[91] Bodl. Tanner MSS. 286, fol. 23; 115, fol. 206.
[92] *Works,* p. xxvii; Tanner, *Historical Register,* p. 183.
[93] D'Ewes, I, 145, 218.
[94] Ibid., I, 121; B.L. Harl. MS. 646, fol. 42.

John Hacket's remarks about Herbert's using one of the King's speeches for analysis when he was lecturer in rhetoric have usually been quoted in part and out of context. Hacket, who probably knew Herbert better than anyone else at Cambridge did, intended praise, not blame. Particularly, of course, he meant to praise the ability of King James as a speaker. In writing about James's address to both houses of Parliament when they convened in 1624, Hacket described the King's speech, remarking on Herbert in an aside intended to compliment both James and Herbert:

his Majesty Feasted them with a Speech, then which nothing could be apter for the Subject, or more Eloquent for the matter. All the helps of that Faculty were extreamly perfect in him, abounding in Wit by Nature, in Art by Education, in Wisdom by Experience. Mr. *George Herbert* being Praelector in the Rhetorique School in *Cambridg anno* 1618. Pass'd by those fluent Orators, that Domineered in the Pulpits of *Athens* and *Rome,* and insisted to Read upon an Oration of King *James,* which he Analysed, shew'd the concinnity of the Parts, the propriety of the Phrase, the height and Power of it to move Affections, the Style utterly unknown to the Ancients, who could not conceive what Kingly Eloquence was, in respect of which, those noted Demagogi were but Hirelings, and Triobulary Rhetoricians. The Speech which was had at the opening of this Parliament; doth commend Mr. *Herbet* [sic] for his Censure: Which yet I Engross not here; for the Reader that is Conversant in Books will find it often Printed.[95]

Herbert fulfilled some of the duties of orator even before 21 October 1619, when he was named deputy to Sir Francis Nethersole, who at the same time was granted leave to go abroad on the King's business.[96] When the Earl of Buckingham was created marquis on 1 January 1618, it was Herbert who wrote the official letter of congratulation.[97] Eighteen months later he wrote to Sir Robert Naunton, a former orator and now a secretary of state, to accept his help in protecting the Cam if the Bedford fens were to be drained.[98] In the same letter to Danvers in which he first mentions the oratorship, he tells of a Latin oration of an hour's length that he is to make "presently

[95] Hacket, I, 175. Note that the misprint "*Herbet*" is corrected in the ERRATA, II, 231.

[96] Grace Book E, p. 310. [97] *Works,* p. 604. [98] Ibid., pp. 456–457.

after *Michaelmas.*"[99] Such experience must have made him a natural choice for the post of deputy in Nethersole's absence.

From the first he had the support of the master of his own college for the permanent appointment, and he actively sought the support of his predecessor[100] and of his stepfather, even as he protested, "I hope I shall get this place without all your *London* helps, of which I am very proud, not but that I joy in your favours, but that you may see, that if all fail, yet I am able to stand on mine own legs."[101]

Whether Herbert conceived of the orator's duty when he first came to the office in the terms he later used to instruct Robert Creighton as his successor is doubtful. When he wrote to his stepfather about the prospects, his emphasis was rather different: he stressed the "commodiousness . . . beyond the Revenue," the public orations to royalty, the place above the proctors and next to the doctors, setting it all forth with keen expectation and ingenuousness.[102] He continued the impression of great enthusiasm for the outward trappings of the oratorship in a second letter written shortly thereafter.[103] A third letter to Danvers shows that Herbert, caught up in his own busyness, had apparently begun to feel some assurance about being elected. But he undoubtedly "worked the heads" (to use his own phrase) and had his way, since he was elected orator in the Senate meeting on 21 January 1619/20.

When we come to read the letters Herbert wrote as orator, however, the question naturally arises whether politic servitude did not quickly pall. Using the language of encomium and compliment expected in such official correspondence must rather shortly have become mere performance of duty. In all the Epistolae Herbert strikes few notes that are anything but

[99] Ibid., p. 369.

[100] Herbert and Nethersole were obviously good friends. In this same letter Herbert writes of him, "He and I are ancient acquaintance, and I have a strong opinion of him, that if he can do me a courtesie, he will of himself." When Nethersole wrote to introduce himself to Edward Herbert the following July, he referred to his friendship with both Henry and George Herbert: "Your Lo: brother Mr Henry Herbert my much esteemed friende hath made me beleave that you are pleased to accept my ancient line to him, and you brother Mr George Herbert in as good part that I may have to professe my selfe yo[r] Lo. Seruant also" (P.R.O. 30/53/3).

[101] *Works,* p. 370. [102] Ibid., pp. 369–370. [103] Ibid., pp. 370–371.

conventional courtesy. (The admission to Bacon of the inadequacy of the Cambridge library and the unquestionably more personal tone of the letter to Bishop Andrewes are the notable exceptions among the Cambridge Latin letters; but of course the letter to Andrewes was no part of Herbert's public duty.)

The surviving letters and orations represent only a fraction of Herbert's whole effort. The letters date mostly from the seventeen months between May 1620 and October 1621;[104] the three orations were crammed into less than eight months in 1623.[105] These representatives, however, probably provide a fair gauge of what was expected of the orator and of the limits placed on the office by tradition: official thanks for favors past or pending, artful flattery, and formal academic compliment. On the whole, the letters and the first two orations are good demonstrations of the advice Herbert later gave Creighton—to think of Alma Mater as a sober and respected matron; to recognize the proper standing of the university; to write for the university, not for oneself; to restrain the display of learning in one's letters.[106]

But in the third oration Herbert allowed himself to speak much more freely and at greater length than in the letters and the other orations, especially in his vigorous championship of the cause of peace. After the expected compliment of Charles, just returned brideless from Spain, Herbert contrived to weave into the praise of that young man a supposed desire of the Prince's for peace. In full knowledge that Charles and Buckingham had returned home determined on war, Herbert courageously extolled the blessings of peace. However impolitic his words, he had good reason to oppose the sort of professional soldiering that had cost the lives of his brothers William and Richard; and he spoke memorably on that October day in a gathering of subjects overjoyed that the Spanish alliance would not develop.

[104] Orator's Book, Cambridge University Archives.

[105] A note in B.L. Harl. MS 7041, fol. 38^{v}, tells a little about the circumstances under which Herbert gave the second oration before King James, on 12 March 1622/23: "but his majesty was pleased to stay there, while the orator Mr Herbert did make a short Farewell Speech unto him. Then he called for a copy of the vicechan^{s}: Speech, & likewise for an epigram the orator made."

[106] *Works,* pp. 470–471.

Herbert's Financial Status at Cambridge

One of the problems that Herbert faced at Cambridge (and indeed for most of his life) was a shortage of funds. Aside from the stipends paid him at Trinity, and later from university sources, his sole income was the thirty-pound annuity allowed him in 1603 by his brother Edward,[107] an amount that was not always readily forthcoming.[108] From Herbert's remarks to his stepfather in Letter V,[109] we realize, however, that his family considered this amount entirely sufficient to meet his needs. In this particular letter Herbert was repeating his request ("yet I had rather fly to my old ward") that his annuity be doubled at his time of need to help him toward the point where he might take a benefice, when he would "surcease all title to it." (In the light of his later remark to Henry, in Letter XII[110]—"the best-bred child hath the best portion"—the idea is not at all inconsistent with his notions about the care of his nieces in their formative years.)

Whether a student's allowance is sufficient to his needs is a matter on which opinion will always vary. Herbert obviously thought that thirty pounds was insufficient to meet his expenses when he was on the point of entering the study of divinity and buying the many and expensive books he found essential. A few years earlier, young Robert Wynn's tutor, a Mr. Holt, had written that "the expenses of a young gentleman living in very good sort are £20 per annum."[111] Yet the expectations of tutor and of pupil might understandably vary. Not much later (in 1618) young Simonds D'Ewes of St. John's, receiving an allowance of fifty pounds, considered that he needed sixty instead.[112]

From Herbert's Letter III to Sir John Danvers it is clear that

[107] L.M. 2014/103.

[108] Magdalene Danvers to Sir Edward Herbert, 12 May 1615, P.R.O. 30/53/10.

[109] *Works*, pp. 366–367. [110] Ibid., pp. 375–376.

[111] *Wynn Papers*, p. 481, quoted by B. Dew Roberts, *Mitre and Musket: John Williams, Lord Keeper, Archbishop of York, 1582–1650* (London: Oxford University Press, 1938), p. 16. Robert Wynn, however, was still an undergraduate, not undertaking the study of divinity.

[112] John Howard Marsden, *College Life in the Time of James the First, as Illustrated by an Unpublished Diary of Sir Symonds d'Ewes, Baronet and M.P.* (London: John W. Parker and Son, 1851), p. 16.

his poor health increased the demands on his funds, both for special diet in his rooms (two days a week normally, and even more during Lent) and for the cost of a few days now and then at Newmarket for a change of air from that of Cambridge.[113]

What additional money came to Herbert through Trinity College and later through the university? The bursars' accounts that survive list payments of 3*s.* 4*d.* quarterly (or one mark yearly) from the third quarter of 1609 through the fourth quarter of 1614.[114] In 1613, when Herbert became a Bachelor of Arts, the payment rose to 10*s.* quarterly (£2 yearly). The following year, when he proceeded Master of Arts, the payments rose again, to one mark quarterly (£2 13*s.* 4*d.* yearly). As a lector domestic he received £2 13*s.* 4*d.* yearly. In addition to the usual quarterly payments of 13*s.* 4*d.* he received in 1618 and after, along with the other masters and scholars, he was given a special single payment (designated "liberat") of 33*s.* 4*d.* His total income from college sources at that time rose to £7 for the year.

Herbert's official stipend as orator, paid from university funds, was £4 yearly, but it included provision for the payment of special fees to the orator.[115] Throughout Herbert's tenure the stipend was paid in two parts ("Pro dimidio stipendii"); shortly after he relinquished the post, however, the account for the year ending at Michaelmas 1629 shows a change in this practice: the entry for the orator's stipend reads, "Pro integro stipendio Oratoris," the entire £4 being paid at one time.

It is hard to estimate the additional revenue Herbert may have received; he himself expected that the oratorship would bring about £30 a year.[116] A grace passed by the Senate on 17 February 1613/14, for example, required that everyone who should be admitted to answer the questions or to incept in Arts

[113] *Works,* pp. 364–365.

[114] Trinity College records generally begin each year near Lady Day and fall by quarters thereafter. Records for 1611, 1613, 1617, 1619, and 1620 are lacking. Payment to Herbert and to Hacket is identical throughout the extant bursars' records.

[115] University Audit Book, 1545–1659, pp. 480, 481, 482, 488, 490, 501, 502, 508, 517, 525, 526, 533, 535, 543, 548, 550, 556, 557, 564, 565, 574, 585, 591, Cambridge University Archives.

[116] *Works,* p. 369.

was to pay the orator 12*d.* in addition to fees formerly charged.[117] Fees paid the orator for the writing of special letters might vary considerably: when, between Michaelmas 1617 and Michaelmas 1618, the orator was paid for writing letters "to my Ld Chancellor, Ld Marquesse, & Sr Robert Nanton," the amount allowed was 20*s.;* but "for wrighting the Letters to my Ld. Chauncello^r^" only a short time later, the fee was a mere 2*s.* 6*d.*[118] Such sums would not quickly make up the £26 above the stipend that Herbert anticipated.

In the light of figures like these, it is clear that Herbert's major source of income during the first eleven years at Cambridge continued to be the annuity allowed by his elder brother and that the outlay cited in Letter III of four or five shillings for a book, and sometimes as much as ten shillings,[119] represented rather a staggering onslaught on Herbert's slender means. Even the annuity amounted to only £2 10*s.* monthly. We may readily understand Herbert's gratitude for any help given him under such circumstances in gathering the books he needed for his studies. The aid of his brother Henry and the possibility of his sister Elizabeth's paying the cost of some books must have been particularly welcome. Books garnered with such help are treasured especially, as every student knows: Herbert's concern for "those infinite Volumes of Divinity"[120] is perhaps therefore additional evidence of his seriousness of purpose at the time he was beginning to lay the platform of his future life.

[117] C. H. Cooper, *Annals of Cambridge* (Cambridge: Warwick, 1842–1908), III, 60. See also II, 446; and *Stat. Acad. Camb.,* p. 372 (cited by Cooper).

[118] University Audit Book, pp. 481, 482.

[119] *Works,* p. 365. [120] Ibid., p. 364.

CHAPTER 4

Westminster and Chelsea (1624–1628)

Herbert in Parliament

Save for the unresolved matter of his taking orders as deacon, Herbert might well have continued in the familiar round at Cambridge. His decision to leave there—probably, as he then understood it, for a limited time that might afford him objectivity and perspective—may have resulted from any one of several causes, or from a combination of them. Cambridge was possibly the worst place he could have chosen to live, and his duties there did not normally allow enough time anywhere else for him to restore his health. The question of taking orders and all its implications about his spiritual state, his readiness, and his future life could not ever have been far from his thoughts. After the death of his brother Richard in 1622, when Edward and Henry were both in France, George was not only the eldest son of the family left in England, but quite possibly the only one; and his mother's uncertain health, along with her responsibility as coguardian (with Edward) of the young daughters of Margaret Herbert Vaughan, may have convinced him that his responsibilities to the family could better be carried out in London than in Cambridge. Probably one or more of these considerations influenced Herbert's decision to stand for the family seat of Montgomery borough when the writs were issued for a new Parliament late in 1623/24.

By this time it is unlikely that Herbert cherished many of the "Court-hopes" Walton ascribes to him. His impassioned plea for peace in the oration before Prince Charles a few months earlier could not build a road to favor with a mettlesome young prince bent on waging war. As public orator at Cambridge

. The Parliament of 1624. From British Library Harl. MS. 159, fol. 4. Reproduced by
rmission of the British Library Board.

Herbert knew what sort of compliment and what deference to royalty were expected of him, as surely as he must have realized that his remarks had burned an essential bridge to any future favor at court.

Walton gives the impression that it was the deaths of Herbert's supposed patrons, the Duke of Lennox (on 16 February 1623/24), the Marquis of Hamilton (on 2 March 1624/25), and the King (on 27 March 1625), that led to the failure of his "Court-hopes";[1] but it is likely that Herbert entertained no such hopes even at the time he consented to stand for the seat that had been held in 1614 by his stepfather and would be held by his brother Henry in 1626. His career in Parliament appears rather to have been a time of transition for him, at the end of which he requested a leave of absence from Cambridge. He did not return to academic life, although he continued to hold the post of orator until 1628.

On 28 December 1623/24 King James had ordered John Williams, the Lord Keeper, to send out writs for a new Parliament.[2] The Parliament of 1623/24 was summoned to meet on Thursday, 12 February; and on that day 250 members were sworn. On the following Monday, 100 more were sworn before word was received of the death of the Duke of Lennox, the Lord High Steward. The Parliament was therefore postponed, actually convening instead on Thursday, 19 February.[3]

Sir William Herbert, knight, had been chosen to represent the county of Montgomery and George Herbert, gentleman, to represent the borough.[4] Whereas in James's first Parliament young Edward Herbert, who sat for Merioneth, had served on

[1] Walton, p. 276.

[2] John Hacket, *Scrinia Reserata: A Memorial Offer'd to the Great Deservings of John Williams, D.D.* . . . (In the Savoy: Printed by Edw. Jones for Samuel Lowndes, 1693), I, 173.

[3] For the complete account of this session, see *Journals of the House of Commons,* I, 670–815.

[4] House of Commons Reports and Papers, *Members of Parliament* . . . , Part I: *Parliaments of England, 1213–1702* (London, 1878), p. 462. See also W. R. Williams, *Parliamentary History of Wales from the Earliest Times to the Present Day* (Brecknock: Edwin Davies and Bell, 1895), pp. 148–149; A. H. Dodd, "Wales's Parliamentary Apprenticeship (1536–1625)," *Transactions of the Honourable Society of the Cymmrodorion* (1942), pp. 69–70.

ten committees,[5] George Herbert served on only one, its main responsibility being to consider accusations against men who were schoolmasters or masters of colleges. During this session a schoolmaster was accused of popery; and unspecified charges against John Richardson, master of Herbert's own college, were eventually dismissed. The only charges considered by this committee that are recorded in detail are those against Dr. Anyan, of Corpus Christi College, Oxford.[6]

Whatever the reasons that had led Herbert to stand for Parliament, delusions about the glories of public office were not among them. The fall of his friend Bacon that had begun with a parliamentary inquiry in 1621 was too recent a reminder, and Herbert would have been fatuous indeed had he not gone to Westminster with his eyes open. But not all his knowledge of the workings of the university and of the King's court (and his secondhand knowledge of the world of affairs) could prepare him for what he was to observe in this one session of Parliament; and some years later he was to comment in *The Country Parson,* "no School to a Parliament."[7]

The time of Herbert's service in Parliament was one of crisis in the affairs of the Virginia Company of which Herbert could not have been ignorant when he went to Westminster. Through his stepfather, an active supporter of the company, he should have known more of its affairs than many of the shareholders themselves; and Nicholas Ferrar and various relatives of Herbert's interested in the venture probably also conveyed to him something of their growing concern over the fate of the colonies that Herbert later described as "not only a noble, but also as they may be handled, a religious imployment."[8] Because of his own idealistic view of the undertaking

[5] Dodd, p. 27. Dodd says that Edward Herbert appeared not to take his parliamentary responsibility seriously and cites an encounter of 1610, when Herbert met the Speaker on the stairs, "put not off his Hat, put out his Tongue and plopt with his Mouth" (although on 18 July he disclaimed any "Intent of Scorn").

[6] *Commons Journals,* I, 692, 707, 713, 777, 791, 793, 796. The account of the report of this committee in B.L. Harl. MS. 159, fols. 123^{v}–124, says that Dr. Richardson had been accused by a Dr. Waterhouse.

[7] *Works,* p. 277. [8] Ibid., p. 279.

(reflected earlier in "The Church Militant") and the undoubtedly strong reaction of some of those closest to him, Herbert must have been gravely troubled about the probable outcome of the struggle between the Crown and the company.

By the autumn of 1623 the members struggling to preserve the Virginia Company must have realized that their cause was doomed. Perhaps the basic reason was the widespread misunderstanding of the twofold task that the company had set out to accomplish: to establish a colony and to carry on trade with that colony, transform a wilderness into a thriving source of trade and profit. Neither the faction that centered around the former governor, Sir Thomas Smith, and supported by the Earl of Warwick, nor the faction of the Earl of Southampton, Sir Edwin Sandys, and Sir John Danvers grasped sufficiently the problems of establishing a colony. Willing hands were needed; but until the willing hands could provide shelter and sustenance, supplies had to be sent from England—clothing and food and guns and nails—not just once, but repeatedly, until the colony could begin to supply its own needs and to produce commodities for trade with the mother country. In the meantime each additional pair of hands, however willing, became merely another mouth to feed, and another body to clothe and shelter and sometimes nurse through sickness, or bury.

Investors accustomed to more ready returns on their money were not satisfied; and often those who saw in the Virginia Company the opportunity to establish a colony and to encourage the spread of religion and learning responded by sending out yet more colonists, no matter at what time of year, without sufficient supplies to carry them through until the next harvest. Despite the best of will and effort it was impossible to direct the affairs of the company in a way satisfactory to all the members. The Ferrars and their associates, who were generally in control of the company after 28 April 1619,[9] when Sir Edwin Sandys replaced Sir Thomas Smith as treasurer, worked tirelessly in the interests of the company, with John Ferrar serving as dep-

[9] Wesley Frank Craven, *The Dissolution of the Virginia Company: The Failure of a Colonial Experiment* (New York, 1932), p. 87.

uty treasurer from April 1619 until he was succeeded by his brother Nicholas on 22 May 1622.[10]

Following the great massacre in the colony on 22 March 1622, the division between factions within the company increased. James himself—influenced by Count Gondomar (or so Nicholas Ferrar's biographers have generally felt)[11]—commissioned a pamphlet by Nathaniel Butler, the former governor of Bermuda, who had visited the Virginia colony. This pamphlet, published in the spring of 1623 as *The Unmasked Face of Our Colony in Virginia,* proved to be mainly an attack upon the Sandys administration. A. L. Maycock sums up the opposition as it appeared to the Ferrars: "These three forces—the Crown, the Spanish interest and the Warwick faction—were united in an effort to destroy the Virginia Company."[12]

There had been other unmistakable indications of royal opposition. After consideration of Butler's pamphlet by the Privy Council on 10 April 1623, Nicholas Ferrar worked feverishly with Southampton, Lord William Cavendish, and Sir Edwin Sandys to draw up a reply to the council. Despite its excellence, it could not save the company from dissolution. One of the clerks of the Privy Council told Southampton: "It will avail nothing, for it is already determined that your patent is to be taken away and the Company dissolved."[13] The following week the council announced the King's intention of setting up a royal commission to consider the administration of both the Virginia colony and the Bermudas;[14] and in the subsequent inquiry, legal assistance having been denied, it was Nicholas Ferrar who appeared repeatedly before the council.

All the records of the Virginia Company were confiscated on 22 May, and at the same time the Privy Council ordered that all

[10] A.L. Maycock, *Nicholas Ferrar of Little Gidding* (London: S.P.C.K., 1938), p. 92.

[11] See, for example, [Jane F. M. Carter], *Nicholas Ferrar: His Household and His Friends,* ed. T. T. Carter (2d ed.; London: Longmans, Green, 1893), p. 64; Craven, pp. 9–12; Maycock, p. 95; and "Life of Nicholas Ferrar by Dr. Jebb," in *Nicholas Ferrar: Two Lives by His Brother John and by Dr. Jebb,* ed. J. E. B. Mayor (Cambridge: University Press, 1855), pp. 207–209.

[12] Maycock, p. 95. Butler's account is in the P.R.O. (C 01/3, No. 36).

[13] Maycock, p. 96. [14] Ibid., p. 97.

mail sent from Virginia must be delivered to the council unopened.[15] Early in October the company was asked whether it would surrender its charter and accept another instead. On 3 November a writ of quo warranto against the company was issued that in effect questioned its right to exist as a company and to conduct the business it had been conducting.[16]

When the records of the company were restored, Nicholas Ferrar, rightly anticipating that they would be confiscated a second (and final) time, supervised the copying of the court books by six clerks.[17] The originals were again confiscated in June 1624 and have not been seen since.[18] The copies, completed barely in time, were delivered to Southampton for safekeeping and passed eventually into the hands of William Byrd of Westover and are now in the Library of Congress.

Against such a background the members of the company could hardly hope to avert the dissolution; yet they tried, and came close to bringing the whole matter before the House of Commons late in May.[19] At this point, however, James intervened directly and forbade the Commons to take any action. The hundred or more members of the Virginia Company who sat in the Parliament of 1623/24 could find no way to prevent the inevitable dissolution; nevertheless, when the session drew to a close, some of them must have been keenly disappointed that their best efforts had not sufficed.

Probably Herbert's only service in Parliament was during this period extending from February through May of 1624. Although the printed returns name Herbert as burgess for Montgomery in the first Parliament of Charles I,[20] it is unlikely that he served any part of the term. Although a Mr. Herbert is mentioned as a committee member, there is no record in the *Commons Journals* for 1625 of Mr. George Herbert (a distinction

[15] Ibid., pp. 98–99. [16] Ibid., p. 99.

[17] Jebb, p. 214. These copies, now in the Library of Congress, have been published as *The Records of the Virginia Company of London,* ed. Susan Myra Kingsbury (Washington; Vols. I, II, 1906; III, 1933; IV, 1935).

[18] Maycock, p. 100. [19] Craven, pp. 319–322.

[20] *Members of Parliament,* p. 467. *Coll. Mont.,* II (1869), 312, however, lists one Lewis Powell as burgess for Montgomery in the Parliament of 1625. It is impossible to draw any conclusions from the original returns at the P.R.O. (C. 219/39, Part II, fol. 249), which are erratically faded and unreadable even under ultraviolet light.

carefully made in the records of the preceding Parliament). There is no reason to suppose that Herbert took part in the Parliament of 1625, despite the inclusion of his name in the printed lists of members, where it may well have appeared by default. The absence of any record after May 1624 of "Mr. Geor. Herberte" (the style typical in the records of 1623/24) strongly suggests that Herbert served only in this first session. The second session, prorogued three times,[21] never actually took place, and writs for a new Parliament were issued early in Charles's reign.

"Many businesses away"

Within two weeks of the prorogation on 29 May, Herbert was granted a grace by the Senate at Cambridge ("on account of many businesses away," as Canon Hutchinson translates it).[22] His service in Parliament had expended more than the seventy days of leave allowed the orator each year, and other responsibilities, particularly within his family, still required his being away from Cambridge. It is probable that from the time this leave was granted, on 11 June, Herbert was occupied in family business and in his own considerations about taking orders.

Any "Court-hopes" that may have existed when the session of Parliament opened had surely been dispelled before it closed. Even though Herbert might have felt satisfaction because the master of his college had been cleared of the charges brought against him, nothing could alleviate the crushing defeat of the Virginia Company in the face of royal opposition, nor the death of earlier idealistic views represented in *W:*

> Religion stands on tiptoe in our land
> Ready to pass to the American strand,
>
> . . . . .
>
> Then shal Religion to America flee:
> They have their time of Gospel euen as wee.

Chief among the "many businesses away," probably, was the responsibility for his three young nieces, daughters of his sister Margaret (the widow of John Vaughan of Llwydiarth),

[21] S. R. Gardiner, *History of England from the Accession of James I to the Outbreak of the Civil War* (rev. ed.; London: Green, 1883–1884), V, 234, 264, 306.

[22] *Works,* p. xxx.

who had died on 14 August 1623, naming her mother and her brother Edward as guardians for the girls, Dorothy, Magdalene, and Katherine. Edward Herbert at the time of her death was abroad for the second embassy to France and would not return to England for another year, and his mother in that state of imperfect health and cheer in which she spent her last years. By the spring of 1624 Lady Danvers could not have been expected to travel to Wales to make arrangements for her three granddaughters (and certainly not during the hot, dry summer that followed),[23] and Herbert's stepfather was undoubtedly caught up in the aftermath of the demise of the Virginia Company. It would not be surprising therefore if George, the eldest of the surviving younger brothers, and the one particularly close to his mother, undertook to make arrangements for the care of his nieces, the two elder at this time probably adolescents, the youngest still a child of eight at the most.

The conclusion therefore is that in the last months of 1624 Herbert was turning his back on worldly preferment, including further service in Parliament. Walton's elaborate explanation of the death of "all of Mr. *Herbert's* Court-hopes" following the death of King James in 1625 is both inaccurate and untimely: some months earlier Herbert had decided to follow the expected course after his studies in divinity and take orders in the Church. Although his service in Parliament may have represented nothing more than filling the family seat when no other male Herbert was available, the school of Parliament apparently helped Herbert to see that the lines of his life did not lie in that direction.

Deacon and Prebendary

The question of when Herbert entered holy orders has long troubled his biographers and clouded discussions of his life before July 1626, when, as a deacon, he became canon of Lincoln Cathedral and prebendary for the church of Leighton Bromswold (Leighton Ecclesia) in Huntingdonshire. The question is of some importance because, for Herbert, taking orders meant setting aside opportunity for secular advancement. Although he failed to meet the requirements of the Trinity Col-

[23] Maycock, p. 111.

lege statute by taking orders in 1623, it is now clear that he was prepared to enter orders late in 1624.

A document that has recently come to light in the Lincolnshire Archives Office shows that Herbert, not wanting to wait out the year normally required of candidates for the diaconate, had applied to the Archbishop of Canterbury for a faculty that would grant him permission to be ordained at any time by John Williams, Bishop of Lincoln.[24] Herbert made this application during his six-month leave from the oratorship at Cambridge, at a time when he must certainly have been considering his future course. Although originally he may have expected to attend the second session of Parliament (first prorogued until 3 November),[25] apparently a matter of greater importance resolved itself during his leave.

It is at this point that John Williams, now Lord Keeper, Dean of Westminster, and Bishop of Lincoln, emerges as an influential figure in Herbert's life. The first record of the part he played is the dispensation of the Archbishop of Canterbury, dated 3 November 1624, granting permission for Herbert to be ordained deacon at any time by Bishop Williams, without letters dimissory from the bishop of his own diocese.

Both provisions of this dispensation are important: without it, Herbert could not have been ordained unless he waited a full year after declaring his intention; nor could he have been ordained by Williams without this or other episcopal permission. Had it been only a matter of being ordained by Williams, then his own bishop, rather than the Archbishop of Canterbury, would have written letters dimissory for him. The matter of time must therefore have been important enough for Herbert to request this permission of the archbishop himself. Williams, it is clear, believed in adhering strictly to the require-

[24] Letters Testamentary and Dimissory, 1624/1, Lincolnshire Archives Office. I am indebted to Dr. Mary Finch, deputy archivist, who discovered this document and generously allowed me to give the first published notice of it, in "George Herbert, Deacon," *Modern Philology,* LXXI (February 1975), 272–276.

[25] As a matter of fact, the second session of this Parliament was never held. On 1 October it was postponed until 26 February 1625, then on 19 January further postponed, and finally superseded by the new Parliament called by Charles to meet on 17 May 1625. See *Members of Parliament,* p. 462; Gardiner, V, 234, 264, 306.

ment of the probationary year, as he showed in a comment in reply to the remarks of a particular prebendary of Westminster about one of the singing men: "This man was made a Deacon sooner than he ought to have beene, that is, within his yeare of probation."[26] The dispensation permitted Herbert's immediate ordination; the ordination itself would effectually end Herbert's career in Parliament and close off most routes of secular preferment—unless, like Williams, he could find a way of combining the sacred and the secular.

It is difficult always not to suspect worldliness in the churchman turned statesman—and perhaps more difficult with John Williams, who seems to have been one of the unhappy men whose motives always appear suspect to those who do not know them well. Whatever first brought them together, probably when Williams was at St. John's and Herbert at Trinity, they seem to have become good friends, certainly by the time Williams gave Herbert his first ecclesiastical preferments. Welsh origin may be a part of it, but only a part; the man who served as Lord Keeper, Dean of Sarum, Dean of Westminster, Bishop of Lincoln, and Archbishop of York knew ability when he saw it—as, for example, when he took Hacket to be his chaplain (as he himself had earlier been chosen chaplain by Sir Thomas Egerton).

Hacket's final assessment of Williams, then, is of particular interest. His account of Williams' life in *Scrinia Reserata,* written during the seven years after Williams died, concludes with this judicious evaluation:

> I need not admonish my Readers, for they find it all the way, that my Scope is not so much to insist upon the memorable things of one Man's Life; as to furnish them with reading out of my small store, that are well-willers to Learning, in Theological, Political, and Moral Knowledge. Yet in those Observations I have not set down a *Cyrus,* a feigned Subject, but wrought them into the true Image of this Prelate. . . . Some are cheated with Wit now-a-days after the *French* fashion, and had rather Men should be commended in Romances of Persons, that were never extant, than in such as lived among us, truly deserved

[26] Ivor Bowen, "John Williams of Gloddaeth," *Transactions of the Honourable Society of the Cymmrodorion* (1927–1928), p. 76.

Glory, and did us good. My Subject is real, and not umbraick; a Man of as deep and large wisdom as I did ever speak with. . . . He was constant to that Religion wherein he was catechized, and instructed in it more perfectly in *Cambridge.* A punctual observer of the ancient Church Orders, whereof he was a Governour, and a great decliner of innovations, holding to it, that what was long in use, if it were not best, it was fittest for the People. He tasted equally of great Prosperity and Adversity, and was a rare example in both . . . not elevated with Honour, nor in the contrary state cast down. His Enemies lik't nothing worse in him than his Courage, and he pleased himself in nothing more: Of a stately Presence, and a Mind suitable to it. Some call'd it Pride and Haughtiness. . . . They twitted him that he was lofty and supercilious. Underlings will never forbear to object it to Men in places of Preheminence, when there is more of it in themselves. . . . Yet I concur with others, who knew this Lord, that Choler and a high Stomach were his Faults, and the only Defects in him. And it had been better for him, if he had known a meek temper, and how to be resisted. Otherwise his Vertues were super-excellent. A great Devotee to publick and private Prayer: There did not live that Christian that hated Revenge more than he, or that would forgive an Injury sooner. Most Munificent, Liberal, Charitable above his Means, for he died in a Debt of 8000 *l.* though his Heir, Sir *Griffith Williams,* had enough in Mannors and Moveables to pay it. He loved to do things Praiseworthy. *Nulla est tanta humilitas quae dulcedine gloriae non capiatur,* Valer. lib. 8. cap. 13. Justice, Charity, Temperance, tender Bowels of Compassion, enchased all his Life and Carriage with wonderful gracefulness. His Skill in the Tongues, his Skill in the course of all Academical Arts, in all History, in all the parts of Divinity, must needs be excellent: for he had a piercing Wit, a sound Judgment, a strong Memory, and with all these concurred indefatigable Industry. Yet by the employment of a great Office, but much more by the Iniquity of troublesome Suits, Imprisonments, fatal Wars, and most of all by the embezelling of his Notes and Papers, Posterity is little beholding to his Pen; but it owes greatly to his good Works. *Et post mortem non opuscula sed opera pensanda,* Sidon. lib. ep. 8. ep. I. I will part with him now, as *Xenophon* did with *Socrates* in his apology for him. . . . That is, to a word, considering the Wisdom and Gallantry of the Man, I cannot choose but remember him, and when I remember him, I cannot but praise him. *Se quisque ut vivit & effert.* Manil. I. 2. But Praise be given to God for all his good Gifts. *Amen.*[27]

[27] Hacket, II, 229–230.

This is the considered judgment of the man who probably knew Williams best, who by the time he wrote it had passed far beyond mere youthful admiration. As a contemporary of Herbert's, Hacket was probably consulted by both Williams and Herbert; and his respect for Williams must surely have played a part in Herbert's decision to be ordained deacon and to accept the preferments that Williams could offer.

As a matter of fact, early in the second part of his work Hacket relates in some detail Williams' principles about young men wanting to be ordained and his careful examination of those he considered appointing to livings in his charge. Hacket, having already described some of Williams' other habits and practices as bishop, goes on to mention not only Herbert, but nine other Trinity men to whom Williams offered preferments:

> The Ordinations of this Bishop past thirty Years ago, are famous in the Discourse of divers yet alive, who call to mind with what Judgment they were prepar'd, and examin'd: how the Bishop preach'd himself sometimes at that Solemnity: with what due Ceremony it was done: with what Grace and Gravity: with what bounty he feasted them: with what civility he took the most into his acquaintance: That I may truly say of him as Dr. *Saravia* doth of *Samuel, de Christian. Obed.*, p. II. . . . He had [left] to be the great Magistrate, the Lord-Keeper, but he was like *Samuel,* when he had acquitted his Government, he liv'd in Estimation like the chief of the Prophets, and most belov'd of the Sons of the Prophets.
>
> . . . And if he would ordain none that were unlearned, what manner of Men were they like to be, whom he presented to Dignities and Cures upon his own Collation? It is a mighty Trust to be a Church-Patron, no less than to be a Feoffee for Christ. Which this Bishop executed with that Conscience, that neither Friends, nor Favour, nor Consanguinity sway'd him: Least of all Lucre; for he was so clear from *Simony,* and so well understood, that I think he was never tempted to it. *Castus quem nemo rogavit.* Commonly he found out such to take his Patronage, as never sought him. Such whose Worth was great, but Humility had obscur'd them. . . . His, whom he made his, were such as commended him that gave: for they were among the best that could receive. Such as deserv'd to sit at the Helm, yet some of them that survive, in these days have scarce a Room in the Pump. Let no more be named but a Handful, whom the Bishop gather'd out of one Society, *Trinity* Colledge in *Cambridge,* and guess at all by their proportion. Dr. *Simson,* the Author of the great Chronology, Dr. *Warr,* Mr. *G. Herbert,*

Dr. *Meredith,* Mr. *H. Thornedick,* Dr. *Creicton,* Dr. *Fearn,* Mr. *J. Duport,* Mr. *A. Scattergood,* Mr. *C. Williamson.* . . . Here are ten *Nestors* in one Militia, according to *Agamemnon's* Wish. These, and far more that might be rank'd in the same File, were his Donees, such as God might reap Glory by them.[28]

No surviving record tells whether Herbert returned to Cambridge at the end of his leave on 11 December, or ever again. His deputies in the oratorship, first Herbert Thorndike and later Robert Creighton, probably received his annual stipend and the fees for individual letters, inceptions, and whatever other acts they performed in his stead. Although he had been accustomed to making do on a limited income, finding himself without his accustomed academic income must have left Herbert in immediate need of funds.

Williams, who had helped bring about Herbert's ordination at this time, was in a position to present the new deacon to a portion of the rectory of Llandinam, Montgomeryshire,[29] a hamlet only a few miles from Herbert's birthplace. Herbert's grandfather had owned land and messuages there and had made a bequest of four pounds a year toward the support of a schoolmaster there.[30] The venerable church, formerly a monastic one, had been the mother church of Arwystli, and the portions survived from monastic days. As executor of the estate of Eleanor Panton, widow of John Panton, patron for the turn by arrangement with the Bishop of Bangor, Bishop Williams made Herbert comportioner of the rectory of Llandinam on 6 December 1624, just before Herbert might otherwise have returned to his duties at Cambridge. Herbert held this preferment until the end of his life.

Herbert's ordination as deacon probably took place soon after the faculty from the Archbishop of Canterbury was issued, before the end of 1624. He would therefore have been in orders nineteen or twenty months before Williams made him a canon of Lincoln Cathedral. It is also possible that his taking

[28] Ibid., II, 42. The omission of "left" is noted in the ERRATA, II, 231.

[29] H. Ince Anderton, letter to *Times Literary Supplement,* 9 March 1933. See also A. I. Pryce, *The Diocese of Bangor in the Sixteenth Century* (1923), pp. 41, 43, and Appendix C. Herbert need not have been in orders to be named comportioner.

[30] *Coll. Mont.,* XXI (1887), 240.

orders set the example for Nicholas Ferrar (rather than Ferrar for him, as is often assumed), who was ordained deacon by Laud at Westminster Abbey on Trinity Sunday 1626. Herbert had not long set forth into the affairs of the world; Ferrar, having been longer involved, could not remove himself so readily.

Unlike Donne, Herbert could not expect that ordination would open the way to royal favor that might advance him in the Church: James, whom he might once have considered his chief probable benefactor, was ageing and sick; and Herbert's associations among some of the chief figures in the Virginia Company would not have recommended him to James at this time. Bishop Williams, moreover, his own secular tenure none too certain, was obviously encouraging Herbert to place his hopes in ecclesiastical preferment. The events of the following year would bear out the wisdom of Williams' advice.

Herbert's circumstances at the expiration of his leave differed markedly from his earlier state. Although his ordination regularized his continuing as a fellow, there is no evidence that he resumed his normal duties as fellow or as orator, or that he took any further part in university life at Cambridge. (It should be remembered, however, that the college records for the period are not complete.) On 7 May 1625 it was Herbert Thorndike, rather than Herbert, who made the oration in Great St. Mary's at the university commemoration of James's death: "Mr Thorndike then Deputy Orator did make an Oration, wch being ended, the company departed to ye severall Colleges."[31] It is possible that Herbert at this time was still visiting the "Friend in *Kent*" to whom Walton implies he repaired after James's death[32] (although in the context—part of the elaboration of "my friends die"—Walton intended chiefly to account for Herbert's decision to enter holy orders, which had to be worked in before July of 1626).

The plague was raging in London during the summer after James died, and Donne, who had been ill during the spring, was staying at the Danvers home in Chelsea from late June through December of 1625.[33] Probably Herbert joined him

[31] B.L. Harl. MS. 7041, fol. 38v. [32] Walton, p. 276.

[33] R. C. Bald, *John Donne: A Life* (Oxford: Clarendon Press, 1970), pp. 470, 472, 496.

there during the course of the summer; despite the appearance of his name in the official printed lists as member for Montgomery borough for the Parliament held in Oxford from 12 May to 12 August,[34] Herbert would have been ineligible to serve because he had been ordained deacon. (His name does not appear in the *Commons Journals* for this session.) Donne's sole reference to their encounter in the household of Herbert's mother is tantalizingly brief: "Mr *George Herbert* is here."[35]

Trying to imagine how these two witty, devout men met and talked can furnish us with the best of imaginary conversations. Two brilliant, resourceful poets, neither likely to give of himself easily, both capable of exciting great admiration in their hearers, both accomplished speakers, quick, alert, mercurial—what sort of conversations *did* they have in the handsome house and the stately Italian gardens? Their acquaintance, begun probably in Herbert's childhood, must have deepened over the years when Herbert followed Donne's example in writing devotional verse and when they met from time to time at Charing Cross or Cambridge or Chelsea. They shared many interests and attitudes, among them the deep interest of their witty and generous hostess in matters of religion and of the Church, and at least some qualities and interests of their host (especially in the promise and disappointment of the Virginia Company), a fairly traditional theology, and now a common vocation. And indeed it is likely that Herbert talked with Donne about the course of his life, the Dean of St. Paul's at this stage probably being a man better able to comprehend and advise about his future than the Dean of Westminster. Donne and Herbert had known each other long enough to speak with complete candor.

From the time he left Cambridge until he settled into the rectory at Bemerton, Herbert had no habitation of his own. While Parliament was in session, he probably stayed in the Danvers household at Charing Cross or in lodgings in Westminster; but until the death of his mother in 1627, a Danvers house, whether in Charing Cross or in Chelsea, was probably his only home. Apparently he visited sporadically with relatives, perhaps with Bishop Andrewes and Bishop Williams, with the

[34] *Members of Parliament,* p. 467.
[35] *Letters to Persons of Honour* (1651), quoted by Bald, p. 276.

"Friend in *Kent,*" certainly with Sir Henry Herbert at Woodford, then with his stepfather's brother, the Earl of Danby, at Dauntesey House, and (after his marriage) with his wife's family at Baynton House.

Setting up house in the seventeenth century was not just a matter of having a roof over one's head, but of being able to maintain the roof and all that it sheltered; and until he went to Bemerton Herbert did not have even the income necessary to establish and maintain a house so much more modest and unpretentious than most others he had known. Until he was past his mid-thirties, then, Herbert was never head of his own house or of his own table, but rather a part of the establishments of his family and of their connections.

Sir Henry Herbert's marriage to Susan Slyford Plomer, widow of Edmund Plomer, citizen and merchant taylor, which took place between 1 March and 1 August 1625, brought him a dowry of five thousand pounds and houses at Woodford and Kilbourn in Essex.[36] J. B. Leishman's suggestion that it was in 1626 rather than in 1629 that Herbert lived with his brother at Woodford (which would settle a puzzling point) is probably right.[37] Herbert is unlikely to have joined the newly wed pair immediately upon their marriage in 1625 or for some months thereafter; but Sir Henry's election to the parliamentary seat formerly held by his elder brother may have played as much a part in Herbert's removal to Woodford as Sir Henry's own illness[38] and the "sharp *Quotidian Ague*" that Walton says seized George Herbert in his thirty-fourth year. Sir Henry's responsibilities in Parliament, added to his duties as Master of the Revels, probably kept him away from Woodford through most weeks of the session of Parliament that was summoned for 6 February and dissolved on 15 June. Particularly with the birth of their first child at hand, the couple should have found welcome reassurance in Herbert's presence at Woodford. Young William Herbert, born on 1 May 1626, was the first of three children of this marriage known to have been born and bap-

[36] Berry, *Pedigrees of Herts.,* p. 199; P.R.O. PROB 11/144, fol. 67.

[37] Cited by Hutchinson, *Works,* p. xxxiii.

[38] F. G. Fleay, *A Chronicle History of the London Stage, 1559–1642* (London: Reeves & Tanner, 1890), pp. 270–271; Walton, p. 284.

tized at Woodford; he had for his godparents the Earls of Pembroke and of Montgomery, and his grandmother Lady Danvers.[39] Probably during this same spring and summer Herbert was involved in collecting poems for the volume commemorating Bacon, who had died on 9 April.

Herbert's installation at Lincoln in July of 1626 was actually carried out by proxy,[40] perhaps because of his involvement in plans for the ceremonies honoring the Duke of Buckingham as the new Chancellor of Cambridge University. Herbert's last public act as orator of which we now have record was the oration delivered at York House on 13 July, when the installation ceremonies were completed. There is no question that it was Herbert himself who made the oration: "Then [the Vice-Chancellor] signified that the whole Senate of the University had sent their orator, who, in the name of the whole University, was to speak unto him, and desired his grace to be pleased to give him audience. The orator's oration ended, the duke made a speech to the whole assembly."[41]

The procedures for Herbert's installation at Lincoln were being carried out at almost the same time. On 5 July 1626 he was installed by proxy canon of Lincoln Cathedral and prebendary of Leighton Ecclesia.[42] The responsibilities he assumed with this office did not include the cure of souls in the parish of Leighton Bromswold (where Maurice Hughes was vicar), but preaching a sermon annually on Whitsunday in the cathedral, reciting Psalms 31 and 32 privately each day, and fulfilling the other obligations of his septism bond, dated 25 July. Because he was nonresidentiary, Herbert undertook to pay yearly the sum of 42*s.* 10*d.* for septisms, 40*s.* to the vicars choral for their salary for a vicar's stall, and 3s. 2*d.* to the young vicars choral

[39] Rebecca Warner, ed., *Epistolary Curiosities: Series the First* (Bath: Richard Cruttwell, 1818), pp. 3–4.

[40] Chapter Act Book, A.iii.9, fol. 160^v, Lincolnshire Archives Office.

[41] See the accounts in B.L. Harl. MS. 390 and in [Robert Folkestone Williams], ed., *The Court and Times of Charles I* (London: Henry Colburn, 1848), I, 126–128, quoting Joseph Mead's letter to Sir Martin Stuteville. References to the orator and the deputy orator are usually very specific in giving the appropriate title.

[42] Chapter Act Book, A.iii.9, fol. 160^v, Lincolnshire Archives Office. A Commonwealth evaluation of the prebend (D.iv.63; signed by a William Dugdale) sets the "antient reserved Rent to the Prebendary" at £18.

and choristers for ministrations. He also agreed to preach or cause to be preached within Lincoln Cathedral "one lawful and laudable sermon on the feast day of Pentecost called Whitsunday" or pay 10s. for each sermon preached by his deputy.[43] Herbert's name appears for Whitsunday 1629 on a list of preachers made by a later dean, Michael Honywood.[44]

The two-year period between the close of the Parliament of 1623/24 and Herbert's installation at Lincoln Cathedral in 1626 marks one of the most important turning points in his life. Although Herbert had not yet found the ultimate "Imploiment" he had been seeking for some years, he had permanently removed himself from the way of secular preferment, at a much earlier time than has generally been supposed. Leighton Bromswold had not yet assumed the full proportion it would have later in his life; and the final decision, to enter priest's orders and undertake the cure of souls, was still nearly four years away; but there could be no retreat from the events that culminated in his installation at Lincoln Cathedral in July of 1626.

Visits to Leighton, Little Gidding, and Lincoln

The usual assumption has been that Herbert neither visited his prebend nor fulfilled his obligation for the Whitsunday sermon by preaching it himself. His installation by proxy as canon of Lincoln Cathedral and prebendary of Leighton Ecclesia and

[43] Dj.30.1, unnumbered, Lincolnshire Archives Office. The bond is signed and sealed by John Pregion, or Prigeon, the principal registrar of the time, although most other bonds were then made by the prebendary in person. Although the records for 1629–1632 are lacking, Accounts of the Common Fund of the Dean and Chapter show payments of 42s. 10d. from the prebend of Leighton Ecclesia for 1626, 1627, and 1633. Again I am indebted to Dr. Finch for answers to my inquiries, for detailed explanations, and for the opportunity to see all these documents at first hand. For further information about these fees and other practices in the chapter at Lincoln see also Andrew Clark, ed., *Lincoln Diocesan Documents, 1450–1544* (London: Published for the Early English Text Society by Kegan Paul, Trench, Trübner, 1914); and Kathleen Edwards, *The English Secular Cathedrals in the Middle Ages* (2d ed.; Manchester: Manchester University Press, 1967). The regulation about the payment of septisms by nonresidentiary canons appears in Christopher Wordsworth's *Statutes of Lincoln Cathedral,* abridged by Henry Bradshaw (Cambridge: University Press, 1892–1897), III, 164 and 656n.

[44] D.vii.3D/1, Lincolnshire Archives Office, Dean and Chapter (a reclassification of the same document cited by Hutchinson as D.vi.28).

the possibility of having a deputy preach the annual sermon have combined to support the assumption. But it is far more likely that Herbert several times made the long journey north to Lincoln whenever he could fulfill his responsibilities in person. This appointment, unlike that at Llandinam, provided the opportunity for his taking an actual part in services by virtue of his position. Herbert's personal ties would also have encouraged such visits. Even during the busy days at Cambridge he had ridden two hundred miles to Lincolnshire and back ("in a way I knew not, in the midst of much business, and all in a Fortnight") to see his younger sister Frances;[45] and after 1626, when the Ferrars were permanently settled at Little Gidding, he could have had the pleasure of a visit with them as well. Leighton also lay close to the Bishop of Lincoln's palace at Buckden and to the residence of the Dowager Duchess of Lennox.

The first of the visits of the prebendary for Leighton Ecclesia must have taken place after the middle of July 1626; the last was likely that of Whitsunday 1630. Herbert would first have appeared at Leighton Bromswold to be inducted into corporal possession of the prebend, probably soon after his oration at York House.

The intent of the letters mandatory decreed by the dean and chapter at Lincoln on 5 July, when Peter Walker acted as Herbert's proxy at the installation, was apparently carried out shortly thereafter by Owen Evans, clerk, and Maurice Hughes, the vicar at Leighton, in the presence of Bartholomew Warner, clerk, and other reliable witnesses.[46] It is entirely possible that Nicholas Ferrar was present at his friend's induction; and it is likely that this visit included a stay at Little Gidding before Herbert returned south. (There would have been no reason to go on to Lincoln itself in 1626, Whitsunday being long past.)

Dr. Mary E. Finch, deputy archivist of the Lincolnshire Archives Office, writes in explanation of the induction:

> It seems reasonable to assume that Herbert's induction took place in Leighton Bromswold, and that it was in person. It is certainly most unlikely that it took place in Lincoln, as there would be no point in the

[45] *Works*, pp. 369, 371.

[46] Chapter Act Book, A.iii.9, fol. 160v, Lincolnshire Archives Office.

Chapter sending letters mandatory to some Huntingdonshire clergy to do it if this were so. If Herbert had been going to Lincoln at all, he would have been installed in person there instead of by Peter Walker, proxy. However, even when a prebendary elect appeared at Lincoln to be installed in person, it seems to have been usual at this period for the Dean and Chapter to issue letters mandatory for him to be inducted into corporal possession of the prebend on the spot by local clergy. In such cases, one assumes it took place in the prebendal church. This was on a par with induction to a benefice: first the Bishop instituted, then sent a mandate to the Archdeacon to have the new incumbent inducted into corporal possession of the living. Induction is like livery of seisin—the symbolical handing over of actual possession of the church, glebe lands etc.[47]

The only surviving record of a visit of Herbert to Lincoln is the appearance of his name in Dean Honywood's list for the sermon on Whitsunday 1629. But the absence of other corroboration does not preclude other visits by Herbert to Leighton, Lincoln, or both. Too often the circumstance described by Barnabas Oley has been misinterpreted to assert that Ferrar and Herbert met only once in their lives; but they almost certainly would have met at Cambridge, and they could hardly have avoided meeting when they were both serving in Parliament, or when Herbert's stepfather took so active a part in the affairs of the Virginia Company, in which Ferrar served as deputy treasurer after 1622. What Oley wrote in 1652 was this: "Yet saw they not each other in many years; I think scarce ever but as members of one university, in their whole lives."[48] "Scarce ever" simply is not "never."

Even Walton, who knew nothing of Herbert's close ties to the Virginia Company or of his service in Parliament, does not preclude the possibility of Herbert's having visited Ferrar: "Mr. *Farrers* and Mr. *Herberts* devout lives, were both so noted, that the general report of their sanctity gave them occasion to renew that slight acquaintance which was begun at their being Contemporaries in *Cambridge;* and this new holy friendship was

[47] Letter dated 26 June 1973.

[48] Barnabas Oley, Introduction to *Herbert's Remains* (London: Printed for Timothy Garthwait, 1652), p. b 11, unnumbered.

long maintain'd without any interview, but only by loving and endearing letters."[49]

Walton's information about the latter part of Herbert's life, probably gathered from Arthur Woodnoth, Ferrar's cousin, ought to have been among his most accurate. But again, a friendship "long maintain'd without any interview" is not necessarily always maintained without any interview. Although (for one example) Herbert might have been sent the proposed wording for the brass plates set up in the hall at Little Gidding and might have written his answer urging that Mrs. Ferrar's words be installed above the chimney piece for all visitors to read,[50] his part in this feature of the house at Gidding suggests an actual visit. One further circumstance virtually assures an actual visit by Herbert.

Both Ferrar's niece Susanna Collett and her husband, Joshua Mapletoft, vicar of Margaretting (or Margetting) in Essex, took a particular interest in Herbert and in his writing, as we know from several of the Ferrar letters. At the time of Herbert's death Susanna's copy of the first of the Little Gidding Story Books was in the rectory at Bemerton, and she had earlier lent Herbert her copy of one of the Little Gidding Harmonies, which Arthur Woodnoth delivered to him in October 1631.[51] Less than three weeks after Herbert's death Woodnoth wrote to Ferrar: "My Cosen Mapletoft hath her story book returnd of wch I conceue his weakenes gaue him not time to peruse it only his first letter after the receapt of it he told me he liked it exceeding well."[52] Seven months after Herbert's death Joshua Mapletoft complained to Ferrar that not enough copies of *The Temple* had been printed and asked whether Ferrar could let him have some for his friends: "Touching Mr Herberts booke it hath ye most generall approbation y^{t} I haue knowne any as it well deserues I haue been importuned by diuerse freinds for some of y^{m} London affords none & complaint att Cambridge y^{t} so few coppyes were printed. If you haue store I shalbe beholding for such a supply as you may afford."[53]

[49] Walton, p. 312. [50] Maycock, pp. 149, 150.
[51] Arthur Woodnoth to Nicholas Ferrar, 13 October 1631, F.P. No. 1092.
[52] 21 March 1632/33, F.P. No. 1118. [53] 10 October 1633, F.P. No. 796.

Whether through Susanna and Joshua or through her younger sister Judith and her husband Solomon Mapletoft, certainly the Mapletoft family was responsible in some way for the preservation of *W* from the general destruction the Puritans wrought at Little Gidding.

Susanna Mapletoft, the first of the Collett daughters to marry and leave Little Gidding,[54] had been sent the first Story Book,[55] a record of the discussions of the Little Academy in the winter of 1630/31, after her sisters Anna and Mary had completed it as a gift for their grandmother. The dedication of this Story Book to old Mrs. Ferrar bears the date of 2 February 1631. Mrs. Ferrar's acceptance of the book urges Anna and Mary to send it along to Susanna: "As for yor Book I kindly accept it: & although I haue heard you very jealously deny the communicating it with any yet because I suppose you esteeme yor sister Mapletoft all one with yo^{r}selues, I would haue you send her this Book which I doubt not will be both of Profit and comfort to her. God continue & encrease you in euery good way & thing till you come to Perfection in Christ Jesus. Amen. Yo^{r} Mother Mary Farrar."

The sisters readily accepted their grandmother's suggestion and appended their own letter to Susanna:

To our Dearest Sister.
With the same Loue, y^{t} is giuen by our most Honoured Grandmother, doe wee make ye Conveyance of this Book vnto you, our Dearest Sister. Professing faithfully, y^{t} we esteeme our Paines as well employed in thus parting with it to you, as wee should haue done in keeping it for our selues; so much doe wee Loue & prize the Grace of God, y^{t} is in you, & the Gracious Benediction of God, wch wee haue receiued by yor meanes. A most worthy & Faithfull Brother. To whose good judgement wee doe freely submitt this Little work, Beseeching him to giue vs Notice of what hee there shall find amisse. And so beseeching God to perfect his goodness in you by ye full Restitution both of Inward & Bodily Health wee rest.
2 Februarie 1631 Your Faithfull Sisters

[54] Susanna Collett to Susanna Mapletoft, 24 November 1628, Bodl. MS. Top. Hunts. e. 1, letter 15.
[55] B.L. Add. MS. 34657.

That Susanna Mapletoft even thought of sending this essentially private record to Herbert during his sickness argues that there was a strong bond of friendship between them; and that the others approved bears out the regard. This book, then, is the one that Arthur Woodnoth mentions as being at Bemerton at the time of Herbert's death.

Since Susanna was married during the summer of 1628,[56] Herbert could not have met her at Gidding after that summer. Before 1625 Susanna had been living with her parents at Bourn; in 1625 the new community was hardly ready to receive its members, let alone visitors. The family finally settled at Gidding early in the summer of 1626. If Herbert met Susanna Collett during a visit at Gidding, therefore, 1626 and 1627 are the most likely times, with the early summer of 1628 (when Whitsunday fell on 1 June) as a last possibility. Since the illness of his mother apparently kept Herbert from preaching the Whitsunday sermon in 1627, 1626 is the probable time for a meeting between Susanna Collett and Herbert.[57]

Herbert's visit to Leighton for his induction in 1626 may have led to the writing of one of his most autobiographical poems, "The Crosse," which almost certainly refers to the church at Leighton Bromswold. Although it is likely that Herbert wrote English poems during much of his adult life, undoubtedly there were periods of more concentrated composition when leisure, real or enforced, or need set him back at the task of representing Christian experience as he came to know it in its many varieties. Few of these poems can be dated exactly or read for direct biographical statement (or even implication); but among those few it is almost impossible to overlook Herbert's remarks about himself and his family and about a particular church, especially in the first two stanzas of "The Crosse."

The speaker here finds himself in the presence of a cross representing a "place, where I might sing, / And serve thee," where his "wealth and familie might combine / To set thy honour up, as our designe." If indeed this poem refers to an actual

[56] Maycock, p. 159; Nicholas Ferrar to Susanna Collett, 5 July 1627, F.P. No. 490; Nicholas Ferrar to Susanna Mapletoft, 4 June 1629, F.P. No. 498.

[57] See Epistola XVII, written a week before Whitsunday 1627 from Chelsea.

church, among the three churches Herbert undertook to rebuild, the only cruciform church is the splendid stone church of Leighton Bromswold.

At the time Herbert was made prebendary, this church had been unfit for public worship for perhaps twenty years, and services had been held in the manor hall of the Duke of Lennox.[58] To Herbert, with his sense of what was fitting and proper in everything related to the worship of God, it was as intolerable for a church to remain in this state as it was to Mrs. Ferrar to find the church at Little Gidding used to store hay and house pigs. If we take the first stanza of "The Crosse" to be autobiographical—and it is hard to see how else it might be taken—it would not be unfair to suppose that Herbert immediately formed the intention of rebuilding this church and enlisting his family's help to that end:

> What is this strange and uncouth thing?
> To make me sigh, and seek, and faint, and die,
> Untill I had some place, where I might sing
> And serve thee; and not onely I,
> But all my wealth and familie might combine
> To set thy honour up, as our designe.

Walton's account of the year 1626 (though misprinted 1629) as the time when Herbert's illness was first identified as a "supposed Consumption"[59] supports the likelihood that "The Crosse" was written about 1626. The poem continues:

> And then when after much delay,
> Much wrastling, many a combate, this deare end,
> So much desir'd, is giv'n, to take away
> My power to serve thee; to unbend
> All my abilities, my designes confound,
> And lay my threatnings bleeding on the ground.

Walton's remarks about Herbert's health in the two sections related to Leighton emphasize both his weak body and his (probably) dejected spirits;[60] and these comments verify the next stanzas of the poem, in which Herbert speaks of his agues,

[58] Maycock, p. 273. See also John Ferrar's account in Blackstone, p. 58.
[59] Walton, p. 284. [60] Ibid., pp. 278–280, 284–285.

stresses the irony of the circumstance that has both given him the opportunity to sing and serve God, and taken away his ability to perform these duties, echoing several parts of the letter Walton says was sent to Lady Danvers in 1622,[61] especially "*For my self,* dear Mother, *I alwaies fear'd sickness more then death, because sickness hath made me unable to perform those Offices for which I came into the world, and must yet be kept in it.*" The consonance between Walton's account and the frustration of purpose Herbert repeatedly mentions in the poem is not in any sense the sort of paraphrase found elsewhere in Walton (notably in the embroidery of "my friends die"). Again, Walton's source is likely to have been Arthur Woodnoth, not only because of the help the Ferrars gave in the restoration of the church at Leighton, but also because in the discussions between Herbert and Woodnoth in 1631, when Woodnoth was considering entering holy orders, Herbert's own account of the uses and frustrations of one's talents would almost inevitably have been brought forth in illustration. The figures based on working at cross-purposes with God are perhaps most memorable in "Affliction" (I) ("Thus doth thy power crosse-bias me") and in "The Crosse." In the earlier poem, the figure is based on cross-biasing in the game of bowls; in "The Crosse," the contrarieties become ropes wound at right angles about the poet's heart. The earlier conclusion stating his manful willingness to be rejected by God if his love is not real gives way here to the submission of the will that he evidently found difficult to achieve but expressed notably in the last line, "*Thy will be done.*"

Probably "The Crosse" should be dated at the time before the plans for the re-edification of Leighton church had been developed and when Herbert was still feeling great discouragement over his inability to carry out the task he had undertaken. His discussions with his mother (who died in June of 1627), his vow that "he would Re-build that Church,"[62] and the account of the names of early benefactors all indicate that Herbert planned from the first to see to this rebuilding. The actual restoration, both raising the money and seeing to the repairs, could not be completed for some years; indeed, it was not to be completed during Herbert's lifetime. The amount of money

[61] Ibid., p. 284. [62] Ibid., p. 279.

needed was not large: John Ferrar estimated "at the least upon two thousand pounds";[63] and it was not until the summer of 1632 that the major work of restoration was actually begun.[64] Any earlier efforts to raise funds seem not to have borne much fruit.[65]

Upon his return from the first visit to Leighton we may suppose that Herbert proceeded to his brother Henry's house—if, that is, Walton is right in stating that in "the 34*th* [year] of his Age, Mr. *Herbert* was seiz'd with a sharp *Quotidian Ague,* and thought to remove it by the change of Air; to which end, he went to *Woodford* in Essex, but thither more chiefly, to enjoy the company of his beloved Brother Sir *Henry Herbert,* and other Friends then of that Family."[66] Who the "other Friends then of that Family" were we can only guess—perhaps cousins like Thomas Lawley or family connections like Robert Harley or even the youngest brother Thomas, the sea captain, who had served some months before as captain of the *Dreadnought* on the expedition to Cadiz.[67]

This period of illness, during which Walton says Herbert "there became his own Physitian, and cur'd himself of his Ague, by forbearing Drink, and not eating any Meat, no not Mutton, nor a Hen, or Pidgeon, unless they were salted; and by such a constant Dyet, he remov'd his Ague,"[68] may well be the time when Herbert set himself to write "The Crosse," to make some tentative effort toward the restoration of Leighton, and to translate Leonard Lessius' Latin version of Luigi Cornaro's *Trattato de la vita sobria.*[69] The lively old Italian, eighty-three when he wrote his work, argued for the temperance and sobriety that Herbert uses in his title, urging a spare diet strictly weighed. Some of the ideas of Cornaro found followers both at Little Gidding and at Margetting, as we may see in some of Joshua Mapletoft's questions to Ferrar about diet,[70] and in the translations of Valdesso and Lessius with which Herbert's

[63] Blackstone, p. 58. [64] Maycock, p. 274.

[65] See [Nicholas Ferrar], "The Printers to the Reader," in *Works,* p. 4.

[66] Walton, p. 284. [67] *CSPD,* 1625–1626, p. 111. [68] Walton, p. 284.

[69] See *Works,* pp. 564–566, for notes showing that Herbert worked from the Latin version rather than the original.

[70] 10 October 1633, F.P. No. 796.

translation was published at Cambridge in 1634 as the *Hygiasticon.*[71]

Herbert shortened the treatise as he translated, but occasionally added an English phrase to clarify or emphasize Cornaro's intent. In his hands Cornaro emerges as an affable, devout, and still rather voluble advocate of discipline and order in life, qualities for which Herbert always showed considerable respect.

Probably Herbert remained at Woodford through the winter and until his mother's illness in the spring of 1627 called him back to Chelsea. In the absence of any record of his activities during this period, we can only assume that the canon of Lincoln Cathedral continued his studies in divinity and his pursuit of the devout life, wrote some poems, played some music, explored ways of carrying out the restoration of the church at Leighton, and perhaps collected some of the "outlandish" proverbs in which he and Henry took delight.

Lady Danvers' Death: Memoriae Matris Sacrum

Nothing specific is known of the state of Lady Danvers' health from the time of her illness in the spring of 1622 until her illness and death in June of 1627. She may well have been dispirited, even depressed, after the death of her son Richard at the siege of Bergen-op-Zoom in 1622, the death of her daughter Margaret Vaughan in the following year, and her husband's discouragement over the failure of the Virginia Company; and as she advanced into her mid-sixties she may have suffered physical infirmities as well. If marked changes in her personality and her outlook came about, however, there is nothing in the verses her son George wrote later that even hints at them.

Herbert apparently went to stay at Chelsea in May of 1627 and from there wrote the letter of advice to his deputy orator, Robert Creighton, that constitutes a virtual resignation of his

[71] John Hodgkin, letter to *Times Literary Supplement,* 28 June 1917. John Ferrar's first wife, Ann, was the sister of Thomas Sheppard, who had been one of the principals in the purchase of the manor of Little Gidding. See also Maycock, p. 8n, and "A Ferrar-Collett Pedigree."

post as orator (though Creighton would not be named to the post officially until the January meeting of the Senate at Cambridge).[72] His apologies for his rusty Latin should not be taken seriously; although he had not been writing much Latin prose recently, Latin syntax and style had been bred into him for years, and only the year before he had been composing his own contribution to the Latin memorial verses for Bacon. The speed with which he composed the memorial verses for his mother shortly thereafter argues no diminution of his earlier abilities in Latin composition.

The time and place of composition of the *Memoriae Matris Sacrum* can be stated with assurance: between the time of Lady Danvers' death (shortly before 8 June 1627) and 7 July, when the poems were entered with Donne's memorial sermon (preached at Chelsea on 1 July) in the Stationers' Register; the place, probably the Danvers house in Chelsea. There is no more reason to suppose that Herbert actually wrote from the little country house he mentions in Number VII (unless by chance it was the summerhouse in the garden) than to believe his protestations to Creighton some weeks earlier about the rustiness of his Latin. The reference to the Thames in Number XVIII certainly gives the impression that Herbert was seeing the moonlight reflecting on the lapping waters of the Thames along Chelsea Reach as he wrote.

The reader accustomed to Herbert's restraint and understatement in English verse may at first glance at the *Memoriae* doubt that he is dealing with the same poet. The extended praise of Lady Danvers and the excesses of grief, particularly in the Latin verses, may dim the perception of attitudes, methods, and devices typical of Herbert's English verse. It is in the terser Greek verses that Herbert's typical control is more readily noticed, particularly in the emphasis on mind rather than flesh in Number XIV:

> The soul's weak wall alone, the spirit's blind urn,
> Seek at this grave, my friend.

[72] *Works,* pp. 470–471. If we accept Hutchinson's date of 6 May 1627, which was the Sunday after Ascension Day, it is obvious that Herbert would not have been able to fulfill in person his obligation for the Whitsunday sermon at Lincoln Cathedral a week later.

The mind's tomb is a star, its light
  Can, as is fitting, only have a shining house.
Now you see that the boundless beauty of her brilliant face
  Was not perishable, was not of the body but of the mind—
Her mind that once through her body shone and now through
  Heaven, as through a window, shines.

But in the Latin verses as well, once we are able to see beneath the excess typical of Latin elegy, elements of Herbert's usual restraint become apparent. The concluding acceptance of Number VIII has much of the quiet power of the conclusion of "Love" (III) or "The Crosse":

Then, my cloak being grasped in a friendly way,
  Somebody whispers in my ear:
"This was once your Lord's drink."
  I taste and approve the wine jar.

The concluding figure in Number III of climbing a sunbeam recalls both the silk twist in "The Pearl" and the sunbeam at the end of "Mattens":

Why do you shine, O sun? . . .
. . . . .
Surely you shine for her: that's the reason you shine,
  And you count her holy joys as gain for yourself.
But if you cannot send Mother down from heaven,
  And if you are absolutely at rest and motionless,
At least double your beams, that my hand their twists
  May grasp and I may seek Mother in heaven.

Yet the general tone of the Latin poems is unquestionably fulsome. It is not surprising that Herbert, long steeped in the traditions of Latin verse, should have found in his second language a release he apparently never allowed himself in English. He had been too young at the time of his father's death to retain much memory of him; in effect, Magdalene Herbert was the only parent he was to know until her marriage (when Herbert was fifteen) to a man in age more like an elder brother than a father. During his formative years, then, Herbert had only one parent, who (he acknowledges here) had made it possible for him to mourn her in verse, because she had taught him to write and had educated him. More than that, her influence in the development of his religious belief and practice had probably been paramount. The thirteenth Latin poem, "Epitaphium," may originally have been intended as Herbert's conclusion—

> Here lies the praise and triumph of womanhood:
> Modest maiden, faithful wife, strict parent;
> The fiery contention of great and poor alike.
> Those her proud bearing won, these her pious deeds.
> Thus, at once high and humble, she united opposites,
> Taking joy in earthly and celestial things.

—almost as though the five Greek verses that follow were an afterthought, now rounded off by the final Latin poem as a kind of envoy, ending:

> Driven by a fierce scourge, I've been unable to refuse;
> Mother's great honor demands song.
> Alas, I must write. You've conquered, O Muse! But listen,
> Foolish one, I write this one time that I may ever silent be.

The whole series of poems progresses from grief to acceptance, accompanied by a growing sense of restraint, and the sure and certain hope of resurrection shines through the formal Latin phrases.

The death of Herbert's mother closed an era in his life, ended the strongest relationship he had known. A journey to Gidding not long afterward to talk with Ferrar, with whom he had much in common from association at Cambridge, from efforts in Parliament to save the Virginia Company and continue its influence in the New World, and from serving God in the diaconate, would have been well within the bounds of possibility.

The Manor of Ribbesford

Two weeks after the entry of Donne's memorial sermon and the accompanying *Memoriae* in the Stationers' Register, the manor of Ribbesford with other lands in Worcestershire was granted by the Crown to Edward Herbert, George Herbert, and their cousin Thomas Lawley.[73] Before the end of the year,

[73] *CSPD,* 1626–1627, p. 265.

Hutchinson tells us, ownership was transferred to Sir Henry Herbert for the sum of three thousand pounds (probably paid from part of the dowry that the widow Susan Plomer brought him at their marriage).

For George Herbert, accustomed to subsisting on such modest funds as his annual allowance of thirty pounds, academic stipends, portions from Llandinam and Lincoln, and orator's fees, his share in such a sum of money must have been an extraordinary windfall, giving him for the first time in his life some measure of financial independence. Usually Herbert's resignation of the oratorship (effective at the time of Creighton's appointment as his successor on 28 January 1627/28)[74] has been interpreted as showing that he no longer had to accede to his mother's wishes and could therefore please himself. As valid a reason may be that he now had funds of his own that enabled him to make changes in the direction of his life. Apparently he invested some of this money with Philemon Stephens (the printer who had published Donne's memorial sermon and Herbert's verses for his mother), as he seems to have done later with the money left him by his niece Dorothy Vaughan. Some of it probably went toward building churches—at Leighton Bromswold and later at Fugglestone and at Bemerton. Some money remained in Stephens' hands at the time of Herbert's death.[75]

The period of Herbert's life that began with his membership in Parliament ended much differently from what he and his family might have expected. Herbert was now in deacon's orders, as he should have been sooner, according to the requirements of the Trinity College statutes; but he was now cut loose from the ties of family and college that had heretofore been his stay. At the time he gave over the oratorship (and apparently all other connections with Cambridge), it was by no means clear what way might open next.

[74] C.U.R. 45, Cambridge University Archives, note by Registrary Romilly under "Orator," giving 28 January 1628 as the date of Robert Creighton's election as orator. The note is part of a list of orators drawn up by Romilly and dated 25 March 1856.

[75] P.R.O. PROB 11/163, fol. 25 (transcribed in *Works,* pp. 382–383).

CHAPTER 5

Wiltshire: Dauntesey, Baynton, and Bemerton (1628–1633)

Removal to Dauntesey

London and Cambridge had been the two focal points of Herbert's life since 1601, but the year 1628 dissolved arrangements long familiar and changed the scene to Wiltshire. The significance of the removal there cannot have been apparent when it occurred; but Herbert was to spend the rest of his life in Wiltshire.

The first great change took place on 28 January, when the Senate at Cambridge elected Herbert's deputy, Robert Creighton, as orator. No form of resignation is known to survive, but Herbert had obviously given whatever notice was necessary and thus had ended the most continuous association of his life outside his own family. He had been orator for eight years in all, though it is doubtful that he spent more than the first four in residence.

The next change from earlier ways came with Herbert's move from his stepfather's house at Chelsea to that of Henry Danvers, Earl of Danby, at Dauntesey, near Chippenham in Wiltshire. When he went to stay with his stepfather's elder brother, Herbert probably had no notion that he would not leave Dauntesey until he was about to become a married man.

Still another change occurred on 10 July, when Sir John Danvers married Elizabeth Dauntesey and thereby came into possession of the estate of Lavington in Wiltshire,[1] where he

[1] At some time in this period Arthur Woodnoth became a kind of manager for Danvers' business affairs, which not even Woodnoth's skill was able to keep under control. When Woodnoth later considered leaving Sir John's service to take holy orders and asked Herbert's advice, Herbert wrote him a series of reasons why

continued to lay out elaborate gardens with as much enthusiasm as he had shown earlier in Chelsea. Even in the absence of any record of their future communication, we may assume that the two men continued to see each other from time to time, since Lavington was no great distance from either Dauntesey or Bemerton, though visits to Chelsea were probably rare. Only a few days before his death Herbert would appoint his stepfather the overseer of his will.

The move to Dauntesey brought Herbert into circumstances far more rural than he had known at Chelsea and into the household of the Earl of Danby,[2] for whom he may have served as a resident chaplain during the ensuing months. As a deacon he could have read, in the church that all but adjoins Dauntesey House, the same daily offices that Nicholas Ferrar was reading in the chapel at Little Gidding.

Herbert apparently found Dauntesey to his liking: the open countryside would offer ample occasion for riding (of which he seems to have been fond), and the riding in turn for reflection; he was among congenial people, and freed alike from the anxieties over his mother's health and the cares of the great world; above all, he was no longer burdened by the sense of uncertainty about returning to Cambridge. On the whole, his new surroundings benefited him, improved his health, lifted his spirits, and encouraged him before the year was out to think of marrying.

Among the several dwellings of George Herbert, only two now standing can be identified with certainty: Dauntesey House and Bemerton Rectory. The house at Dauntesey has been considerably altered since Herbert's time, even in its external facing. The Earl of Danby is said to have offered Herbert any apartment in the house he might choose, "as might

he should not do so ([October 1631], F.P. No. 714). See also Arthur Woodnoth to Nicholas Ferrar, 13 October 1631, F.P. No. 1092. The birth of the first child of Sir John's second marriage, a daughter, is mentioned in another letter from Woodnoth to Ferrar, 7 May 1629, F.P. No. 1068.

[2] There seems little reason to question the authenticity of the verse attributed to Herbert, carved on the Earl of Danby's tomb in Dauntesey Church, which could well have been written long before it was required (and does not actually mention Danby's name). Clearly it was intended for a tomb; the "must sleepe" of line 2 suggests at least that the sleeping had not begun when the verse was written. See *Works,* pp. 208–209, 550–551.

best sute with his accommodation and liking";[3] and despite the numerous changes and additions since that day, we can be certain that any apartment Herbert chose would look forth on a pleasant prospect of meadow or wood, or church or farm buildings or stream. And no matter how extensive the other changes, one feature remains certain: the proximity of the church, the north door of which today opens on the garden of the house. In this church, with its memorable painting of the Doom, and in that at Edington, which became his parish church at the time of his marriage in the following year, Herbert would undergo and resolve some of the conflicts that must be overcome before he could eventually proceed to Bemerton and to the priesthood. Here and at Baynton House he would come to know that the scholar and the orator must dwindle to a country parson.

Further Writing of English Poems

Before the last great watershed of his life, however, Dauntesey must have played another part. Between Cambridge and Bemerton Herbert composed probably almost half the poems we now find in *The Temple.* Some of them were probably written at Chelsea, others at Woodford, perhaps some at the home of the unidentified "Friend" in Kent; but Dauntesey House, where Herbert was to find the last uninterrupted leisure he would know, is the most likely place for the greater part of the concentrated literary effort that altered and fleshed out the ground Herbert had laid in *W*. In the spring of 1629 he married and removed to Baynton House, and the following year he made the final move, to Bemerton, where the round of duties would leave little time for writing and less for concentration of the sort necessary for writing poetry.

Without attempting here to account for all the changes and additions that occurred between *W* and whatever antecedent of *B* Herbert sent to Ferrar (which are discussed in the final chapter), we may assume that many of them resulted from Herbert's spiritual growth and greater understanding, developed through suffering and adversity. Two of the finest of the added poems, "The Collar" and "The Bunch of Grapes,"

[3] Walton, p. 285.

address themselves to the question of the reward to be found in God's service, the former with its famous quiet ending betokening the submission of the will, the latter with its combined awe and joy in God's gift to man:

> Joy, I did lock thee up: but some bad man
> Hath let thee out again:
> And now, me thinks, I am where I began
> Sev'n yeares ago: one vogue and vein,
> One aire of thoughts usurps my brain.
> I did toward Canaan draw; but now I am
> Brought back to the Red sea, the sea of shame.
>
> . . . . . .
>
> But can he want the grape, who hath the wine?
> I have their fruit and more.
> Blessed be God, who prosper'd *Noahs* vine,
> And made it bring forth grapes good store.
> But much more him I must adore,
> Who of the Laws sowre juice sweet wine did make,
> Ev'n God himself being pressed for my sake.

One stage of Herbert's poetic development may be traced in his changes in *W* itself, before he set it aside in favor of a much expanded volume with a closely related, but subtler sense of order. While *W* was still the focus of his English verse, he made a number of revisions, generally a change of word or phrase only, although "Perfection" was revised more thoroughly and its pointed ending underlined by its new title of "The Elixir." But this first revision was not yet "The Elixir" as we know it; if Herbert added the triumphant final stanza here and dropped two rather pedestrian ones, he also kept a dull first stanza:[4]

> Lord teach mee to referr
> All things I doe to thee
> That I not onely may not erre
> But allso pleasing bee.

The original third stanza (which he canceled) merely repeated the theme of the poem without adding anything of clarity or grace:

[4] See Helen C. White's excellent discussion of the stages of this poem, in *The Metaphysical Poets* (New York: Macmillan, 1936), pp. 189–194.

He that does ought for thee,
Marketh y^{t} deed for thine.
And when the Divel shakes ye tree,
Thou saist, this fruit is mine.

The original conclusion was discarded in favor of the one we now know; again, the aptness and succinctness of the later version are immediately apparent:

But these are high perfections:
Happy are they that dare
Lett in the light to all their
actions
And show them as they are.

This is y^{t} famous stone
That turneth all to gold
For y^{t} wch God doth touch &
owne
Cannot for less be told.

But the revision was not yet complete. As this stage Herbert let stand the original opening, but at some later stage, before he drew up the original of *B,* he brought the entire poem under fine control with a new first stanza:

Teach me, my God and King,
In all things thee to see,
And what I do in any thing,
To do it as for thee.

But the conception of order already established in *W* precluded further development beyond minor revision; and on the basis both of order and of making place for additional poems Herbert abandoned the little manuscript volume he had used for some years and went on to revise the order and enlarge the scope of the final version.[5]

One other poem may be mentioned as almost certainly having been written about the time Herbert was living at Dauntesey or at Baynton House, the poem in which he draws near to the priesthood, but has not yet become a priest. "The Priest-

[5] At what point Herbert began to expand the concept of order he had earlier developed for *W* it is impossible to say. Since most of what we know of his handwriting at different periods is of necessity based on his signatures and little else, the evidence is sorely limited. Nonetheless, it is of some significance that in the changes in "Perfection" he is still using the secretary *e,* though writing in an italic hand otherwise. In the Latin poems in *W* he uses the secretary *e* (particularly, but not exclusively for final *e*) and the Greek *e,* with an occasional italic *e.* In later years he sometimes returned to the secretary *e* when he was under stress; see the marriage bond and the will and also Appendix B, below.

hood" clearly deals with the question whether Herbert is worthy to serve at God's altar:

> Blest Order, which in power dost so excell,
> That with th' one hand thou liftest to the sky,
> And with the other throwest down to hell
> In thy just censures; fain would I draw nigh,
> Fain put thee on, exchanging my lay-sword
>   For that of th' holy Word.
>
> . . . . . .
>
> But th' holy men of God such vessels are,
> As serve him up, who all the world commands:
> When God vouchsafeth to become our fare,
> Their hands convey him, who conveys their hands.
> O what pure things, most pure must those things be,
>   Who bring my God to me!

Many of the poems added to the expanded volume that Herbert finally compiled record the varied experiences of the soul in progress between the supposed submission of the will in "Obedience" (Number 80) and the final revision of "The Elixir" (Number 156) that marks the transition to the final upward movement to the Last Things. Thereafter there are no more false starts or wanderings or sudden descents to despair. It is reasonable to suppose that many of these added poems were composed during Herbert's first two years in Wiltshire, when he had both good health and the greatest degree of leisure he was to know for the remainder of his life.[6]

Herbert's Marriage

> I will not Marry; or if shee be mine,
>   She and her Children shal be thine.

So the bachelor Herbert had written in "The Thanks-giving" in answer to his own question, "But how then shall I imitate thee, and / Copie thy fair, though bloudie hand?" Whether during his Cambridge days Herbert expected to remain single cannot be determined from this one poem. There is no question that he thought highly of the single state, even for a parish priest, as he made clear in chapter ix of *The Country Parson:*

[6] I discuss the development of the final plan of *The Temple* in "The Williams Manuscript and *The Temple,*" in *Renaissance Papers, 1971*, pp. 59–77.

"The Country Parson considering that virginity is a higher state then Matrimony, and that the Ministry requires the best and highest things, is rather unmarryed, then marryed. But as the temper of his body may be, or as the temper of his Parish may be, where he may have occasion to converse with women, and that among suspicious men, *and other like circumstances considered,* he is rather married than unmarried. Let him communicate the thing often by prayer unto God, and as his grace shall direct him, so let him proceed."[7]

Aside from these two passages, Herbert did not comment on marriage or on the relationship between men and women. Yet he seems to have entertained a high opinion of women, having grown up in the household of a most remarkable and accomplished woman, with his sister-in-law Mary, who came into that household when he was still a child, and with three sisters to whom he was obviously devoted. (He rode two hundred miles from Cambridge to Lincolnshire to visit Frances, wrote and sent greetings to Elizabeth when she was sick, and showed the most sensitive consideration for Margaret's three daughters.) From the tone of his remarks to his brother Henry in Letter XII, we may assume that he considered a Christian family a household of God's servants.[8]

It is worth noting, however, that Herbert often mentions the temptations of the flesh: although the term "affections" (meaning passions) appears only once (in "Christmas"), "passion" (in the fleshly sense) appears nine times, "lust" fourteen times, and "flesh" or "fleshly" forty-one times (not always exclusively in connection with the passions of the flesh). Contrasts between flesh and spirit are marked in two *W* poems, the rejected version of "The H. Communion" and the original "Church-Musick."

In the final portion of chapter ix and in chapter x of *The Country Parson* Herbert sets forth some of his ideas about a parson's wife. Like Eve, she is to come to God through her husband. She is to be known for her good works, and to play a separate but important part in the parish, especially in caring for the sick and the poor. She is also to superintend the household and the accounts, to train up the children and the maids. All

[7] *Works,* pp. 236–237. [8] Ibid., pp. 375–376.

these remarks were written after Herbert had been married two or three years and may therefore convey some impression of the woman he married and the kind of relationship that existed between them.

For a man who had protested a good ten years before, "My stuffe is flesh, not brasse," Herbert had waited a long time to marry. One reason for the delay was undoubtedly his uncertainty about his own future. Until he had determined whether to remain at Cambridge and take orders or to leave the university, there could be no question of marriage. Another reason was surely his inability to support a wife.

But early in 1629 Herbert had severed the connection with Cambridge, had been in deacon's orders four years or more, was assured of the incomes from Llandinam and Leighton Bromswold, and had probably begun to feel some assurance about the income from his portion of the price of Ribbesford. His health had apparently improved, and with improved health probably came increased hope. In all, Herbert felt that the time for marriage had come.

Walton's account of Herbert's marriage is so idealized as to be almost ludicrous. If Sir John Danvers, Jane's cousin, had been Herbert's stepfather for twenty years, it would be strange indeed if Herbert had never seen Jane Danvers until three days before he married her. But Walton was merely being Walton, embellishing his own picture without regard to how it made his subject look.

What we know of Jane Herbert must be pieced together at best. Walton accords her high praise, once he gets past the platonic courtship,[9] but his version is beyond the point of belief for ordinary mortals. Aubrey was both complimentary and waspish about her: "My kinswoman was a handsome *bona roba* and ingeniose," he wrote, adding that after her second marriage she condemned a folio work of Herbert's in Latin "to the uses of good houswifry."[10] The term *bona roba,* as it is generally interpreted, is about the last one would expect to see applied to the wife of George Herbert; nor does Aubrey's use of it in re-

[9] Walton, pp. 285–287.

[10] John Aubrey, *Brief Lives,* ed. Oliver Lawson Dick (Ann Arbor: University of Michigan Press, 1957), p. 137.

ferring to Lady Digby clarify the meaning. Probably George Duyckinck's interpretation (which follows Florio's usage) approximates what Aubrey intended for both women: "He seems to mean by it a full, well-rounded figure."[11] Aubrey's second term, "ingeniose," at that time might compliment Jane Herbert's intellectual capacity or her amorous propensity. This young woman, whom Barnabas Oley terms "a loving *and* vertuous Lady,"[12] was the favorite daughter of Mr. Charles Danvers of Baynton House, which lies less that twenty miles from Dauntesey.[13] Considering the habits and the hospitality of county families, it is hard to believe that the courtship was carried on by proxy until three days before the wedding, particularly when one examines the extant documents. All the records call Walton's account into question.

Herbert's wedding took place on 5 March 1629 in the priory church at Edington, which had become the parish church for Baynton.[14] The date fell on the third Thursday in Lent, an unusual time for a wedding.[15] Both the allegation and the bond are dated after the beginning of Lent, Ash Wednesday having fallen on 18 February. The allegation, filed on 23 February by one William Sadler of Dauntesey, is written in a clerk's hand and describes Herbert as being "aged xxx^{tv} yeers or therabout[es]" and Jane as "aged xx^{tv} yeers or therabout[es]."[16] The bond, dated 26 February (one week before the wedding), names the groom as "Georgius Herbert de Dantsey . . . Armiger."[17] Were we to accept Walton's version, we would have to believe that Herbert would not yet have laid eyes on his

[11] George L. Duyckinck, *The Life of George Herbert* (2d ed.; New York: General Protestant Episcopal Sunday School Union, 1858), p. 94n. Florio's use reads "as we say good stuffe, that is a good wholesome plum-cheeked wench" (*Oxford English Dictionary*). In his account of John Selden Aubrey also refers to the Countess of Kent as "ingeniose."

[12] *Herbert's Remains* (London: Printed for Timothy Garthwait, 1652), p. c 5^{v}, unnumbered.

[13] For Danvers family relationships, see F.N. Macnamara, *Memorials of the Danvers Family* (London: Hardy and Page, 1895).

[14] The Edington Parish Registers are lost, but the date may be verified in the transcripts at the Salisbury Diocesan Record Office.

[15] [Douglas] Macleane, "George Herbert and Bemerton," in *The Festival Book of Salisbury*, ed. Frank Stevens (Salisbury, 1914), p. 105.

[16] The allegation is in the Salisbury Diocesan Record Office.

[17] The bond is in the Salisbury Diocesan Record Office.

bride, but was apparently certain enough of being accepted to record the allegation and the bond.

The names of two of Herbert's future brothers-in-law also appear in this bond: Edward Michell, husband of Jane's sister Joan; and Henry Danvers, their brother. The bond itself, its wording a set formula used in other bonds of the time, binds Herbert and Michell to John, Bishop of Sarum, for one hundred pounds of lawful English money.[18]

Mr. and Mrs. Herbert lived at Baynton House with Mrs. Charles Danvers (now a widow) and Jane's brothers and sisters for a year or more after the marriage, through the time of Herbert's hesitancy about accepting the rectory of Fugglestone-with-Bemerton, offered to him late in the winter or early in the spring of 1630.

Presentation, Institution, and Induction at Bemerton

There is no way to reconcile Walton's account of Herbert's presentation to the living of Fugglestone-with-Bemerton with the facts officially recorded. The living, says Walton, fell vacant when Dr. Walter Curle (or Curll), the incumbent, was made Bishop of Bath and Wells, about three months after Herbert's marriage (therefore about June 1629). The presentation fell to the King rather than to the patron, the Earl of Pembroke, because it was Charles who had advanced Curle to his new rank. Walton goes on to say that "*Philip,* then Earl of *Pembroke* (for *William* was lately dead) requested the King to bestow it upon his kinsman *George Herbert*"; but it is just at this point that the account falls apart, because William Herbert, the third Earl of Pembroke, did not die until 10 April 1630, and there was not therefore time for Herbert to "fast and pray often, and consider, for not less than a month," as Walton says he did,[19] if Philip were actually the Earl of Pembroke who recommended him to the King. That Herbert's installation and induction at Bemerton took place after Philip had succeeded as fourth earl therefore has nothing to do with the nomination. The presen-

[18] The amount is the same as that of the fine imposed on any parson who performed a marriage without proper banns or license (Miss Pamela Stewart, assistant archivist, Salisbury Diocesan Record Office, 13 July 1973).

[19] Walton, p. 287.

tation is dated 16 April;[20] Herbert was actually inducted on 26 April.[21] If Herbert is to be allowed his month for fasting and praying and deciding on acceptance, then it was clearly William, the third earl, who spoke for him.

Walton's source for the information about this period of Herbert's life was undoubtedly Arthur Woodnoth, whom Walton did not know well (and in fact called John in the first edition of the biography), and by the time Walton finally came to write about Herbert, Woodnoth had been dead the better part of thirty years. Walton may therefore have filled a gap in his notes with what appeared likely. The Chancellor of Oxford, William, the third earl, would have had particular reason to note the intellectual gifts of his young kinsman, as Walton had mentioned earlier.[22] And he might very well have made some appeal to Charles on his cousin's behalf during one of Charles's visits to Wilton. (Aubrey writes, "King Charles 1st did love Wilton aboue all places: and came thither every sommer.")[23]

Presentation to the living of Fugglestone-with-Bemerton conferred upon Herbert the responsibility for the cure of souls in a parish that extended from Wilton House on the west to the parish of Fisherton Anger on the east. This dual rectory included the parish church of Fugglestone St. Peter and the chapel of Bemerton St. Andrew, the former located to the north of the grounds of Wilton House, the seat of the Earls of Pembroke, the latter just across the road from Bemerton Rectory. The church probably dates from the thirteenth century, the chapel from the fourteenth. Both they and Bemerton Rectory were in need of extensive repair.

According to Walton's account, Arthur Woodnoth went to visit Herbert at Baynton House during the month when Herbert was considering whether to accept the living that had been offered him, and the two men then went on for a visit at Wilton House.[24] It is impossible to sift the truth from the details Walton records (to lend verisimilitude?): the King and the Court

[20] P.R.O. C 66/2543.
[21] Herbert's subscription is in the Salisbury Diocesan Record Office.
[22] Walton, p. 271. [23] Bodl. Aubrey MS. 2, fol. 31.
[24] Walton, pp. 287–288.

were not there, nor at Salisbury; Laud had no reason for being close at hand for consultation and persuasion; in fact, not even the account of the tailor hastily summoned "to take measure, and make him Canonical Cloaths, against next day," reads true. For Herbert, appropriate dress was part of the preparation for worship (as we may see in his many uses of the figure of dressing as proper preparation, not the least of these being his description of the priest's preparation in "Aaron"); and if he had any notion that he was about to accept the living at Bemerton, it is likely that he would already have seen to the proper "Canonical Cloaths" himself.

Herbert was instituted on 26 April by John Davenant, Bishop of Salisbury. The subscription reads:

> Ego Georgius Herbert diaconus in artib[us] magister ad rectoriā de Fulston S[ti] Petri & Bemmerton in Comitatu Wilt. Dioces. Sarū admittend[us] & instituend[us] hisce articulis singulisq[ue] in ijsdē contentis volens & ex āiō subscribo & consensū meū ijsdē p[re]beo 26 die Apr. 1630.
>
> Georgius Herbert[25]

The induction at Bemerton followed the same day, with Woodnoth still in attendance, waiting outside the door of St. Andrew's when Herbert was shut into the church to toll the bell and to pray, and finally, after some time had passed, looking through a window to discover Herbert lying prostrate before the altar.[26] Walton undoubtedly had the details from Woodnoth and may have taken notes after he talked with him. Woodnoth perhaps gave him some slight basis for the lengthy passage that follows, supposedly recording what Herbert said to Woodnoth that night. But for this passage and many others in which Walton ostensibly reports conversation, readers need to keep in mind the caveats of David Novarr.[27]

[25] Salisbury Diocesan Record Office. [26] Walton, pp. 288–289.

[27] *The Making of Walton's "Lives"* (Ithaca: Cornell University Press, 1958), especially pp. 301–341. Walton began with preconceived interpretations, oversimplified the character of Herbert to parallel the kind of duality he had earlier found in Donne, and used the life of Herbert as a vehicle for his own leanings and preferences. See also John Butt, "Izaak Walton's Methods in Biography," in *Essays and Studies by Members of the English Association,* XIX (Oxford: Clarendon Press, 1934), pp. 67–84.

Ordination as Priest

Walton is not entirely truthful in his remarks about Herbert's ordination as priest; he may indeed have held back a part of the truth (and a part that should have been perfectly obvious to him) in order to make Herbert appear the more zealous for ordination: ". . . but as yet he was but a *Deacon,* and therefore long'd for the next *Ember-week,* that he might be ordain'd *Priest,* and made capable of Administring both the Sacraments."[28] The words are accurate enough, so far as they go; but, as is often true of Walton, what he does not say is at least as important as what he says.

Although both the presentation and the institution took place in April, Herbert was not ordained priest until 19 September.[29] If he longed for the coming of the next Ember week, so that he might be ordained priest, it is strange indeed that he let pass the ordination at Salisbury on Trinity Sunday, which that year fell on 23 May. Not only were twelve other men made priests at this ordination, but Herbert's own curate, Nathanael Bostocke, was among them.[30] It is odd indeed that the curate should be in priest's orders when the rector was only a deacon.

Certainly Herbert's parish had every right to expect that he would be ordained priest at the earliest possible opportunity. Fugglestone-with-Bemerton, though it has often been described as a poor country parish, was a good living, nearly double the value of the neighboring Wilton, for example; and Herbert could be offered this dual rectory only because his predecessor, the Bishop of Rochester,[31] who had been very active in the chapter at Salisbury Cathedral, had been advanced to the bishopric of Bath and Wells. It was not the sort of parish for which a patron would normally nominate a candidate not fully prepared in every way to perform priestly duties. Both parish and patron must therefore have expected Herbert's ordination during the next Ember days.

[28] Walton, p. 293.

[29] Herbert's subscription at ordination is in the Salisbury Diocesan Record Office.

[30] The subscriptions of all these ordinands are in the Salisbury Diocesan Record Office.

[31] *Victoria County History of Wiltshire,* p. 47, n. 31.

The point is important, because the variance from Walton's account might appear to call in question the degree of Herbert's commitment during his early months at Bemerton. As long as he was only a deacon, he could (like Ferrar) read most of the daily offices, but could not give absolution nor administer the Sacrament. In some parishes of Herbert's time, the Sacrament was administered only the required three times a year, but Herbert favored more frequent celebrations,[32] which Bostocke could probably have managed readily enough on the few occasions after his own ordination (and before Herbert's) when he would have been required to celebrate at both churches. Far more important in Herbert's daily round were the offices of Mattins and Evensong, which Walton tells us Herbert said faithfully each day at the canonical hours of ten and four, each of them including words of absolution that could be spoken only by a priest. Since all that summer Bostocke, the only ordained priest, was dutifully off at the other end of the parish, at Fugglestone, saying the daily offices and giving absolution, one can readily understand that the cumulative frustration of never being able to pronounce the absolution or administer the Sacrament would indeed have intensified Herbert's longing for the arrival of the next Ember days. Other local clergy doubtless celebrated the Communion on Whitsunday at both St. Peter's and St. Andrew's, as Bostocke would do after his ordination; but it was in the daily offices that Herbert's not yet being a priest would have proved the greater handicap, and a continuing reminder that he was not yet fully "dressed" to serve at God's altar.

Once Herbert had been instituted and had accepted the responsibility for the cure of souls, there could be no further impediment through his own admitted tendency toward delay; the reason for the lapse in time until his ordination must therefore have been one not readily in his control. In the face of the obvious practical disadvantages, to say nothing of the piety and eagerness that Walton ascribes to him, such delay could result only from weighty and extraordinary causes. With Herbert, the possibility of sickness can never be wholly discounted; but there

[32] *Works,* p. 259.

is another explanation that is much more likely in this period when Herbert was generally in the best health he had known for years.

Because both churches were being repaired and the rectory at Bemerton probably was not yet habitable, perhaps Bostocke carried the greater responsibility for daily offices and Herbert came from Baynton for Sunday services, or perhaps lodged at Wilton during his visits to the parish. Given Herbert's strong conviction that the parson belongs in the parish,[33] probably nothing less compelling than his prior commitment at Lincoln would have drawn him from his parish and from the ordination on 23 May 1630.

In that year Whitsunday, the day on which Herbert was responsible for the sermon at Lincoln Cathedral, fell on 16 May. It would have been simple enough for him to arrange for a deputy to take his place; but I suggest that instead he had decided that this was the time to perform this duty in person for the last time and then to urge Nicholas Ferrar, a deacon living less than five miles from Leighton Bromswold, to accept the responsibilities of the prebend in his stead. The demands of parish life at Bemerton would have been one of his reasons, the delay in raising sufficient money to complete the repairs at Leighton another. If, more than ten years earlier, Herbert had considered that a journey of two hundred miles in a fortnight exceeded normal expectation,[34] it may have seemed disproportionate to him to continue to take time for yearly journeys nearly twice as long. The stewardship of time is not the least important of Christian obligations; and for Herbert, prone to delay (and ready enough to admit his propensity), there should have been some appreciation of the value of the time he had already let pass by, wasted, and a concomitant resolve to make the most of the time remaining to him.

Since Herbert could not be fully resident in his parish until the repairs to the rectory had been completed, and since in the meantime he had secured a resident curate, he may well have felt that the parish was better provided than during Curle's incumbency and that a journey north to divest himself of the responsibilities of the prebend of Leighton Ecclesia would in the

[33] Ibid., pp. 250–251. [34] Letter VIII, ibid., p. 271.

long run serve the interests of the parish at Bemerton by freeing him of responsibility elsewhere. Although no record now known affirms that Herbert traveled to Lincoln or Leighton or Little Gidding in May of 1630, the probability remains as a link between his earlier efforts as prebendary and the rather impressive accomplishment in raising funds and rebuilding Leighton church that would ensue.

The first of Herbert's two letters to Ferrar about the restoration of Leighton church (which Canon Hutchinson dates in March 1631/32 because of the date of the receipt of Arthur Woodnoth's letter to Nicholas Ferrar about working with Sir Henry Herbert to raise money for Leighton)[35] suggests something of Herbert's concern about the rebuilding and his past unsuccessful efforts: "God knowes, I have desired a long time, to doe the place good, & have endeavoured many wayes, to find out a man for it. And now My gratious Lord God, is pleased to give me you for the Man, I desired, for wch I humbly thank him, & am so far from giving you cause, to apology, about your counselling me herein: that I take it exceedingly kindly of you."[36]

Both Nicholas and John Ferrar tell of Herbert's urging Nicholas to accept the responsibility for the prebend in his stead:

As for worldly matters, his love and esteem to them was so little, as no man can more ambitiously seek, then he did earnestly endeavour the resignation of an Ecclesiasticall dignitie, which he was possessour of. But God permitted not the accomplishment of this desire, having ordained him his instrument for reedifying of the Church belonging thereunto, that had layen ruinated almost twenty yeares. The reparation whereof, having been uneffectually attempted by publick collections, was in the end by his own and some few others private free-will-offerings successfully effected.[37]

Mr Herbert (who ever styled him Brother Ferrar) understanding that his Prebend of Layton lay within two miles of N. F. earnestly (intreated) him, to accept of that Prebendship, as most fitted for him, at so near a distance. The one urgeth it with much earnestness, the other as eagerly put all off—At the last he found the way to divert to a much

[35] F.P. No. 1119, received on 25 March 1632. [36] *Works*, p. 378.
[37] [Nicholas Ferrar], "The Printers to the Reader," ibid., p. 4.

righter end his Brother Herbert's good Intentions, by a Proposition he had made to him—wch was, that seeing the fair Church of Layton was fallen down a long time, & lay in the dust, the vicar & Parish fain to use my Lord Duke's great Hall for y^{r} Prayers & preaching; & tho' there had been gotten a Brief for the repairing of it, the Cost estimated to be at the least upon two thousand pounds, & collections yet made, the money being not above [*space*] pounds, could no way help the matter. N. F. very earnestly hereupon assaults his Brother Herbert, to sett to the work,/ & to try, what he could doe amongst his Friends, towards so good a work: N. F. promising all the assistance he could in that kind—he would undertake, his Brother J. F.—should very carefully prosecute the business (if once begun) by three times a week attending the workmen, & providing all Materials—At last Mr Herbert sett upon it, to sollicite his Friends, & spared not his own Purse: So God in the end blessed both y^{r} Endeavours, that a handsome & uniforme (& as the Country termed it) a fine neat Church was erected, Inside & outside finished, not only to ye Parishioners own much comfort & joy, but to the admiration of all men, how such a Structure should be raysed, & brought to pass by Mr Herbert, & performed with [*space*] pounds charge.[38]

The time when Herbert urged Ferrar to replace him as prebendary was, then, after earlier efforts at raising the amount of money needed had proved insufficient, but well in advance of the summer of 1632, when the work was regularly supervised by John Ferrar.[39] Particularly in John Ferrar's account ("The one urgeth . . . , the other as eagerly put all off") the use of the present tense conveys a sense of immediacy, as if John Ferrar had heard the arguments back and forth between the two deacons. That a large part of the money had been raised by the summer of 1632 also supports a date no later than 1630 for this interchange: if even the wealthy typically gave as the Earl of Pembroke and the Duchess of Lennox did, it would have taken many months to raise nearly two thousand pounds from gifts of fifty or a hundred pounds at a time. But George Herbert, Woodnoth, and Sir Henry Herbert prepared a book of some sort to show to prospective donors—probably something more than a bare list of names, and perhaps a prospectus that

[38] John Ferrar, "A Life of Nicholas Ferrar," in Blackstone, pp. 58–59.

[39] See the account in A. L. Maycock, *Nicholas Ferrar of Little Gidding* (London: S.P.C.K., 1938), pp. 270, 273–275.

included drawings. (After Sir Henry had persuaded the Duchess of Lennox to give one hundred pounds, Herbert wrote to Ferrar, "She liked our Book well.")[40]

The accounts of Leighton by the early biographers are cumulative: Nicholas Ferrar first; then Barnabas Oley, depending in part on Ferrar; and then Izaak Walton, depending almost wholly on his predecessors, with some additional information (such as the names of donors) from Arthur Woodnoth. But Nicholas Ferrar remains the authority. (John Ferrar's account was not generally known until the nineteenth century, when J. E. B. Mayor published it in *Nicholas Ferrar: Two Lives by His Brother John and by Dr. Jebb.*)

If, then, Herbert did undertake the long ride to Lincoln to preach the Whitsunday sermon at the cathedral and to try to persuade Ferrar to become prebendary in his place, we have a reasonable explanation of his failure to be ordained at Salisbury at the earliest possible opportunity, on Trinity Sunday, as well as a basis for understanding why he "long'd for the next Ember-week."[41]

Herbert's subscription at his ordination as priest reads:

> Ego Georgius Herbert in artib[us] magister diacon[us] ad sacros presbiterat[us] ordines admittend[us] et instituend[us] ōib[us] hisce articulis singulisq[ue] in ijsdē contentis volens & ex āiō subscribo & consensū meū ijsdē p[re]beo 19° die septemb. 1630. A.D.
>
> Georgius Herbert[42]

Bemerton Rectory

Walton's statement that Herbert had "to rebuild almost three parts" of the rectory at Bemerton[43] probably makes the condition of the rectory sound worse than it was. William Lewis, the rector under whom the terrier of 1616[44] was prepared, died in 1620 and was succeeded by Walter Curle, who chose to live "at *Minal,* 16 or 20 miles from this place."[45] It is rather difficult to

[40] *Works,* p. 379. [41] Walton, p. 293.

[42] Salisbury Diocesan Record Office. [43] Walton, p. 291.

[44] Salisbury Diocesan Record Office. A terrier is a description or inventory of lands attached to a living.

[45] Walton, p. 291. Walton's information came by word of mouth; in writing, the place becomes Mildenhall. Miss Stewart tells me that for a time at least Curle also maintained a residence in Salisbury Close.

believe that a house built a good five hundred years ago and substantial today would have fallen into utter ruin ("fall'n down, or decayd," says Walton, who of course never saw it in that state) in a mere ten years. Three parts (three-fourths?) of the rectory may well have required repair and redecoration, but probably most of the inconveniences were those of a house that has stood vacant for the better part of ten years—mustiness, damp, dust, birds, mice, broken windows, perhaps even a roof in need of repairs—in that state not the sort of place in which to set up one's first home, but certainly not a house requiring major rebuilding.

Repairs to the churches came first, of course, but we may suppose that by the autumn of 1630 Jane and George Herbert had settled into their first home, in Bemerton Rectory. Letter XII, which Canon Hutchinson supposes to have been written to Sir Henry Herbert about this time, establishes that Herbert was now installed in the rectory, had brought Dorothy and Magdalene Vaughan to live with him, and was concerned for the welfare of their younger sister. That Herbert was "beggarly" because he had spent £200 in building and had "nothing yett"[46] strongly supports this date. For the year 1630 he later paid his first fruits ("Geo. Herbert per ii^{as}") of £10 16*s.*[47]

Hutchinson has remarked on the delicacy and good sense Herbert showed in this letter[48] in writing Sir Henry about their orphaned nieces. The letter says a great deal also about his kindliness and insight—in acknowledging, for example, that he could be no real companion to the two older girls then living with him, in recognizing how much solace they gained through their own companionship, but beyond all else, in understanding the loneliness of the youngest sister. Even before he was well settled at Bemerton or had any assurance of his income there, he decided to bring her into his household, even though his brothers, much more able to afford the expense, declined to take such responsibility. His sensitivity to the plight of the youngest niece in her isolation and lack of incentive causes him to cite one of the *Outlandish Proverbs* (Number 953)

[46] *Works,* pp. 375–376.
[47] P.R.O. E. 341/11, fol. 6^{v} (Remembrancer's Account Books).
[48] *Works,* pp. xxxv–xxxvi.

in a way altogether typical of Herbert in its wry and practical observation that reminds us that both brothers shared a delight in such astringent proverb lore: "For the time of breeding is the time of doing children good; and not as many think who think they have done fairly, if they leave them a good portion after their decease. But take this rule, and it is an outlandish one, which I commend to you as being now a father, 'the best-bredd child hath the best portion.' "[49]

Without question, the household at Bemerton kept in rather close touch with that at Baynton. Even in the midst of settling into these new surroundings, Jane Herbert and the Vaughans probably visited back and forth with the Danvers family. Dorothy Vaughan, the eldest of Herbert's nieces, must have had many happy days at Bemerton with her uncle and his wife and her own sisters, but obviously she came to know Jane Herbert's family as well during the months she lived in Bemerton. Probably several of Jane's sisters were near the ages of her sisters and herself. When she later made her will, in August 1632,[50] she left a legacy of £5 to Mrs. Danvers, Jane's mother; 30*s.* to Amy Danvers; and 20*s.* each to Jane's sisters Anne, Mary, and Joan (Mrs. Michell), and to her sister-in-law, her brother Henry's wife. If proportion in legacies means anything, these bequests are much smaller than those to her own relatives. She left £100 each to her two sisters and to her uncle George, £40 to her cousin Beatrice, and £10 each to Jane Herbert and to her uncle Edward; but Jane Herbert's family, though she knew them scarcely two years, meant enough to her that she wanted to remember them, and to have them remember her, through memorial rings.

[49] Ibid., p. 376.

[50] P.R.O. PROB 11/162, fol. 101. I assume a date in August for the writing of the will chiefly because wills in this family (and in many others of the period) usually were not written until death was imminent. From Dorothy Vaughan's signature it is clear that she must have been very ill when she attempted to sign the will. Although her burial is not mentioned in the parish registers at Bemerton, it appears in the transcript, signed by Bostocke, in the Salisbury Diocesan Record Office: "Dorothe Vahhan gentle woman was buryed the xvth day of August." The will was not proved until 19 October 1632, perhaps because Herbert had hoped to carry out in person his duties as executor; but Bostocke and the second curate, John Hayes, actually conveyed the will to London for probate. This will, like Herbert's, is in Bostocke's hand; here, Herbert wrote the word "Witnesses" and subscribed as the first witness.

Head of his own household and table for the first time at the age of thirty-seven, Herbert settled into a new home less pretentious than those he had known at Charing Cross and at Chelsea, at Dauntesey and probably at Baynton House. In addition to Jane and George Herbert and the three Vaughan sisters, the household included four maidservants and two menservants. Because of Herbert's tenure at Bemerton, this rectory that might readily pass unnoted with a hundred others has taken on a special significance in the English church.

The rectory as Herbert found and restored it was basically of the type known as the English hall. Despite extensive additions at both the east and west ends and lesser ones on the north, it is still possible to trace the original outlines, particularly from the great fireplace (now a part of the kitchen) and the heavy beams. To the east of the hall would have been a second room; and to the west, stores, pantries, outbuildings, and tithe barn. Probably a staircase to the north gave access to the rooms above.

The most favorable exposure of the house is to the south, across what was probably an orchard in Herbert's time,[51] but is now lawn sloping down to the River Nadder. Herbert's bedchamber, immediately above what is now the drawing room, commanded a view of lawn, trees, river, and the water meadows beyond. The spire of Salisbury Cathedral is visible from the bottom of the garden, just at the edge of the river. Glebe lands probably extended both east and west, with footpaths along the river bank to the cathedral close and across the meadows to Harnham and Netherhampton. The characteristic view cannot have altered greatly: the view to the south in our day, as it was in Herbert's, is one of rural quiet and peace. Lorries may thunder on Lower Road between rectory and church; but to the south all is tranquillity.

[51] Two trees said to survive from Herbert's time were a part of the rectory garden until recently. The fig tree, about which the legend appears to be slighter, survives. The medlar apparently died about the turn of the century, but (according to records kept at the rectory) in 1906 a small shoot appeared, and the following year Kew Gardens planted a whitethorn beside it, to which the shoot was inarched in 1908. It became a handsome, gnarled tree and flourished until 1973, when the roots were attacked by honey fungus. Since that time quince grafts have been tried.

The Country Parson

It would be a mistake to regard Bemerton as in any sense a retreat from the problems of the world. Aside from the few surviving letters of this period, probably the best guide to Herbert's life at Bemerton is his *A Priest to the Temple; or, The Countrey Parson His Character and Rule of Holy Life* (completed, according to the prefatory letter, in 1632). This work, brought to its present form during the last year of his life, may well be an expansion of the rules Herbert set for himself at the time of his induction at Bemerton.[52] If it may be taken as "the Form and Character of a true Pastour . . . a Mark to aim at,"[53] it may be accepted as the model Herbert intended to follow, whether or not the realities of circumstance allowed him to follow it in every detail. The goal is one he acknowledges in his introduction: "I will set [my mark] as high as I can, since hee shoots higher that threatens the Moon, then hee that aims at a Tree."[54] The title is probably based on that given to his English poems after his death; but most students long since have referred to it by the homelier subtitle appended at its first publication in 1652, *The Country Parson.*

The work may be considered as an expanded and somewhat idealized "character," the lengthiest of this type that became popular during the earlier seventeenth century; but it rarely departs from the immediate experience of its author in the parish of Fugglestone-with-Bemerton. The parishioners Herbert attempted to help are generalized, recognizable in most other country parishes, as Sir Toby Belch is generic; but like Sir Toby, each of Herbert's charges is also recognizable as an Englishman (or an Englishwoman), closely tied to the bit of ground from which he sprang. They are not often lovable; frequently they are willful, stubborn, even exasperating. The parson for his part is persevering, firm, charitable, patient, but constantly ready to teach his people "how Gods goodnesse strives with mans refractoriness; Man would sit down at this world, God bids him sell it, and purchase a better."[55] The parson's task is most often to bring his parishioners to deal better with God and with their fellows. Often Herbert comes close to

[52] Walton, p. 289. [53] *Works,* p. 224. [54] Ibid. [55] Ibid., p. 272.

the proverb lore he loved, garnered, and used in other works. Many passages might be quoted for their working knowledge of human nature; this selection demonstrates also his good sense, forthright diction, and economical phrasing in describing his parson:

Accordingly his voyce is humble, his words treatable, and slow; yet not so slow neither, as to let the fervency of the supplicant hang and dy between speaking, but with a grave livelinesse, between fear and zeal, pausing yet pressing, he performes his duty.[56]

Sometimes he tells them stories, and sayings of others, according as his text invites him; for them also men heed, and remember better then exhortations; which though earnest, yet often dy with the Sermon, especially with Countrey people; which are thick, and heavy, and hard to raise to a poynt of Zeal, and fervency, and need a mountaine of fire to kindle them; but stories and sayings they will well remember.[57]

The Country Parson, as soon as he awakes on Sunday morning, presently falls to work, and seems to himselfe so as a Market-man is, when the Market day comes, or a shopkeeper, when customers use to come in. His thoughts are full of making the best of the day, and contriving it to his best gaines.[58]

He keeps his servants between love, and fear, according as hee findes them; but generally he distributes it thus, To his Children he shewes more love then terrour, to his servants more terrour then love; but an old good servant boards a child.[59]

For meat was made for man, not man for meat.[60]

If the Parson were ashamed of particularizing in these things, hee were not fit to be a Parson: but he holds the Rule, that Nothing is little in Gods service: If it once have the honour of that Name, it grows great instantly.[61]

The Countrey Parson is not only a father to his flock, but also professeth himselfe throughly of the opinion, carrying it about with him as fully, as if he begot his whole Parish.[62]

[56] Ibid., p. 231. [57] Ibid., p. 233.
[58] Ibid., p. 235. [59] Ibid., p. 241.
[60] Ibid., p. 242. [61] Ibid., pp. 248–249. [62] Ibid., p. 250.

In judging, he followes that, which is altogether right; so that if the poorest man of the Parish detain but a pin unjustly from the richest, he absolutely restores it as a Judge; but when he hath so done, then he assumes the Parson, and exhorts to Charity.[63]

More particularly, and to give one instance for all, if God have given me servants, and I either provide too little for them, or that which is unwholsome, being sometimes baned meat, sometimes too salt, and so not competent nourishment, I am Covetous.[64]

Country people are full of these petty injustices, being cunning to make use of another, and spare themselves.[65]

Neverthelesse, he somtimes refresheth himselfe, as knowing that nature will not bear everlasting droopings, and that pleasantnesse of disposition is a great key to do good; not onely because all men shun the company of perpetuall severity, but also for that when they are in company, instructions seasoned with pleasantnesse, both enter sooner, and roote deeper.[66]

Do well, and right, and let the world sinke.[67]

But his family is his best care, to labour Christian soules, and raise them to their height, even to heaven; to dresse and prune them, and take as much joy in a straight-growing childe, or servant, as a Gardiner doth in a choice tree.[68]

The thrusting away of his arme makes us onely not embraced.[69]

The fruit of this blessing good *Hannah* found, and received with great joy, I *Sam.* I. 18. though it came from a man disallowed by God: for it was not the person, but Priesthood, that blessed; so that even ill Priests may blesse.[70]

Herbert probably worked at *The Country Parson* during most of his time at Bemerton. It is an expandable kind of book, one that he did not expect to be complete in itself, but to be added to by others. The earlier portions define, limit, and classify; but after the seventh chapter ("The Parson preaching")

[63] Ibid., p. 260. [64] Ibid., p. 265. [65] Ibid.
[66] Ibid., pp. 267–268. [67] Ibid., p. 270. [68] Ibid., p. 275.
[69] Ibid., p. 283. [70] Ibid., p. 285.

the chapters take up whatever subject has most recently come to mind, probably as Herbert's experience with his parish grew.

From this book drawn from his experience as priest, we may gather some impressions of the parish, the parishioners, and the patterns of life at Bemerton as Herbert came to know it. Among this cluster of villages in the parish, the houses were concentrated at Fugglestone and at Bemerton; some dwellings stood within what has since been enclosed as Wilton Park, and certainly some also in Quidhampton, between the two churches. Herbert had known villages and villagers all his life, at Montgomery and Wroxeter, in Charing Cross and Chelsea, at Royston and Buckden, at Woodford and Dauntesey. At Bemerton his parishioners included masters and men, cottagers and landowners, gentry and perhaps nobility, to all of whom he spoke frankly and directly, but always charitably, considering of what sort the person was and what was required to reach him. Throughout this book he shows great understanding and great compassion toward the poor, the repentant, the sick, and the unfortunate, his sternness being reserved for the haughty, the selfish, the lazy, and the uncharitable. No good man, however impoverished, had anything to fear from this parson; but no man of rank went unrebuked when rebuke was in order. Herbert's birth, breeding, and past life did not set a gulf between them, because he labored constantly to teach them, to comfort them, and to bring them to an understanding of God's love.

Herbert's following of the use of the Church of England is implicit in many of his chapters, particularly in "The Parson praying," "The Parson preaching," "The Parson on Sundays," "The Parson's Church," "The Parson Catechizing," and "The Parson in Sacraments." It is clear that Walton, having found his cue in the remarks of Ferrar and of Oley, borrowed extensively from these chapters in his long digressions on Herbert's teaching and practice at Bemerton.

To suit his own impressions and purposes, Walton, in fact, was all too willing to expand a remark or even a slight hint from Ferrar or Oley, or to inflate a short phrase from a poem into a full-blown and sometimes plausible incident. David Novarr and John Butt have demonstrated many of Walton's shortcomings and distortions; I shall merely emphasize their findings.

A long portion of Walton's account of Herbert at Bemerton is the homily on Herbert's manner of praying, preaching, teaching, and catechizing[71]—perhaps based in part on information Walton had from Woodnoth, but written so earnestly and zealously that it is obvious that Walton is expatiating on some of his own preferences and contrasting them to the parlous practices he saw on all sides after the Restoration.

One passage in particular I would call in question. Herbert notices that Edmund Duncon is a priest and asks him to pray with him; Walton represents their conversation thus: "*Sir, I see by your habit that you are a Priest, and I desire you to pray with me;* which being granted, Mr. *Duncon* ask'd him, *what Prayers?* to which, Mr. *Herberts* answer was, *O Sir, the Prayers of my Mother, the Church of* England, *no other Prayers are equal to them! but, at this time, I beg of you to pray only the* Litany, *for I am weak and faint;* and Mr. *Duncon* did so."[72] What other prayers *would* a priest of the Church of England pray? And particularly, why would one Anglican priest have to ask another, "*what Prayers?*"? The conversation would hardly ring true even if the speakers had been two laymen. It seems likely that the whole passage is merely Walton's means of working in a paraphrase of the opening of "The British Church":

> I joy, deare Mother, when I view
> Thy perfect lineaments and hue
> Both sweet and bright.
> Beautie in thee takes up her place,
> And dates her letters from thy face,
> When she doth write.

But if we may forget Walton's homiletics for a time and try instead to draw our own conclusions about Herbert at Bemerton as in life he was, we find that he must have known many months of good health when he was free to grow into the round of parish life and the Christian year before ill health

[71] Walton, pp. 295–303.

[72] Ibid., p. 308. The Litany in the Prayer Book of Herbert's time occupied nearly six pages; Evensong, even with two lessons and the Athanasian Creed, would scarcely have required much more time.

forced him to lessen his efforts, to employ a second curate, and finally to become *"only a hearer"*[73] at the daily offices at St. Andrew's. That this second curate, John Hayes, had come to Bemerton before 19 October 1632 (the date when he and Bostocke took Dorothy Vaughan's will to London for probate) sets one limit to the time by which Herbert felt the need of further lightening of his responsibilities in the parish.

Even so, he must have had two good years or more after his arrival at Bemerton, during most of which he was fully resident, taking Sunday services and daily offices, catechizing diligently, preaching and teaching, exhorting and loving his people in accordance with his concept of his duties in the parish. Walton dwells at length on Herbert's sickness and death; George Herbert Palmer's arbitrary rearrangement of Herbert's poems according to an assumed chronology shows Herbert's life as ending in despair and defeat. But Herbert himself always conceived of his service to God as one of joy—of reverence, holy fear, humility, but also the joy he expresses in such poems as "Praise" (I), "Christmas," "The Starre," "Sunday," "The Call," and "Easter." Anyone who would understand Herbert's attitude in worship and service should recall such comments on the Christian tradition as that A. L. Maycock made about Nicholas Ferrar and Little Gidding:

> What was lacking in Puritanism and what was the conspicuous quality in the life and spirit of Little Gidding was, quite simply, that supernatural joy which is the very essence of true devotion, which rests in the knowledge of God's infinite mercy in utter simplicity of heart and lives in the consciousness of his innumerable benefits to us and to all men, a joy deep and serene, peaceful and untroubled, altogether unaffected by the trials and troubles of this present life. If we would understand the place that joy should hold in the life of the Christian, we need only consider that the early fathers of the Church counted sickness or despondency as one of the capital sins: and as a corollary we may recall the dictum of St. Francis de Sales that "sadness is always unprofitable and in contradiction to the service of God."[74]

[73] Ibid., p. 307.
[74] A. L. Maycock, *Chronicles of Little Gidding* (London: S.P.C.K., 1954), p. 11.

Such joy was the spirit of Herbert's life at Bemerton; and anyone who fails to grasp his "grave livelinesse"[75] would do well to read in *The Country Parson* the chapter "The Parson on Sundays" or Herbert's two prayers for use before and after sermons, or the almost playful opening of "The Bunch of Grapes" or his address to rhetorical devices in "The Forerunners":

> Farewell sweet phrases, lovely metaphors.
> But will ye leave me thus? when ye before
> Of stews and brothels onely knew the doores,
> Then did I wash you with my tears, and more,
> Brought you to Church well drest and clad:
> My God must have my best, ev'n all I had.
>
> Lovely enchanting language, sugar-cane,
> Hony of roses, whither wilt thou flie?
> Hath some fond lover tic'd thee to thy bane?
> And wilt thou leave the Church, and love a stie?
> Fie, thou wilt soil thy broider'd coat,
> And hurt thy self, and him that sings the note.

Herbert and the Music at Salisbury

The familiar round of the parson's duties established the sense of order that Herbert loved. Regularly he enriched it by attending Evensong at Salisbury Cathedral twice weekly and playing (and perhaps singing) in private musical gatherings afterward. Having been blessed from childhood by hearing regularly some of the greatest liturgical music in an age of very great liturgical music—of Tallis and Tye, Byrd and Gibbons—he must have welcomed the opportunity to feast his soul on the choral music of the singing men of Sarum.

Herbert's attitude toward music in general, or even toward such liturgical services, cannot be interpreted solely from the poem "Church-Musick," which appears in *W*[76] and was therefore probably written at Cambridge. Herbert loved music all his life, probably secular consort as well as sacred music; and all

[75] *Works,* p. 231. Note also Herbert's remark (p. 241) "Sunday is his day of joy."
[76] Fol. 32.

his life he sang, played, and perhaps even composed music. (Some impression of the extent of his musical knowledge may be drawn from his brother Edward's lute book, now in the Fitzwilliam Museum, Cambridge.)

Walton is so emphatic in his remarks about how Herbert found *"his Heaven upon Earth"* in prayer and cathedral music[77] that it is difficult to assess the extent to which an unfortunate series of events in 1629 and 1630 interfered with the quality of music in the cathedral. It may indeed be true that the service music at Salisbury did not attain the standard one would desire of so old and great a foundation. There is record enough of the altercation that began in 1629 with the death of John Holmes, tutor of the choristers, when Holmes's widow refused to vacate the Choristers' House for Giles Tomkins, formerly the organist of King's College, Cambridge, who had been chosen by John Bowle, Dean of Salisbury, to replace Holmes. (Dulcibella Holmes not only hoped to see her son-in-law, James Clark, one of the vicars choral, made permanent tutor of the choristers, but brought about deadlocked arguments in the chapter that eventually came to the attention of the Archbishop of Canterbury and of King Charles.)[78] To what extent this continuing internal strife affected the performance of music at the cathedral services it is now impossible to say, because the extant records are inconclusive.

At the time of Laud's visitation of Salisbury in 1634 the membership of the choir consisted of "six vicars chorall which are to be in holy orders, seaven singing men, which are not required to be in holy orders and six choristers, of which seaven singing-men, one is teacher of the Choristers, and another organist"[79]—eighteen singers all told and an organist.

Giles Tomkins apparently came to Salisbury in April of 1629 expecting to teach music to the choristers; by 16 July he had served a full quarter as a lay vicar, the dean having admitted him to this post while the arguments about his becoming the tutor of the choristers continued.[80] By 13 October no choristers remained at the cathedral, and the dean proposed appointing

[77] Walton, p. 303.
[78] Dora H. Robertson, *Sarum Close* (2d ed., Bath: Firecrest, 1969), p. 176.
[79] Ibid., p. 187. [80] Ibid., pp. 178–183.

other boys to sing in their places. Tomkins' petition in Chancery of 5 November 1629 has survived, though not the answer to it;[81] but at last, in December 1630, Tomkins was able to move into the Choristers' House and properly undertake his duties as choristers' tutor in music.

A further passage in the replies to Laud's visitation inquiry of 1634 elicited this comment about the music of the choristers:

> All save Doctor Seward answere that they conceave that the Choristers have not ben well ordered and instructed in the arte of singing, but their teacher doth promise to looke better unto them, and they have not ben catechized and instructed as they ought in the principles of religion, by the defaults of the master of our Gram'er schoole and of their teacher in singing. Dr. Seward for his parte answereth in these words. The choristers are as well ordered as their poore meanes and maintenance will afford. I never knew them better; the number of them is furnished. One Gyles Tompkins hath the charge of instructing them in the art of singing, which he protesteth he doth carefully and I believe he doth. He hath been blamed lately for leaving them without a guide and teacher once or twice when he went to waite at the courte, but he promiseth he will doe noe more so, yet protesteth that they all saue two sing their parts perfectly, and neede noe teacher in his absence. Our schoolemaster of our free schoole I conceave is to instructe them in their catechisme, as in the latine tongue, yet Mr. Tompkins protesteth that he takes that care and paynes likewise.[82]

Yet, difficult as it may be to assess these remarks, it is certain that Herbert, an accomplished musician, considered the services and music at Salisbury worth his twice-weekly visits. That the singing men of Sarum sang the burial office for Herbert at Bemerton[83] conveys the impression that it was choral music that transported him from earth to heaven. When, therefore, Rosalie Eggleston suggests that in Herbert's time the music for services at Salisbury Cathedral was in complete shambles, I think she has overlooked some of the facts.[84]

Instrumental music—of organ, cornets, and sackbuts—apparently continued without interruption. To provide vocal

[81] Ibid., pp. 184–185. [82] Ibid., pp. 187–188.

[83] Aubrey, *Brief Lives,* p. 137.

[84] Rosalie J. Eggleston, "A Study of Some Relationships between Late Renaissance Music and *The Temple* of George Herbert" (Ph.D. dissertation, University of New Mexico, 1969), pp. 178, 182.

music, six vicars choral, six lay vicars, and one organist—the adult members—continued their normal course. Even if there had been no boy choristers at all, the thirteen men would surely have been capable of singing both plainsong and the services that Herbert went to hear. (By the time of Herbert's death, however, boy choristers were once again a regular part of the choir; Aubrey mentions Francis Sambroke, an attorney, who had sung as a chorister at Herbert's burial.)[85]

The thirteen men included Humphrey Henchman as precentor, Edward Tucker as organist, and of course Giles Tomkins as teacher of the choristers.[86] After Evensong in the cathedral, Herbert went on, probably with some of these singers and other friends, to "sing and play his part, at an appointed private Musick-meeting."[87] The music was probably both sacred and secular. The singing may have been madrigals or solo songs to the accompaniment of a lute; the instrumental music was probably for a consort of viols. Possibly Herbert sang here some of his own poems, accompanying himself on the lute; the unusual number of poems in trochaic meter included among the seventy-six new poems that he added to the original of *B* suggests that some of them may have been intended for such setting and performance. If his Salisbury companions heard Herbert sing his own texts, they were among the few who knew him, during his lifetime, as an author of English verses.[88]

There is no certainty about where these meetings were held, but the general impression is of a house within the close. As precentor, Henchman lived in the South Canonry, and the meetings may well have been held there.[89] But no matter what the place: in music Herbert found one of his chief earthly joys, one that enters his poetry not only in his specific musical terms, but also in musical effect or heightened consciousness of sound.[90]

[85] Aubrey, *Brief Lives,* p. 137. [86] Robertson, pp. 175, 185.
[87] Walton, p. 303.
[88] Aubrey, p. 137. H. Allen of Dauntesey told Aubrey that Herbert "had a very good hand on the Lute, and that he sett his own Lyricks or sacred poems."
[89] Eggleston, p. 183.
[90] Amy M. Charles, "George Herbert: Priest, Poet, Musician," *Journal of the Viola da Gamba Society of America,* IV (1967), 27–36.

Arthur Woodnoth's Visits to Herbert

Another less frequent variation in the daily round at Bemerton came with the visits of Arthur Woodnoth, a cousin of Nicholas Ferrar's who was a goldsmith in Foster Lane. He acted as a purchasing and forwarding agent for all the Ferrars, buying cloth or paper or cheese or ginger beer or anything else the household at Little Gidding needed. After Sir John Danvers' second marriage he served as some sort of business manager for that rather extravagant gentleman; and at one time he talked with Herbert about leaving this service to enter holy orders. Perhaps through his close association with the Ferrars, perhaps because of handling matters for Sir John Danvers, especially at Lavington, Woodnoth visited Herbert both at Baynton House and, later, at Bemerton.

Aside from Ferrar's unsigned preface to *The Temple,* Arthur Woodnoth was probably Walton's first source of information about Herbert's life. That Walton talked with him and made notes of what Woodnoth told him establishes that Walton had begun collecting material about Herbert far earlier than the "late retreat from the business of this World"[91] that he mentions in his introduction of 1670, because Arthur Woodnoth's will, written on 18 February 1644, was probated on 17 March 1644.[92] The dates are written in Old Style; and Woodnoth had been dead for many years before Walton completed and published his life of Herbert. The point is an important one to

[91] Walton, p. 258.

[92] P.R.O. PROB 11/192. Another circumstance that has clouded understanding of the relationship between Walton and Woodnoth is the posthumous publication in 1651 of Woodnoth's pamphlet about Sir John Danvers, "An Account and Observation taken by A. W., a true friend and Servant to Sir John Danvers," in *A Short Collection of the Most Remarkable Passages from the originall to the dissolution of the Virginia Company,* which has long led to the assumption that Woodnoth was alive at the time of publication and consequently would have known of Danvers' part in the death of Charles I. But Woodnoth, who never knew Sir John as a regicide and wrote his remarks in support of him simply from his knowledge of the affairs of the Virginia Company, completed his pamphlet in 1644. At most, then, Woodnoth was looking back over ten or fifteen years to provide the information Walton asked. Woodnoth is listed as deputy to the governor of the Bermuda Company on 13 October 1644 in J. M. Lefroy, *Memorials of the Discovery and Early Settlement of the Bermudas or Somers Islands, 1515–1685* (London, 1877–1879), I, 590.

remember when we consider some of Walton's errors in fact or inference, as well as his rather free interpretation and expansion of the notes he had taken during their conversation. And though Walton never knew that Woodnoth and Ferrar were cousins, Woodnoth's close relationship with the Ferrars probably supplied material for Walton's account of them and of life at Little Gidding.

Woodnoth, who was less than a year Herbert's elder,[93] apparently undertook a rather extensive examination of the course of his own life, his purposes, and the best uses of his talents during the time Herbert was at Bemerton. Woodnoth had been active and successful in his chosen craft, had earned a comfortable estate, and had taken more apprentices than the number usual within the Goldsmiths' Company. As he approached his fortieth year, and particularly as he saw Ferrar and Herbert happy and contented in their different ways of serving God, he seems to have pondered for many months whether he himself should also turn from all secular interests and devote his abilities wholly to the service of God. Both Ferrar and Herbert attempted to help him resolve his uncertainties; but for whatever reason, he chose ultimately to remain in secular employment.

The sequence of Walton's references to Woodnoth is confusing because his first one follows the account of Herbert's being made prebendary of Leighton (therefore after 1626), but Walton then drops back to permit Woodnoth to deliver to Herbert's mother the letter dated from Trinity College on 25 May 1622.[94] The other remarks about Woodnoth are therefore rather difficult to date. It would be useful to know, for example, at what point he "did therefore set limits to himself as to desire of wealth."[95]

Woodnoth had been made free of the Goldsmiths' Company

[93] Wybunbury Parish Registers, P37/1/1, Cheshire Record Office. Woodnoth was baptized on 24 April 1592. The pedigree of the family of his father, John Woodnoth, gentleman, is included in *Ormerod's History of Cheshire* (1858), III, 508. See also the 1613 *Herald's Visitation* (Lancashire and Cheshire Record Society), LVIII, 263–266. Of the seven sons of John Woodnoth apprenticed to members of the Goldsmiths' Company, only Arthur and his elder brother John were apprenticed to Richard Keane (or Keine).

[94] Walton, p. 279. [95] Ibid., p. 280.

on 31 March 1615 (three years before his apprenticeship would normally have ended).[96] But he never wholly gave over his own craft, as we may see from the Apprentice Book at Goldsmiths' Hall: Woodnoth took apprentices in 1617, 1622, 1626 (Nicholas Collett, Ferrar's nephew), 1627, 1631, 1632, 1634, 1637, and 1641; Martin Johnson was made free of the company on 28 March 1645, not long after Woodnoth's death, and William Bressie, Woodnoth's last apprentice, in 1650. At no time after 1617 was Woodnoth without any apprentice, and for most of the time he had two or three apprentices working under him. While he may have set limits on the amount he needed to earn to "preserve a competence for himself," it is clear that his intention of "dedicat[ing] the remaining part of his life to the service of God" was not accomplished by giving up his activity as a goldsmith at the sign of the Bunch of Grapes in Foster Lane.

Whether Woodnoth was at home or traveling, he wrote to Nicholas Ferrar rather often. From the extant letters, it looks as though he intended to write weekly; but occasionally he would write on several days in succession, and at other times (probably because of letters now lost to us) there may be a gap of weeks or even months. A loyal, able, reliable, and warmhearted man, he wrote to his cousin about matters small and great, practical and pedestrian, but sometimes spiritual, because Ferrar served most of his relatives as a spiritual director and mentor in establishing rules for daily life. Woodnoth had therefore mentioned in a number of letters his uncertainties about how he might best employ his talents; and the two men apparently agreed finally to consult Herbert for his advice about Woodnoth's future, which by this time Woodnoth perceived as a choice between continuing to serve Sir John Danvers and entering holy orders. Either course might require him to leave his craft.

Whatever the reason, Ferrar and Herbert did not advise Woodnoth to seek ordination. Although Ferrar never says plainly that Woodnoth is too readily subject to discouragement, if not actual melancholy, he implies such a possibility in several

[96] Goldsmiths' Company, Apprentice Book No. 1; Wardens Accounts and Court Minutes, Part I, 26 July 1611–22 January 1617.

of his letters.[97] It is possible too that both Ferrar and Herbert felt that Woodnoth had created a false dilemma, partly because of his discouragement over what he interpreted as his own ineffectual efforts to keep Herbert's free-spending stepfather from running headlong into bankruptcy.

When Woodnoth arrived at Bemerton, then, late in September or early in October of 1631, he was seeking Herbert's counsel.[98] Having given him "my Cosens booke" (apparently a concordance), Woodnoth then delivered a letter from Ferrar and "undertooke to explaine by telling him it concerned my self and so proceeded to a more playne demonstration of my desyres of his aduise and counsell." Their discussions were interrupted by the canonical hours of prayer and by a visit to Wilton; but Herbert eventually wrote out, in two parts, the document that Woodnoth enclosed in this letter to Ferrar.

In his comments (labeled at Little Gidding, "Mr Herberts reasons for Arth. Woodenoths Liuing wth Sr Jhon Daūers")[99] Herbert urges Woodnoth not to leave Sir John's employ, but to cultivate constancy and long-suffering; he suggests, moreover, that Woodnoth may have been more successful than he realizes in restraining Sir John and that things that may not have improved during his presence might grow worse in his absence. He also commented, Woodnoth said, that "we were much troubled about words for the Name of a Diuine wold satisfy all when in truth I might doe the office tho I wanted the tytle for to be a prompter of good to Sr John was to be a good Angell to him Nay was to doo that which God himself did."

This advice is of particular importance as the only prose exposition (apart from passing remarks in the letters and in *The Country Parson*) of Herbert's attitudes toward Christian faith, practice, and vocation. For Woodnoth, who had been troubled

[97] Several times Woodnoth retreated to Wiltshire, apparently to think over his problems. See especially Sir John Danvers to Arthur Woodnoth, 14 September 1631, F.P. No. 223; John Ferrar to Arthur Woodnoth, 16 July 1632, F.P. No. 376; Nicholas Ferrar to Arthur Woodnoth, 19 April 1630–17 May 1630, F.P. Nos. 505–509; and Nicholas Ferrar to Arthur Woodnoth, 27 October 1630, F.P. No. 521. F.P. Nos. 508 and 521 are available in Blackstone, pp. 255–257.

[98] Arthur Woodnoth to Nicholas Ferrar, 13 October 1631, F.P. No. 1092.

[99] F.P. No. 714; *Works*, pp. 380–381; Blackstone, pp. 269–270 (with partial facsimile).

for many months about handling Sir John's business affairs, this assessment and counsel must surely have been helpful in offering a steadier view of the circumstances he was attempting to control.

Lady Anne Clifford

The same letter from Arthur Woodnoth to Nicholas Ferrar is one of two surviving records of the friendship between Herbert and Lady Anne Clifford, formerly the Countess of Dorset, who had become Countess of Pembroke and Montgomery when she married Philip Herbert on 1 June 1630. Here Woodnoth tells of going to Wilton and spending an hour in solitary thought while Herbert was with the Countess.

Lady Anne Clifford, as she was known during her marriage to the Earl of Dorset and throughout her life, was a remarkable woman in an age that produced a number of women known for their intelligence, wit, and interest in literature, and abilities in managing great estates. She and Herbert arrived as newcomers in the neighborhood of Wilton and Bemerton within a month or so of each other during the spring of 1630. Although there is no evidence to support the assumption that Herbert regularly served as chaplain to the Earl of Pembroke, the two men were members of the same great family and had probably known each other from childhood. Without doubt the rector of Bemerton was a welcome guest at his cousin's great house. From Herbert's own letter of 10 December 1631 to the Countess it is clear that he and she had established a firm friendship. Recently she had sent a cask of metheglin (spiced mead) to the household at Bemerton, perhaps in anticipation of the Christmas season; and Herbert wrote gracefully to thank her on behalf of her "poor Colony of Servants," to say that they would send "some thing not unworthy of those hands at which they aim," to give her in the meantime "a Priests blessing, though it be none of the Court-Stile."[100]

Philip Herbert differed in almost every way from his popular elder brother William, the third Earl of Pembroke, who was known as a patron of literary men. Nothing about Philip Herbert suggests that this son of "Sidney's sister, Pembroke's

[100] *Works,* pp. 376–377.

mother" took the slightest interest in poetry of the sort that had enchanted his mother's circle or that the dedication of the Shakespeare First Folio "to the most noble and incomparable paire of brethren" represented his interests, least of all that he shared his second wife's appreciation of poetry.[101]

But Lady Anne Clifford had decided tastes in literature, as indeed she had in almost everything else, from child-rearing to estate management. Her friendship with Donne had probably formed another bond between her and Herbert. Books by several of her favorite authors are represented in the "Great Picture" of her at Appleby (with a copy originally at Skipton), including Donne, Herbert, Daniel, and George Sandys.[102] Daniel had written a complimentary epistle of nearly a hundred lines to the lady, the beginning and ending of which convey his intended tone:

> Vnto the tender youth of those faire eyes
> The light of iudgement can arise but new,
> And yong the world appeares t'a yong conceit,
> Whilst thorow th'vnacquainted faculties
> The late inuested soule doth rawly view
> Those Obiects which on that discretion waite.
>
> . . . . .
>
> Such are your holy bounds, who must conuay
> (If God so please) the honourable bloud
> Of *Clifford,* and of *Russell,* led aright
> To many worthy stemmes whose off-spring may
> Looke backe with comfort, to haue had that good
> To spring from such a branch that grew s'vpright:
> Since nothing cheeres the heart of greatnesse more
> Then th'Ancestors faire glory gone before.[103]

Aside from the "Great Picture" and the letters of Herbert and Woodnoth, we know nothing of the friendship. But from *The Country Parson* we know that Herbert felt that a priest could

[101] See Tresham Lever, *The Herberts of Wilton* (London: John Murray, 1967), pp. 72–117.

[102] George C. Williamson, *Lady Anne Clifford, Countess of Dorset, Pembroke, and Montgomery* (Kendal, 1922), p. 344; R. C. Bald, *John Donne: A Life* (Oxford: Clarendon Press, 1970), p. 324; *Works,* p. 583.

[103] Samuel Daniel, *Poems and a Defence of Ryme,* ed. Arthur Colby Sprague (Cambridge, Mass.: Harvard University Press, 1930), pp. xxii, 119–121.

never set aside his priesthood, that he must admonish the great as well as the lowly: "Before [chaplains] are in Orders, they may be received for Companions, or discoursers; but after a man is once Minister, he cannot agree to come into any house, where he shall not exercise what he is, unless he forsake his plough, and look back."[104] The Countess was not notably happy in this marriage (and ultimately lived apart from her husband). It may well be that during her hour's conversation with Herbert the Countess received some of the same sort of calm, practical advice that he later gave Woodnoth in the "Reasons."

Last Days at Bemerton

Herbert's apparent return to health during and after his stay at Dauntesey may have been genuine and might have continued had he not drawn so extensively on his newfound strength in his work at Bemerton. But if he had never tested and applied that strength by going to Bemerton, then he would indeed have gone down to the defeat that Palmer implies in his arrangement of the poems—in the decline from "The Happy Priest" to "Restlessness," "Suffering," and "Death."[105] But Palmer, despite his great services to Herbert in many other ways, was here riding out dreary preconceived notions of chronology; and other responsible scholars who have also made close studies of the order that Herbert set for the final arrangement of his poems emphasize the internal unity of Herbert's order and particularly the sense it conveys of the progress of the soul that can end only in the joy that is one of Herbert's chief themes.[106] (The relationship was fixed in his mind as early as the time when he determined the order of the last poems in "The Church" in *W*.) To Herbert, death represented not the ultimate defeat of all earthly efforts but the crown of all earthly expectations.

[104] *Works*, p. 226.

[105] *The English Works of George Herbert*, ed. George Herbert Palmer (Boston: Houghton Mifflin, 1905), vol. III.

[106] See especially Louis L. Martz, *The Poetry of Meditation* (New Haven: Yale University Press, 1954), pp. 288–320; Joseph H. Summers, *George Herbert: His Religion and Art* (London: Chatto and Windus, 1954); and my "The Williams Manuscript and *The Temple*."

Even Walton, though he dwells on the earthly sadness of Herbert's death, particularly on the weeping of Mrs. Herbert and the nieces, emphasizes that Herbert was fully prepared for death, calm in the face of it, looking forward with quiet joy to the blessings and reunions beyond this life.[107] Walton undoubtedly had his account of Herbert's death from Woodnoth; and it was Woodnoth who wrote almost at once to tell Ferrar of the death and burial of their friend: "Vppon friday, about foure a Clock itt pleased God to take vnto his mercy the soule of o^r Deere Deere Brother & frend Mr Harbert whose body vppon Sunday was buried the more particular passages of his sicknes Death and buriall I shall giue yo an accoumpt."[108]

Although in his haste Woodnoth neglected to date the letter, internal evidence establishes Monday, 4 March 1633, as the likely date. The parish registers give the date of 3 March for the burial; the date of death was therefore Friday, 1 March.

Herbert died in the bedchamber overlooking the River Nadder and the water meadows beyond. He had written his will only the preceding Monday, the day after Walton says he rose from his bed to play and sing verses from "The Thanksgiving" ("My musick shall finde thee") and "Sunday" ("The Sundaies of man's life").

The will is in the hand of Nathanael Bostocke and is witnessed by Bostocke and Elizabeth Burden, one of the servants. In it Herbert leaves the bulk of his estate to his wife, save for legacies of books to his curates and money to his servants, provides for a last gift for the restoration at Leighton, and arranges for the payment of various legacies of his niece Dorothy Vaughan, generously dividing his own earlier legacy of a hundred pounds from her between her sisters Magdalene and Katherine and adding four hundred pounds beyond her original bequest. Woodnoth is named executor (as he ruefully tells Ferrar) and Sir John Danvers overseer. From subsequent letters we may be sure that Woodnoth performed his duties con-

[107] Walton, pp. 316–319. Walton twice mentions three nieces, but only Katherine and Magdalene were present, Dorothy having died the preceding August.

[108] F.P. No. 1047, undated (probably 4 March 1632/33). There is no factual basis for the date of 27 February as that of Herbert's death, though the error has been perpetuated in several recent Prayer Books.

scientiously and sensitively, carrying out the oral charge Herbert gave shortly before he died.[109] He also continued to raise money for the restoration at Leighton.

Herbert's funeral followed quickly; like his brothers Edward and Henry he apparently preferred a prompt and simple ceremony.[110] The distance between rectory and church is very short; and in the little church the service for the burial of the dead must have been solemn and impressive, its only ornament beyond the words themselves being the singing of the cathedral choir, some of whom had shared his musical evenings in the past.

That year the third of March was Quinquagesima Sunday, the last Sunday before the beginning of Lent (as Canon Hutchinson has it, "Quinquagesima Sunday, a day singularly appropriate for one whose feeling quickens at every mention in his poems of the Divine love").[111] The propers for that day speak especially of love, compassion, faith, and charity, the epistle being I Corinthians 13. The collect is in every way appropriate to Herbert: "O Lord, who hast taught us that all our doings without charity are nothing worth: Send thy Holy Ghost, and pour into our hearts that most excellent gift of charity, the very bond of peace and of all virtues, without which whosoever liveth is counted dead before thee: Grant this for thy only Son Jesus Christ's sake. Amen."

The grave was not marked, and the exact location is not certain: it is either beneath or to the north of the altar.[112] Excavation in the nineteenth century suggested that Herbert's body had been laid in the grave of his niece; but the evidence is sketchy, and there is little hope now of finding more precise information.

"Thus he liv'd, and thus he dy'd," says Walton, and goes on

[109] Walton, p. 316. Herbert's will is now catalogued as P.R.O. PROB 11/163, fol. 25.

[110] Will of Edward, Lord Herbert of Chirbury, P.R.O. PROB 11/205, fol. 138; will of Sir Henry Herbert, P.R.O. PROB 11/342, fol. 59.

[111] *Works,* p. xxxix. John Ferrar, in his life of his brother, tells how the community at Little Gidding, just about the hour of Herbert's death, heard from one of the Mapletofts the "grievous Newes" that Herbert "was past hope of Recovery" and prayed for him (Blackstone, p. 79).

[112] *A Collection of Papers Relating to the Parish of Bemerton* (Salisbury: Edward Roe, 1893).

to expand too much on the statement. Perhaps the more fitting memorial for this poet who had taught himelf never to say too much is that written by his elder brother a decade or more later:

My brother George was so excellent a scholar, that he was made the publick Orator of the University in Cambridge, some of whose English works are extant, which thô they be rare in their kind, yet are far short of expressing those perfections he had in the Greek and Latin Tongue, and all divine and human literature: his life was most holy and exemplary, in so much that about Salisbury where he lived beneficed for many years, he was little less than sainted: He was not exempt from passion and choler, being infirmities to which all our race is subject, but that excepted, without reproach in his actions.[113]

[113]*Life,* pp. 12–13. The statement about Herbert's benefice, as it is here punctuated, is misleading. (The punctuation is the same in the private edition of the *Life* published at Strawberry Hill in 1764.) This portion of the *Life,* unfortunately, does not survive in manuscript. The sense clearly requires a comma after "beneficed," certainly a longer pause than that after "years."

CHAPTER 6

Little Gidding, Cambridge, and London (1633–1662)

Departures from Bemerton

Immediately after the funeral the anxieties of the winter months had to give way to the variety of activities now required. For Jane Herbert the new way of life meant leaving the home she had known less than three years, breaking up her household, arranging for packing and forwarding of goods, and dismissing most of the servants before returning to her mother's home at Baynton. For the Vaughan sisters it meant going on to another temporary home until further arrangements could be completed—a procedure they must have known all too often during the ten years since their mother's death. For Arthur Woodnoth it meant making some preliminary arrangements at Bemerton, then returning to London to file Herbert's will for probate and to begin whatever other steps were necessary in the process of settling the estate. For all of them it was a sharp break from the companionship of the man they loved and honored and from the time when they might still make some effort toward his comfort; but even during the first raw stages of grief, all of them turned to the various duties required of them.

Woodnoth wrote rather hurriedly to Ferrar on 4 March, the day after the funeral, about Herbert's death and burial and referred to some of the matters at hand:

His will He made but vppon Munday before he dyde and the most imperfect act that euer he did. & to proue wch I shall not neede to say more than this He hath made me his executor and [h]as expressed his Confidence so imposd one me much care and trouble I am afrayd much above my Understanding & strength But by Gods grace yor

aduise (wch I beseech yo^{u} deny me not) I shall I hope in some measure performe his expectation.

This Day they are vppon the praysem^{t} of thinges & to morrow or Wed[n]esday I supose Mrs Herbert will remoue to her mothers Two Neeces Mr Herbert had liuing wth him for whose sakes I suppose He was moued to inioyn my imploym^{t} their goodnes of disposition chalanges much his confidence and in [certain] commãdes more but aboue all my God will now as the case stands exact it from me: I will not be fearefull to make any proposition to yo^{u} who I hope will wth the same resolution refuse w^{ht}so^{er} I propose if yo^{u} think it be meete It is that if they cannot to there satisfaction be acomodated wth a convenient place for a while or longer yo^{u} will pleas to lett them com to Gidding. I am very confident that they will be rather promoters then Hinderers of any good yo^{u} see my confidence & I hope will pardon me wh so^{er} tender of my due respect.[1]

Earlier, when Woodnoth had been unsure about which course in life he should follow, Herbert had invited him to come live in his household and manage his affairs for him[2]—a gesture surely intended to increase Woodnoth's confidence in his own capabilities. Now again, when Woodnoth had just lived through the poignant, ennobling experience of standing at the bedside during the last days of such a friend, Herbert required him to stretch a bit to carry out his responsibilities. Herbert's act was by no means "imperfect" (as Woodnoth termed it), but rather settled upon judiciously. Others could have carried out the responsibilities well; Woodnoth, Herbert knew, would do what was required and more, especially in seeing to the welfare of the young nieces. Sir John Danvers was to serve as overseer; and it was assuredly better for Sir John to oversee Woodnoth than for Woodnoth to attempt to oversee Sir John.

After the long days at the rectory, then, Woodnoth was forced after the burial ceremony into immediate activity. Herbert had obviously placed upon him responsibilities far beyond those stated in his brief will, especially for his wife, for his nieces, and for the restoration of Leighton church. He had probably charged him also about what was to become of his other writings.

The "praysem^{t} of thinges" that Woodnoth refers to was the

[1] 4 March 1632/33, F.P. No. 1047.
[2] Arthur Woodnoth to Nicholas Ferrar, 13 October 1631, F.P. No. 1092.

beginning of the appraisal of what Herbert termed "all my goodes both within doores and without doores both monneys and bookes that properly belonge to me," necessary before the value of the estate could be agreed upon. Some of these "thinges" of course Jane Herbert would be wanting to take with her when she returned from Bemerton to her mother's house.

But there were other papers far more precious than lists of household goods that Woodnoth had to take with him from Bemerton. Some months earlier Herbert had sent to Little Gidding a copy of his translation of Cornaro, we learn from the preface to the *Hygiasticon,* the volume in which it was published in 1634. From the hand of Edmund Duncon, Nicholas Ferrar had received the collection of Herbert's poems we now call *The Temple.*[3] Herbert had in his cabinet other unpublished manuscripts, several of which would ultimately issue from the press: the works we know as *The Country Parson,* perhaps the *Outlandish Proverbs* (under whatever title Herbert used), and the *Musae Responsoriae.*[4] He may also have had the book of early poems we know as *W;* or it may already have been lent to one or another of the Ferrar-Mapletoft connection. It is doubtful that there were any other English poems in Herbert's possession, since he had so recently sent to Ferrar the ones he considered worth publishing. Possibly, however, he still had some stray single papers lying about—like the two prayers appended to the printed versions of *The Country Parson.*

A comment of Ferrar's to Woodnoth later that year makes clear that Ferrar had been entrusted with at least some of Herbert's remaining manuscripts and that he regarded himself as Herbert's literary executor.[5] It is likely therefore that Herbert had arranged to send to Ferrar all his other papers of any liter-

[3] Duncon himself was Walton's source for this famous account, and it is likely therefore to be as accurate as Duncon could make it nearly forty years after the event, albeit an event likely to remain clearly remembered through all subsequent experience.

[4] Like Donne (if we except the *Anniversaries*) Herbert did not publish his English poems during his lifetime. Aside from Latin and Greek poems in the *Memoriae Matris Sacrum,* his only published works were Latin orations and poems—poems in memory of Prince Henry, of Queen Anne, and of Francis Bacon. It is altogether likely that Herbert was either the organizer or the editor of the memorial volume for Bacon.

[5] 2 December 1633, F.P. No. 550.

ary significance. (We do not know at what point Duncon was given the manuscript of *The Country Parson*.) But despite the later remarks of Walton and of Aubrey, it is unlikely that any manuscripts of consequence remained with Mrs. Herbert to be used for pie papers or destroyed at Highnam House during the Civil War.

The "*private Writings*" Walton speaks of[6] may have been devotions or rejected poems; but on the whole it is likely that Herbert, in the last weeks of his life, had chosen the writings he considered ready to publish and had made plans to send them to Ferrar. Anything not sent to him had simply not met Herbert's standard.

Family papers and letters addressed to Herbert, on the other hand, may well have been kept by Jane Herbert during the years of her widowhood, only to be destroyed when Highnam House was burned. It is difficult to account in any other way for the fact that not a single letter addressed to Herbert has survived, or survived even until the days when Aubrey and Walton were writing. Certainly Herbert must have received and preserved many letters important to him at various stages of his life—from Lancelot Andrewes, Francis Bacon, and John Williams; from John Hacket and perhaps Henry Fairfax; from Nicholas Ferrar and Arthur Woodnoth; from his brothers and sisters, his cousins, his stepfather, and his mother. There were probably even letters from Jane herself, written before their marriage or during the days when he was at Bemerton making ready their new home in the rectory. Still, there is no reason to suppose that any of the "*private Writings*" that Jane Herbert took with her lasted even until the middle of the century.

Within a few days Bemerton Rectory would have been almost deserted. John Hayes may have stayed on there, perhaps with one or two servants, until the Earl of Pembroke could present a new rector to the living. Nathanael Bostocke, who had always lived at Fugglestone, already had lodgings there. Herbert had left each curate his half-year's wages—"his halfe yeares wages aforehand," as he states it in his will—and to Bostocke his copy of St. Augustine, to Hayes his "Comment of Lucas Brugensis" (probably among "those infinite Volumes of Divinity, which yet every day swell, and grow bigger" that he had scraped and

[6] Walton, p. 321.

stinted himself to buy during his student days).[7] The daily order of prayer and praise would continue in both Herbert's churches.

Jane Herbert, then, set out for her mother's at the earliest time possible, probably accompanied by Magdalene and Katherine Vaughan. Woodnoth departed also as soon as he could, and by the following Tuesday had had Herbert's will accepted for probate.[8] Shortly thereafter he saw to it that the Story Book that Susanna Mapletoft had lent Herbert was returned to her.[9] During the next few weeks he was probably paying out the bequests of Herbert and those of Dorothy Vaughan that Herbert had not paid earlier. He was also working with Sir Henry Herbert, the Duchess of Lennox, and others to raise money to complete the restoration at Leighton Bromswold.

Publication of Herbert's Works

The Temple

At Little Gidding in the meantime Nicholas Ferrar was having a fair copy of Herbert's English poems prepared to submit to the Vice-Chancellor at Cambridge to be licensed for publication.[10] Ferrar, who knew and respected good printing, chose a procedure perfectly natural to him: a Cambridge man himself, he turned to Cambridge with the works of the erstwhile Cambridge orator, rather than having them printed in London. (Thomas Buck, then the university printer, was known as one of the finest printers of his day.) Apparently the academic imprint was important to Ferrar (now for *The Temple,* later for the *Hygiasticon*); had he chosen to have the works published in London, Sir Henry Herbert would have been the official responsible for allowing their entry in the Stationers' Register. But Cambridge was the choice, even though this choice led to a delay in publishing *The Temple* and perhaps other works that Ferrar expected to follow it. (The reset title page of the second issue of the first edition emphasized the connection with the university by adding the phrase "late Oratour of the

[7] *Works,* p. 365. [8] P.R.O. PROB 11/163, fol. 25.

[9] Arthur Woodnoth to Nicholas Ferrar, 21 March 1632/33, F.P. No. 1118.

[10] No books were actually printed at Little Gidding, though a number were bound there, both large books with leather bindings such as the concordances and the Story Books and dainty little volumes done in blue silk and pearls.

Universitie of *Cambridge,*" which continues in subsequent editions.)

Had the poems Herbert sent to Ferrar already been copied in suitable form, there would have been no need to postpone publication, nor to engage the skill and the time of the copyists, who undoubtedly had other tasks to occupy their days in the workroom at Little Gidding. But since Ferrar found it necessary to have a fair copy made for the licensers and the printer,[11] we must conclude that what he received from Herbert was not in proper form to be submitted for licensing.[12]

[11] I am entirely in agreement with Canon Hutchinson's opinion that *B* was the copy sent to the licensers and used by the printers. See *Works,* pp. li–liii, lxxii–lxxiii. J. Max Patrick's suggestion (in "The Editor as Critic," a paper published by the William Andrews Clark Memorial Library, University of California, Los Angeles, 1973) that Herbert himself may have sent the poems for publication does not give sufficient weight to the information Walton had from Duncon and probably from Woodnoth about Herbert's sending them to Nicholas Ferrar. Arthur Woodnoth, always in close touch with his Ferrar cousins, in 1634 was involved with Edmund Duncon in some plan to publish another work of Herbert's. Walton had his information from Woodnoth within ten or eleven years after Herbert's death. It is clear that Walton had talked with Duncon not long before writing this portion of the life of Herbert. There is no need to question whether Duncon talked to Herbert and nearly forty years later described the meeting to Walton; Walton says explicitly (p. 308): "*This Mr.* Duncon *tells me.*" Patrick omits any mention of John Ferrar's account of how his brother received the poems from Herbert (Blackstone, p. 59):

> And when Mr Herbert dy'd, he recommended only of all his Papers, that of his Divine Poems, & willed it to be delivered into the hands of his Brother N. F. appointing him to be the Midwife, to bring that piece into the World, If he so thought good of it, else to [*space*] The wch when N. F. had many & many a time read over, & embraced & kissed again & again, he sayd, he could not sufficiently admire it, as a rich Jewell, & most worthy to be in ye hands & hearts of all true Christians, that feared God, & loved the Church of England. It was licensed at Cambridge (with some kind of Scruple by some, if I was not misinformed) only for those his Verses upon America &c: But it did pass, with the epistle that N. F. made to it, & (as I take it) hath passed nine impressions, since the first printing of it, as well it hath, & will deserve to doe./

I find no documentary evidence to support any suggestion about the publication of *The Temple* offered in Patrick's essay. A. L. Maycock, late Keeper of the Old Library at Magdalene College, Cambridge, who had worked closely with the Ferrar Papers both when he wrote his biography of Nicholas Ferrar and when (with his wife) he catalogued the collection, readily accepted as fact that *B* was copied at Little Gidding by Ferrar's nieces Anna and Mary Collett (letter of 30 September 1967). He suggested also that Mrs. Collett might have been one of the copyists for *B*.

[12] Despite Walton's description of "*this little Book,*" we must remember that Walton knew Herbert's poems only in their published form—and any of the seventeenth-century editions was, indeed, a little book.

The process of readying a book for publication in the seventeenth century was not really all that different from our own practice. In our day when the typescript (our fair copy) of a book has been accepted by a publisher, that copy becomes the basis for all further work entailed in editing and publishing. Now, if he needs ten copies of the typescript for press readers, editors, designers, and author, the publisher can have them made in a few hours at most; and they will be exact. Both then and now the publisher must be assured that what he accepts is what will be printed.

In Herbert's time, making a fair copy was a matter of countless hours of concentrated work, often under less than ideal conditions of lighting and comfort. A book like *The Temple* would take several weeks to copy and require many hours more for verifying the accuracy of the copy. (Anyone who questions this estimate may set himself the task of typing an exact copy of "The Sacrifice"—or, for an easier beginning, "The Dedication." Or he may undertake to copy the same poems in handwriting, keeping in mind the requirements of spacing, the pecularities of the Little Gidding hand, and the tendency of the brain to absorb too much or too little of the work in process.) The time the licensers would require was unpredictable. And even when the far-off day of their approval arrived, there was still a book of poems in intricately spaced stanzas to be set entirely by hand, again under variable conditions of lighting, to be proofread, and to issue from the press before October 1633, by which time we know it had been published.

The Little Gidding copy of Herbert's poems (the manuscript we know as *B*) is a handsome work, executed in the characteristic Little Gidding hand (requiring some time for the newcomer to learn to read because of its exaggerations of letter forms and its arches and its filled loops). Both its calligraphy and its orthography differ from Herbert's own practice in that they are a bit inflated and pretentious, rejecting the simple and the usual; the entire work is artificial in the best seventeenth-century sense, a product of artifice with perhaps a slight overtone of "It is a pretty poem, Mr. Pope."

Probably the task of preparing the fair copy was entrusted to Nicholas Ferrar's nieces, Anna and Mary Collett, daughters of Susanna Ferrar and John Collett (the Chief and the Patient in the Story Books of the Little Academy).[13] It would be venturesome indeed to guess which sister copied which page; their hands are so similar as to be almost identical.[14] These copyists give the impression of not being deeply involved in the content of what they were copying; many of the errors in the manuscript are the result of mindless inattention. They substituted their own more artificial spellings as they liked; they failed to notice when they had left the meter deficient; but worse, they let their minds wander, and this lack of proper attention led, alas, to the utter loss of one line from "The Size."

The form Herbert chose in this poem of eight stanzas is followed in all but the seventh. Stanza 5 serves well as an example of what Herbert intended:

> Thy Saviour sentenc'd joy,
> And in the flesh condemn'd it as unfit,
> At least in the lump: for such doth oft destroy;
> Whereas a bit
> Doth tice us on to hopes of more,
> And for the present health restore.

Herbert was using a favorite rhyme-scheme, with line lengths running 6 10 10 4 8 8 syllables. But in stanza 7 the copyist failed to catch the pattern, or was distracted; and now we have only the spoiled verse:

> Wherefore sit down, good heart;
> Grasp not at much, for fear thou losest all.
> If comforts fell according to desert,
> . . . . .
> They would great frosts and snows destroy:
> For we should count, Since the last joy.

The line may have been only so simple a one as "On one and all" or "On great and small," but the sense the author intended, the emphasis he chose, are irretrievably lost.

One other gap of a very different sort should be noted. The manuscript is not foliated, but paginated; the title page, how-

[13] Blackstone, p. 99.

[14] For samples of their hands, see Blackstone, pp. 30, 101. A point not often mentioned about the study of scripts of this time is that one learns the hand more quickly by going through the motions of forming the letters as he examines them.

ever, instead of being page 1, is page 10. No numbered leaves precede; the question therefore arises what was written on pages 0 to 9. It was not the table of contents (which comes at the end of this volume). The obvious answer may be the right one: a preface that was replaced in the printed volume by Ferrar's "The Printers to the Reader."

Ferrar supervised the entire procedure and very probably instructed the copyists about how the pages were to be ruled (in red) and the poems laid out, and then painstakingly read over the new copy. When the work was completed, he added the title and the epigraph in his own hand (as H. P. Kennedy-Skipton noted many years ago).[15] We may suppose that it then went off to the vice-chancellor for his approval, a matter to which we shall return.

There is of course no manuscript authority known for the addition of this title and this epigraph: *The Temple,* followed by the quotation from the Prayer Book version of Psalm 29:8, "In his Temple doth euery man speake of his honour." (Ferrar used no subtitle.) In considering whether this title is appropriate to Herbert's thought and whether he is likely to have settled on such a conceit to present his English poems, the reader who knows him well must review Herbert's interpretation and use of the word *temple* in five of the poems in this collection. In none of these does he make any special use of the term, except in "Sion," and even here he rejects the building materials of architecture in favor of upward-moving groans, "quick, and full of wings."[16] In no way does he point toward a title for the entire work or emphasize any figure of constructing a temple. For Herbert, the natural place for the worship of God is a church, not a temple. And during the seventeenth century, the little volume was generally referred to as "The Church"[17]—a designation much less pretentious, and more persuasive as the

[15] *The Life and Times of Nicholas Ferrar* (London: Mowbray, 1907), p. 116. It should be added, however, that Kennedy-Skipton did not differentiate between Ferrar's hand and other Little Gidding hands.

[16] See my discussion in "The Williams Manuscript and *The Temple*" in *Renaissance Papers, 1971.*

[17] See, for example, John Polwhele's poem "On Mr Herberts Devine poeme the Church. Jo. Polw: post mortem author mestris posuit" in Bodl. MS. Eng. poet. f. 16, fol. 11.

sort of title Herbert would have been likely to choose as the culmination of "The Church-porch," "The Church," and "The Church Militant," the section titles he had decided upon early in his poetic career that remained unchanged as he developed the whole collection of his English poems into the work Walton refers to as "this excellent Book . . . which now bears the name of *The TEMPLE:* Or, *Sacred Poems,* and *Private Ejaculations.*" Walton's comment that "this excellent Book . . . now bears the name of *The TEMPLE*" certainly suggests that it had not always borne this name.[18]

The Prose Works

Once the poems had been published as *The Temple,* the influence of the formal title extended to make it apply as well to Herbert's major prose work, which was apparently intended for publication soon thereafter. As matters worked out, however, with difficulties over other publications, Ferrar's death in 1637, and the later disruption of all work at Little Gidding, it eventually fell to Barnabas Oley, a fellow of Clare Hall who was ten or twelve years younger than Ferrar, to see to the publication of *Herbert's Remains,* in 1652. The volume included Oley's unsigned biographical introduction; *A Priest to the Temple; or, The Countrey Parson His Character and Rule of Holy Life; Jacula Prudentum* (1651), with the prayers before and after sermon; Herbert's letter to Ferrar about the translation of Valdesso; Latin poems to Donne and Bacon; and a collection of apothegms. A second edition of *A Priest to the Temple* followed in 1671; and with the passing of "Sad Times" Oley permitted his initials to appear on the title page and his name to be printed at the end of his new "Praeface."[19]

Publication of *The Country Parson* had probably been expected earlier; Oley, trying to avoid unnecessary conflict with the Puritans, toward the end of his introduction called it "*this*

[18] Walton, p. 314.

[19] In this "Praeface" Oley, now able to speak freely, acknowledges that it was Edmond Duncon who had had the manuscript of *The Country Parson:* "*My design in this Praeface is to do a Piece of Right, an office of Justice to the Good man that was possessor of the Manuscript of this Book, and transmitted it freely to the Stationers who first printed it, meerly upon design to benefit the Clergy, and in them, the Church of* England. *He was Mr.* Edmund Duncon *Rector of* Fryarn-Barnet *in* Middlesex."

Tract: which being writ nigh twenty years since, *will be lesse subject to misconstruction.*"[20] The title as Oley set it forth is obviously based on that chosen by Ferrar for the English poems; Herbert probably had intended as his title what we now see as the subtitle. The subtitle, nonetheless, has become the name by which readers usually refer to this practical, witty, and delightful work: *The Country Parson.* (Herbert may have been pointing toward this as a title in his chapter headings: of the twenty-seven headings, twenty-four use the term *parson.*) Given Herbert's determination to keep his utterances on the level of his hearers, *The Country Parson* is far more likely to have been the title he chose than the one under which it appeared in 1652. Needless to say, there is nothing at all here to account for the use of the term *temple* in the title, save the parallel with the title of the book of poems published nearly twenty years earlier.

If Ferrar had intended the companion volumes of *The Temple* and *A Priest to the Temple* (*The Country Parson*) to be published within a short time of each other, his plans were altered; but it is not easy to discern any reason among the extant records. The cause of the delay could hardly have been the cost of publishing the second book, because *The Temple* itself, an immediate success, went through two editions in 1633 and four by the time of Ferrar's death on 4 December 1637. The most likely explanation is the delay Ferrar encountered with the licensers over the *Hygiasticon* (published at Cambridge in 1634 by Roger Daniel, university printer, who had worked with Thomas Buck in publishing *The Temple*). As a matter of fact, Ferrar did not himself see his translation of Valdesso through the press. (It was published posthumously at Oxford in 1638, where it was "allowed" by Dr. Thomas Jackson, a man much respected in the Ferrar circle. Oley praises him along with Herbert and Ferrar in the prefaces to *The Country Parson.*)

At first glance there seems no reason that the *Hygiasticon* should have stirred up any difficulty when it was about to be published. The little volume includes translations of the *Hygiasticon* of Leonard Lessius by one T. S.; *A Treatise of Temperance and Sobrietie of Luigi Cornaro* by Herbert; and *Of the Instruction of*

[20] *Herbert's Remains* (London: Printed for Timothy Garthwait, 1652), sig. c 6^{v}, unnumbered.

Children in the Christian Doctrine of Ludovico Carbone, a translation by Ferrar or possibly by T. S.[21] The first two treatises would have been of special interest to the Ferrars and the Mapletofts, a number of whom were much interested in limiting their diet; but of course it is the third treatise that probably caused offense and led to the licensers' objection. Oley's account of Ferrar affords a clue to the sort of doctrinal difference that led to the licensers' disapproval: *"hee help'd to put out* Lessius, *and to stir up us Ministers to be painfull in that excellent labour of the Lord,* Catechising, feeding the Lambs of Christ: *Hee translated a piece of* Lud. Carbo; *wherein* Carbo *confesseth, that the Heretícks* (i.e. *Protestants*) *had got much advantage by Catechizing: But the Authority at Cambridge suffered not that Egyptian Jewell to be publish'd."*[22]

Even before the *Hygiasticon* was ready for the licensers' consideration, however, a heated and stubborn misunderstanding developed among several of the friends who were involved in the plans for the proposed volume. Though there was much ink spilled about the squabble, the records are incomplete, and the point of it never becomes entirely clear.

What we know of the difficulty is found in several letters of Arthur Woodnoth's and in one of Nicholas Ferrar's, all written between 29 November and 12 December 1633, along with one undated letter of Woodnoth's probably written about the same time.[23] The persons involved, other than Ferrar and Woodnoth, were Edmund Duncon, the clerical friend of the Ferrars; Philemon Stephens, a London stationer; and a Mr. Tabor—possibly James Tabor, the Cambridge University Registrary (an official well acquainted with controversy between London stationers and university printers), or his son John.

[21] See *Nicholas Ferrar: Two Lives by His Brother John and by Dr. Jebb,* ed. J. E. B. Mayor (Cambridge: University Press, 1855), pp. 51 and 302, especially the mention of Ferrar's note at the end of the copy of Carbone that Jebb apparently had before him: "This translation was finished the 15 June, 1634, at the request of Edmund Duncon."

[22] *Herbert's Remains,* sig. b^{v}, unnumbered.

[23] Woodnoth to Ferrar, n.d., F.P. No. 1055; Woodnoth to Ferrar, 29 November 1633, F.P. No. 1131; Ferrar to Woodnoth, 2 December 1633, F.P. No. 550; Woodnoth to Ferrar, 6 December 1633, F.P. No. 1132, Woodnoth to Ferrar, 12 December 1633, F.P. No. 1133. John Tabor wrote Ferrar on 22 August 1634 (F.P. No. 1016).

Ferrar had apparently said he would entrust Herbert's translation of Cornaro to Woodnoth and had authorized him to proceed with arrangements toward publication, then himself proceeded with other arrangements. (So Woodnoth affirms.) Whatever the reason, Tabor (and perhaps Duncon, though in a secondary role) became distrustful of Stephens; and Woodnoth, who had until this time been on friendly terms with all parties, found himself siding with Stephens, yet believing Duncon innocent of any unworthy intent. As Herbert's executor, Woodnoth apparently felt that he was defending some interest or right of Mrs. Herbert's as well. In the undated letter he wrote to Ferrar: "I haue allredy sayd that wthout y^{r} leaue att least nothing of Mr Herberts shalbe printed that I can preuent and I purpose not to leaue that resolution." In the first of the dated letters (29 November 1633) he is troubled by Tabor's change of expression in recent letters and comes as close as he ever does to describing the issue that was causing the trouble:

> yett I cold not but conceaue som-what there was that had changed Mr Tabors expression both in the letter I receaud from Giding wth one since from Cambridg both wch differed much from what I formerly had receaud/ To haue perswaded Mr Tabor to as much as was required I thought my reasons had bin of Valedity since nothing was desyred ether to preiudice him on the worke but rather the Contrary if I mistook not were it to purpose I shold willingly take the matter as farr as from the Deliuering the booke to M^{r} [Dumoneve] or farther and hauinge expressed all particular passages therabouts submitt to the award of any Saynt ether in Heaven or Earth.

Toward the end of this paragraph comes Woodnoth's only remark about Mrs. Herbert's interests: "When Mrs Herbert shall require it I shall then endeavor to giue her the best satisfaction I can."[24]

[24] The next matter Woodnoth takes up may or may not be related to the proposed publishing of the three treatises on health. I am inclined to think there is no direct connection, yet mention it because omission might cause greater confusion. By a rather unusual provision of the will of the Timothy Sheppard who had died in 1613, his bequest of £900 to his two executors, his brother Thomas and his brother-in-law John Ferrar, was to be made up by reducing other legacies proportionately, should his estate prove not to amount to £900 at the time of his death. In November 1633 the matter was being taken up in court, but one Mr. Ireland had informed Woodnoth that they could expect nothing to come of it. Both John Ferrar and Woodnoth refer to Timothy

Nicholas Ferrar's reply of 2 December is surely one of the strongest letters he ever wrote—stern in the earlier part, but full of loving assurance toward the end. He has had a letter from Tabor enclosing one of Woodnoth's that suggests to him that Woodnoth has not given a full account:

hee sent me a letter of yours wch I confess I doe not understand but therby I perceaue there is more in the matter than you haue been willing that I shold understand wherin you haue don amiss for wher y^{o} should haue made known those forceable reasons or at least you should haue accepted their Condition wch I offered at first of receiuing by way of Loue and kyndness what your selfe desyred but you would haue it by right and therin undoubtedly you haue been in [. . .] using first the Tribunall [. . .] are unable to Invest either M$^{[rs]}$ Herbert or you wth any Right in the booke wch was giuen and consigned mee and when I had passed ouer my right there was noe possibility of recalling it on my parte neither. I meane by way of Justice and right. As a way of Loue I made y^{u} offer of obteyning whateuer you would but as I wrott but for you I would not haue intermedled at all for any man Liuinge—Nor would I haue don it for your sake neither but soe I found [my?] mynde distasted soe as I was afrayd you would haue interpreted my refusall amiss—and it would haue added to the discomposure of your affections. And as I began I ended the buisness wth protestacon to doe the uttermost y^{t} freindship can reach unto for satisfaction of yor desyres if y^{o} will desyre it but to say that Mr Steeuens hath right on his syde or Mr Tabor none were an abominable syn being soe much acount in Conscience as for myselfe my deare Cosen I am not quit of any name of Loue or respect toward you in that kynde wch you desyre and intimate but for the preservation therof the execucion of that true Loue wch I beare you.

The advice with which Ferrar begins this letter ("If you will follow my Counsell you shall returne wth your Affection and [speak] reconcilliances in perfect amity wth Mr Duncon and Mr Tabor whose proceedings in this matter of the booke—as much as concerneth you and mee and Mr Herbert himselfe haue been full not onely of Justice but Christian generosity of mynd and of abundant Loue and respect to all and to y^{u} in particular") combined with some of the phraseology to ruffle Woodnoth's feathers still more.

Sheppard as "Mr T. S." This gentleman should not be confused with his brother Thomas nor with Thomas Sheppard the translator.

Woodnoth replied on 6 December. He would gladly forget "that busines of wch there hath bine so much too much sayd allredy." He would return to reconciliation if he knew wherein his fault lay. Ferrar had written of receiving "from Mr Tabor a mournefull letter lamenting his vexation in this matter by the callumnious accusations of Mr Stephens and desyring mee to Learne the true cause." In reply Woodnoth cannot resist a jibe at "Mr Tabors mournfull lamentations of his vexatives" or at "there Christian Generosity so y^{u} call it." But apparently he feels that his grievance is genuine, because he proceeds to a forthright criticism of Ferrar as the one who caused the misunderstanding:

> And now to winde upp this Clew and make upp this bottom att once for all giue me leaue to doe as Chirgants [surgeons] doe in Case bones ar ill sett break them agayne or as in wounds first eate out the Dead flesh to be playne and att once tho wth some payne to bynde upp the wound that it may not Ranckle. Now giue me leaue to tell yo^{u} that yo^{u} are origin really the Author of all this trouble wch will apeare by this kinde of Sylogism. He that makes a Proposition and faylcs in the [per]formance of itt when inconveniencing others com into by that fayling he is Author of. Butt yo^{u} made me the tender of this in thes words I Leaue itt wholly to yor disposall and affirm whilst I expected itt disposed otherwise of itt therefor the conclusion is, yo^{u} are the principal in this trouble/

The conclusion of this passage suggests the possibility that Woodnoth may have been making arrangements with Stephens to publish the translation of Cornaro separately. Had Ferrar indeed changed his mind and "disposed otherwise of itt," Woodnoth's sense of injury would certainly be understandable.

In the final letter of the group Woodnoth writes to enclose another letter—and in an entirely different mood. The salutation runs "Reu S^{r} and my Deere Deere Cosen"; the opening paragraph is joyous and loving. Woodnoth then returns to the disagreement, almost dismissing it: "The busines I vnderstand is now att an End (and the bookes disposed of) and so shalbe my consideration of itt farther then to remitt the money." Whatever accusation Tabor had raised about Stephens still bothers him, however, and he returns to it, again exonerating Duncon of blame:

> . . . and therefore in the behalf of Mr Stephens lett me desyre that Mr Tabor will doo Mr Stephens and himself that right as to express the particular calumny intimated ether agaynst himself or Mr Dunkin. . . . Its true Mr Tabor som weeks since intimated som such thing to be doon by him agaynst Mr Dunkin but if I had had no other motion to haue perswaded me to the contrary his quiett composure wold haue asurd me of his inocency. I haue scarce mett wth a man of a better Temper to Mr Herberts Character and my own obseruance must deliu[er] him and I beseech you till you know otherwise receiu him.

So the matter would seem to have come to an end. There are no extant letters from either Woodnoth or Ferrar for some time thereafter, and we can only assume that plans for the volume to be published by Daniel developed further during the first half of 1634. If we accept Ferrar's date of 15 June for the completion of the translation of Carbone, the publication of the three treatises must have fallen in the latter half of the year.

There has never been any question of Herbert's authorship of the translation included as the second treatise in the *Hygiasticon.* On the other hand, the translation of the first treatise has sometimes been attributed to Nicholas Ferrar, or even to Ferrar with the help of Robert Mapletoft. Surely some of these attributions arise from the circumstance that John Ferrar mentioned that Nicholas had sent "those three Translations of Valdezzo, Lessius, & Carbo to Herbert" for his perusal and that Oley said that Ferrar had *"help'd to put out* Lessius."[25]

A careful reading of the prefatory note "To the Reader," however, tells us several interesting things about this little book. In it T. S., who calls himself "the Publisher of the ensuing Treatises," says that Herbert's translation (*"the middlemost"*) was made first, Herbert *"having at the request of a Noble Personage translated it into English."* This personage is generally believed to have been Bacon, who is quoted elsewhere in the prefatory matter. But Herbert's own interest in the supposed restoration of his health by following a strict diet should not be ignored as another reason for his interest in Cornaro.

Without referring to the Ferrars or to Little Gidding by name, T. S. tells how Herbert *"sent a copie thereof, not many moneths before his death, unto some friends of his, who a good while*

[25] Blackstone, p. 59; *Herbert's Remains,* sig. bv, unnumbered.

before had given an attempt of regulating themselves in matter of Diet." When, "*not long after,*" a copy of Lessius came into their hands, they turned to T. S.: "*It was their desire to have the Translation entire; and finding no just reason to the contrary, I have been willing to satisfy them therein.*" He assumed that Herbert was "*enforced*" to leave out parts of the Cornaro (whereas what Herbert omitted were merely Cornaro's remarks about life and events in Italy in his day). Although there might be objection to "*the old blinde zeal*" of Cornaro or to "*the new and dangerous profession of* Lessius," their works are being published only for what they have to say about temperance: "*That they were both* Papists, *and the one of them a* Jesuite, *is no prejudice to the truth of what they write concerning* Temperance."

Although T. S. dates his preface 7 December 1633, the *Hygiasticon* did not issue from the press for some months. Robert Mapletoft's message of 30 January 1633/34 to Ferrar, that "Lessius will be finished some time tomorrow," does not specify whether he means the translation or the printed text. On 22 August he wrote Ferrar: "Mr Tabor hath expected your p[ro]mised Carbone."[26]

Who was this T. S.? Two possibilities emerge at once from among the Ferrar connection: Timothy Sheppard and Thomas Sheppard, sons of William Sheppard of London (a friend of the elder Nicholas Ferrar), and brothers of the Ann Sheppard who was John Ferrar's first wife and died in 1613. Timothy Sheppard, citizen and haberdasher, may be dismissed at once, because he died before 6 May 1613,[27] when John Ferrar, one of his executors, entered his will for probate. (The other executor was Sheppard's brother Thomas.)

This Thomas Sheppard appears a more likely candidate; and John Hodgkin first suggested him, in 1917.[28] This man, a merchant, witnessed the will of the elder Nicholas Ferrar and received his diamond ring as a bequest. In 1625 he sold the manor of Little Gidding to the Ferrars. From the letters of Arthur Woodnoth and other of the Ferrar Papers, it is clear that he remained in close touch with the family. But did he have the knowledge and the literary ability to translate the rather

[26] F.P. Nos. 829 and 835. [27] P.R.O. PROB 8/15, fol. 75.

[28] *Times Literary Supplement,* 29 June 1917, pp. 309–310, as comment on a letter of F. E. Hutchinson of 8 June, p. 273.

lengthy treatise by Lessius (210 pages as compared with 46 for Cornaro and 24 for Carbone)? Nothing we know of this Thomas Sheppard suggests the slightest interest in literature. In the absence of any positive evidence, he must be set aside.

Yet there was another Thomas Sheppard who would undoubtedly have been qualified to make such a translation, a man likely to have been known among the circle of Ferrar's friends. J. E. B. Mayor includes at the end of *Nicholas Ferrar: Two Lives* an Index of Cambridge Names (by colleges) that mentions more than twenty men of Clare. (Trinity, next in number, yields only five.) Ferrar must have known some of these men from his own days at Clare and others because they were younger friends of his friends. Ferrar may have known this younger Thomas Sheppard from his own connections at Clare, but certainly Barnabas Oley and Joshua Mapletoft would have known the Thomas Sheppard who matriculated from Clare Hall in 1614 and was ordained both deacon and priest at Peterborough in 1622. He also became rector of Graffham in Huntingdonshire, only a short distance from Leighton Bromswold.[29]

Thomas Sheppard of Graffham appears a likely candidate indeed. His education qualified him both to make the translation of Lessius and to form the judgments about possible Jesuit influence already mentioned; he must certainly have known Herbert as a university lecturer and orator and could therefore write of him from his own knowledge as "*Master* George Herbert *of blessed memorie*"; he lived close enough to both Little Gidding and Cambridge to keep in touch during the process of translation and publication. And of course it is not beyond possibility that he was related to the Huntingdonshire Sheppards who had settled in London to become citizens and merchants.

This clergyman may have hinted in his preface at some of the difficulties Ferrar and the others interested in publishing the *Hygiasticon* had encountered. After the preliminary skirmishes Tabor, Stephens, Duncon, and Woodnoth had engaged in (some of which clearly involved Herbert's translation), Fer-

[29] P.R.O. PROB 11/179, fol. 2, is the will of Thomas Sheppard of Hilton, who died late in 1638 or early in 1639, naming the Reverend Thomas Sheppard as his executor, and leaving bequests to him and his son, yet another Thomas.

rar and Sheppard knew well enough what sort of objection was likely to be raised to a volume, however well intended to offer the reader advice about improving his health, that was made up entirely of translations from Roman Catholic authors. The author of the third treatise is never mentioned by name; indeed, the treatise itself is not even named. Sheppard passes over it as lightly as possible, apparently in the hope that it may slip by unnoticed: "*And so I come to the third Discourse: which is added to the other, as a banquet of Junkets after a solid Feast. The Authour thereof was an* Italian *of great reputation, living in the same age which* Cornarus *did.*" (A "banquet" in this sense is a course in itself, obviously not a full meal.) The rest of Sheppard's paragraph about the third treatise continues to emphasize its lightness and the benefit that may be derived from it, "*however it seems to play.*" Yet there is Oley's solemn summation: "*But the Authority at Cambridge suffered not that Egyptian jewell to be published.*"

It may be unfair to interpret the circumstance of Sheppard's referring to the Ferrars without mentioning the name of the family as evidence that he was trying not to ripple peaceful waters; Ferrar, after all, in his preface to *The Temple,* used no proper names save those of Trinity College and of Cambridge University. But this preface, nonetheless, gives the impression of underlining the wholesomeness of the treatises and answering points that have not yet been raised about possible harmful effects—rather too much protestation. And though the *Hygiasticon* was several times reissued in its century (1634, 1636, 1678), the name Ludovico Carbone was not permitted to grace a title page.

Any plan that Ferrar may have had for further publication of his own work or of Herbert's was not to be carried out during his lifetime. Whether Ferrar himself decided to change from the university printer at Cambridge to the one at Oxford we do not know. Barnabas Oley, who may have been charged with the responsibility of seeing Ferrar's translation of Valdesso through the press,[30] was a great admirer of Dr. Thomas Jack-

[30] It is only a small point, but the spelling of Bemerton that Oley uses in *Herbert's Remains* ("Bemmorton") is the same used in Herbert's letter appended to the first edition of Valdesso. There are many ways of spelling Bemerton, but

son, president of Corpus Christi College, Oxford, and may have turned to Jackson for help when the time came to publish the work. In any event, Jackson approved the book for publication, and in 1638 it was published by Leonard Lichfield as *The Hundred and Ten Considerations of Signior Iohn Valdesso,* including Herbert's "Briefe Notes" and the letter he had written to Ferrar on 29 September 1632, when he returned the translation with his comments.

Of all the published works of Herbert, we know least about how the volumes of proverbs came to be printed. There is no reason to doubt that the collections are in large part his own work. The 1032 proverbs of foreign origin published in 1640 as *Outlandish Proverbs Selected by Mr. G. H.* were augmented in 1651 to 1190 proverbs and called *Jacula Prudentum.* (This second edition was included in 1652 in *Herbert's Remains.* Several manuscripts parallel the published collections in various ways.)[31]

Herbert had a natural affinity for the proverb. In his own writing he valued succinctness, especially when it combined with wit in a sudden flash of truth. Perhaps his delight in this expression of folk wisdom developed from his study of languages: Randle Cotgrave's *Dictionarie of the French and English Tongue* (1611), for example, utilized a rich variety of proverbs to illustrate colloquial usage. An even stronger demonstration of Herbert's early interest in proverbs lies in "The Church-porch," an early work in which nearly every stanza includes a proverb or some other mode of terse expression. This interest was to continue throughout his life: in the poems in "The Church" proverbs are sometimes used as *sententiae* (though more often he imitates their terseness in *sententiae*); we should not therefore be surprised to find him quoting an "outlandish" proverb to his brother Henry in a letter written from Bemerton. Henry himself, several years after George's death, copied

---

this unusual one, as far as I recall found only in these two places, strongly suggests that it was Oley who saw Valdesso through the press. He was also instrumental in the publication of the works of Dr. Thomas Jackson.

[31] *Outlandish Proverbs* was included by its publisher, Humphrey Blunden, as the second part of *Witts Recreations* (1640). Hutchinson's discussion (*Works,* pp. 321, 568–573) of the various collections of proverbs admirably summarizes the history of this series.

seventy-two "Outlandishe Prouerbs," all but three of which tally with the proverbs that would be published in 1640. In his letters and particularly in *The Country Parson* Herbert often uses proverbs to underline his arguments or to sum up his points. The 463 proverbs copied into a Little Gidding Story Book (now at Clare College) are evidence that the Ferrar circle shared Herbert's interest.[32] The question, then, is not whether Herbert collected some, most, or all of the foreign proverbs published as *Selected by Mr. G. H.*, but how they came to be printed. For those printed in 1651 and particularly for their inclusion in *Herbert's Remains* the following year, the publisher was Timothy Garthwait, a friend of Barnabas Oley's. Oley must surely have been aware that Garthwait planned to include them in *Herbert's Remains* in 1652.[33] But how the original collection came to be published in 1640 we may never know.

Later Publications

The last work of Herbert published during the seventeenth century appeared after the Restoration when James Duport included in his *Ecclesiastes Solomonis* Herbert's Latin epigrams composed forty years before in answer to Andrew Melville. The *Musae Responsoriae,* the earliest of the four series of Latin poems Herbert wrote, thus became the last to be published, when Duport's book was printed at Cambridge in 1662. Duport, a fellow and vice-master of Trinity, received Herbert's poems from the master of Emmanuel, William Dillingham.[34] Like his friend William Sancroft (who at one time owned *B*), Dillingham took a deep interest in Herbert's works and actually

[32] See John Ferrar's citation of two of these proverbs in Blackstone, p. 303.

[33] See the discussion by Herbert G. Wright, "Was George Herbert the Author of *Jacula Prudentum?*" *Modern Language Review,* XI (April 1935), 139–144. Any hesitancy over accepting the proverbs as Herbert's because they are included with the prayers before and after sermon (on the likelihood that Herbert would not use unauthorized prayers in his church) ignores two facts: that these may well have been unuttered prayers and that Herbert, like his brothers, probably wrote devotions for his own use. In Henry Herbert's two collections of private devotions we find the same sort of prayers and meditations echoing the Prayer Book and Psalms and other biblical passages. Even Lord Herbert wrote private prayers. (See Rebecca Warner, ed., *Epistolary Curiosities: Series the First* (Bath: Richard Cruttwell, 1818), pp. 187–189.

[34] *Works,* p. 588.

translated "The Church-porch" and some of the lyrics into Latin. By this time, of course, the *Musae Responsoriae* were published for a reason quite different from that for which they were written: by 1662 what was significant about them was that they were Herbert's.

Passio discerpta and *Lucus* remained in manuscript until Grosart published them in the nineteenth century. In the meantime William Pickering had published a revised version of "Triumphus Mortis," a long poem in *Lucus* (Number XXXII), from a manuscript (not now known) in his possession. Finally, in 1962, G. M. Story described and reproduced yet another version of "Inventa Bellica" that uses the same title as Pickering's manuscript.[35]

From time to time other poems possibly by Herbert have been brought to light to be examined, but few of them have survived examination and been added to the canon. That no English poem has been so discovered emphasizes once again that Herbert's English poems were not circulated during his lifetime. (Those in commonplace books are invariably from printed sources.) With the probable exception of the epitaph for the Earl of Danby, no English poem found outside the two manuscripts and Walton's *Lives* has been accepted as authentic.

But with the Latin poems it is possible that other academic or occasional verse may be discovered. Herbert, who spent about fifteen years in Cambridge, may well have contributed to other collections than those we now know. One of the last places one would expect to find hitherto unknown poems by George Herbert would be the Vatican Library; but in 1962 Leicester Bradner published two such Latin poems from an anthology given to Prince Frederick, the Elector Palatine, when he visited Cambridge in 1613. A similar volume given to Prince Charles at the same time, if it is ever found, may yield one more Latin poem by Herbert.[36]

[35] "George Herbert's *Inventa Bellica:* A New Manuscript," *Modern Philology,* LIX (May 1962), 270–272.

[36] Leicester Bradner, "New Poems by George Herbert: The Cambridge Latin Gratulatory of 1613," *Renaissance News,* XV (Autumn 1962), 208–211.

Herbert after 1633

Without the devoted work of his friends after his death, Herbert might have passed into the oblivion that is the fate of most other obscure parish priests. Through the diligence and perseverance of Arthur Woodnoth and of Sir Henry Herbert and the careful supervision of John Ferrar, the church of St. Mary at Leighton Bromswold, restored with beauty and dignity, continues to this day as a reminder of Herbert's own work for his prebend. On the other hand, the little church of St. Andrew at Bemerton has become his unofficial memorial simply because it typifies the culmination of his life, his parish priesthood.

But Herbert's friends have served him generously in another way. When he died, George Herbert had no literary reputation: the few Latin (and Greek) works that he had published—orations and memorial verses—are not the stuff on which literary fame is grounded. Had it not been for the constancy and determination of Nicholas Ferrar and Barnabas Oley in seeing Herbert's English works through the press, his reputation as a poet would never have developed, Walton would have had no occasion to write the life of Herbert, and Crashaw and Knevet and Vaughan (and even Christopher Harvey) would have lacked a major inspiration and example for their own verse. And through the years that divide our time from Herbert's, countless thousands of readers would never have heard his particular accents or shared his moments of playfulness, his wit, his understanding of man's obstinacy, or his joy in the morning after a spring rain. With no notion of how far the results of their actions would extend Ferrar and Oley sent Herbert's writings forth to his readers. Through Herbert his readers come to value the beauty of utter simplicity, of order, of controlled diction. No English poet has said more plainly—or more memorably—"*My God, My King,*" or represented so fully the relationship between God and man.

APPENDIX A

Herbert's Lives

Heretofore, for all practical purposes, there has been only one life of Herbert. It has been borrowed and paraphrased repeatedly, but rarely examined objectively. Walton's life of Herbert first published in 1670 is a classic of Christian literature, a winning and persuasive exposition that molded subsequent accounts for nearly three hundred years.

Occasionally someone questioned the received version; here and there a biographer carried on a bit of research that contradicted Walton; but too often, having pierced the surface of this plausible version, they allowed themselves to slide back into general acceptance. Grosart, for instance, having taken firm hold of the matter of the rectory of Whitford, once held by Sir Philip Sidney, failed to carry on to find that Walton had no basis for assigning this sinecure to Herbert. Nor, once Canon Hutchinson had added his brief note in 1945 about Herbert's parliamentary service, did any subsequent student go on to note the contradictions in the published lists of members.

What is most discouraging to the student of Herbert, however, is to find biographers with access to more recent sources persistently repeating Walton's interpretations and errors, whether about Herbert's supposed yearning to be a Secretary of State, or his following the court to further his ambitions, or his supposed dependence on influential friends who might further those ambitions. David Novarr's excellent study of Walton as biographer has been available since 1958 but amateurs and professionals alike persist in repeating Walton—as he was in the beginning and perhaps ever shall be. It would be a welcome change to read a biographical sketch in a new edition or to see a dramatic representation of Herbert's life that took account of recent scholarship. Too often, the voice of Walton drones on in the writings of his successors, lulling us with its reassurances.

Yet the biographer of Herbert inclined to grumble over having to depend so frequently upon Walton alone need only attempt a biography of Herbert *without* Walton. Herbert is no Dr. Johnson, to be approached through alternative sources; refreshing as it might be to set aside Walton's exhortations to piety, he is too often our only source of information; and we must therefore endure his embroideries, his fabricated scenes and conversations, and pick our way with caution and robust skepticism if we are not to succumb to assurances and interpretations that are sometimes a bit too neat and plausible in expanding upon hints he took from his predecessors or in echoing lines in *The Temple* that may or may not have applied to Herbert himself.

There is dross, of course—great buckets of it in Walton's account of Herbert's practices as parish priest, which is clearly intended to encourage other priests after the Restoration to follow this supposed example. But there is little danger that an alert scholar will be taken in if he has learned from the work of John Butt and David Novarr.

Since we must turn often to Walton for material not recorded elsewhere, it is reasonable first to consider his sources. In addition to the published sources available to him or to any other reader of the time (the accounts by Nicholas Ferrar and Barnabas Oley, *The Temple,* and *The Country Parson,* from all of which he drew as he pleased), he had access to several persons connected with Herbert whose recollections would be of value (Arthur Woodnoth and Edmund Duncon, for example). He took his themes from Ferrar and Oley, expanded them in variations on the poems and *The Country Parson,* and filled the intervals as he could with what specific information he could garner.

Walton, who obviously had close access to the Herbert family, preserved copies of documents that would else have perished. Sir Henry Herbert, who lived until April 1673, was one likely source. Walton might have applied to him directly, or through Bishop Morley, for whom Walton served as factor (or agent). Arthur Woodnoth, who had worked closely with Sir

Henry in raising funds for the restoration of Leighton, was another possible avenue. By whatever means he procured the documents, Walton was able to publish the date of Herbert's birth (not entered in the parish registers), the New Year's sonnets of 1610, and (ultimately) ten of Herbert's letters, all but the earliest one complete.

That Woodnoth apparently told Walton that he had been the bearer of the letter of 25 May 1622 to Lady Danvers argues that Walton began work on his biography much earlier than he would have his readers know, and that Walton therefore knew of the existence of this letter before Woodnoth's death in 1645. That he did not publish it and the one to Lady Anne Clifford until after Sir Henry's death suggests that he did not have them in hand in 1670, when the *Life* first appeared. It also raises the possibility that the eight letters of Herbert published in 1670 came not from Sir Henry, but from Sir John Danvers, to whom Woodnoth had had ready access. (Since Walton was not aware that Danvers was one of the regicides, clearly he himself had no direct contact with Sir John during the six years by which Danvers survived Charles I.) These eight letters then, six to Sir John himself and one each to his wife and his stepdaughter, may have come into Walton's hands when he first gathered material for Herbert's biography, as another result of his conversations with Woodnoth. (Walton added another letter in 1674 and yet another in 1675.)

Although both John Aubrey and Thomas Fuller were collecting material during Walton's lifetime for their brief accounts of Herbert (that would not be published for many years), there is no evidence that he was in touch with either of them. And probably Walton never knew that Edward Herbert had written an account of his own life, let alone anything about his brother George.

The interest in Herbert that had waned after the thirteenth edition in 1709 began to revive slowly toward the end of the eighteenth century. Though the sketch of Herbert's life by one D. Warren[1] is based on Walton, it is evidence of the reviving interest no less than are Wesley's adaptations, the remarks of Cowper and Coleridge, and the series of editions by William

[1] Bodl. MS. Engl. hist. e. 318, fols. 30–39.

Pickering. But not until 1858, more than two hundred years after Walton had begun to gather his notes, was a second full life of Herbert published, this time under the sponsorship of the General Protestant Episcopal Sunday School Union and Church Book Society in New York. The little book, written by George L. Duyckinck, largely a repetition of Walton and other published sources, apparently was so well received that a second edition was issued within the year.

For his *Works in Verse and Prose of George Herbert* (1874 and after) the Reverend Alexander B. Grosart followed his practice in editions of other poets and included a lengthy "Memorial Introduction," partly biographical, partly critical. Despite a style that sometimes becomes puffed and pompous, Grosart questioned several of Walton's assertions, particularly about Herbert's reply to Melville, and even burst forth impatiently: "Dear as are 'meek' Walton's name and memory, the truth must at long-last be told, and this mingle-mangle of unhistoric statement and mendacious zeal exposed. There are nearly as many blunders as sentences in the narrative, and the *animus* is as base as the supercilious ignorance is discreditable. Alas that I must say these 'hard things' of anything from the pen of one I so revere (substantially)! Alas that they should be true!" Grosart attempted to bring balance to the picture of Herbert the man, but the influence of Walton was too strong: though Grosart endeavored to imagine what sort of man Herbert was and to include such documents as the will, essentially his biography is yet-once-more Walton.

Following the revival of interest in Herbert that began in the last century, most editions have included some sort of biographical account—sometimes Walton's life, sometimes a summary based on it, generally in the spirit of Walton, rarely with any addition of fact or interpretation. There are occasional exceptions, of course: though the Reverend Robert Aris Willmott added neither jot nor tittle of biography in his introductory sketch in 1861, J. Henry Shorthouse, in his introduction to the Fisher Unwin type facsimile (1882) of the first edition, showed great perspicacity in rejecting Walton's view of how "all Mr. *Herbert's* Court-hopes" died, a view few others have bothered to question:

It has been insinuated, I think with some unkindness, that *George Herbert's* dedication, if not his religion, was the result of disappointed political hopes. That there is any reason for this unkindly suspicion, I fail to see. That *George Herbert's* tastes may have led him towards a courtier's and a statesman's life, need not be denied. Churchmen were often statesmen in those days, and it very naturally seemed to a religious man that he could do God's service in one walk as in another; but the concluding years of *George Herbert's* life, the "Country Parson," and the activity and sweetness that marked his pastoral life at *Bemerton,* amidst ever increasing weakness and approaching death, were not the results of disappointed political hopes. Such years do not follow on such a youth, and such fruit is not grown on such a stock. These verses which have been called, with singular infelicity, "the enigmatical history of a difficult resignation," are in fact the spiritual instinct of a human life consecrated to God amid the pleasures, the temptations, the pains of this world's courts and cities.[2]

But on most other points Walton continued as almost the sole authority for editors and biographers who followed him.

Most developments in the writing of the biography of Herbert since Walton's time have been the result either of sheer accident or of assiduous search on the part of a biographer. Rebecca Warner, for example, apparently had the great good fortune to stumble upon a collection of Sir Henry Herbert's papers at Ribbesford House; through the kind offices of the Ingram family she published them in 1818 in *Epistolary Curiosities: First Series.* Grosart (apparently) simply came across *W* at Dr. Williams's Library and made the first use of it in his edition of 1874. Bishop Daniell, working on the first (unsigned) edition of his biography three hundred years after Herbert's birth, happened to inquire at Salisbury near the time when the records of Herbert's institution and ordination came to light. There is something to be said for being on hand at the right moment.

Most of what Daniell added to the account of Herbert's life, on the other hand, was the result of logical inquiry and hard work. Thoroughly steeped in the spirit of Herbert's writing, he looked into all the places where one might reasonably expect to find records, found many of them, and published them. He hunted out the parish registers at Montgomery and at Bemer-

[2] Pp. xiii–xiv.

ton and Herbert's will in London; knowing Bemerton well already, since he was a Wiltshire parson, he visited Montgomery and Leighton; he settled the matter of whether Herbert held the sinecure of Whitford. Above all, he did more to show the man in the setting of his time than anyone before or since has managed to do. His sometimes florid Victorianism with its use of the dramatic present and exhortations may embarrass some readers today, but we are indebted to him for his care in hunting out the records, for correcting interpretations and perspectives too long unquestioned. Even on matters he was not able to carry through fully (the *Kitchin Booke,* Herbert's ring, the supposed portrait), he set forth information he had gathered that others might explore further.

Although the records of the Herbert family deposited in the Public Record Office and at the National Library of Wales deal mainly with Edward and Henry Herbert and their descendants, it would be perilous not to examine them with care, not least because of parallels they may suggest on such points as education or attitude. Indeed, it would be impossible to write a biography of any one of the ten Herberts of this generation without learning all there is to learn about the other nine—and to be able to pick one's way through the intertwinings of the Henrys and Richards and Edwards among the sons and grandsons whose names and letters and accounts appear both in these collections and in single papers one may encounter unexpectedly.

Lord Herbert's single paragraph about his brother George is a good case in point: in some ways, we learn even more from the portions of the autobiography in which George Herbert's name is not mentioned, where we read indispensable family history or learn about attitudes toward growing medicinal herbs or educating children or practicing horsemanship that were important parts of George Herbert's background. Making a point of reading the originals of Lord Herbert's letters to Sir George More leads to several documents of considerable importance in understanding the life of the family. (And though I still suspect that the Guildford archivists generously let me "discover" Mrs. Herbert's letter to Sir George More, the excitement was none the less genuine.)

For very different reasons the Ferrar records are indispensable in the study of Herbert's life and attitudes, not only for the single paper Herbert wrote for Arthur Woodnoth, but for the interchange and the friendship, the place Herbert occupied in the lives of the Ferrars, reflected in the Story Books and even in letters written after his death. Accordingly, though none of these documents of the Herberts or the Ferrars was intended as a biographical study of Herbert, no complete biographical study of Herbert is possible without them.

Selections from both sets of papers have been published, but the greater number remain in manuscript. The serious student must examine the originals for even so carefully edited a work as Bernard Blackstone's fine miscellany, *The Ferrar Papers.* First-hand reading of documents is particularly important for the documents transcribed in *Old Herbert Papers at Powis Castle and in the British Museum,*[3] a collection of useful records published with the permission and help of the Earl of Powis, but with many misreadings and errors in transcription. (The same may be said of the "Herbertiana," a continuing feature of the *Collections for Montgomeryshire* that includes much information of the sort set forth also in nineteenth-century *Notes and Queries;* but it also offers occasional choice bits.)

Shortly after the turn of this century George Herbert Palmer published *The English Works of George Herbert* (1905) and A. G. Hyde, *George Herbert and His Times* (1906). Both, in their different ways, continue Daniell's effort to show the man Herbert in the setting of his time; both works are generously illustrated; but neither adds new information about Herbert. Palmer, though he allots fewer than fifty pages to the section called "The Life," includes a detailed chronology. His subsequent interpretation in "The Man," like his arrangement of the poems, is determined by some preconceived notions, the most regrettable being that Herbert is a "minor" or "subordinate" poet, known for only a few poems, largely because editors have allowed his poems to remain in their "original chaos" of disorder.

It is difficult to understand how a scholar who had known Herbert's poems all his life could so completely misinterpret

[3] *Coll. Mont.,* XX (1886).

the principle of order that Herbert valued so highly; perhaps the assumption that most of the poems except those in *W* were composed at Bemerton misled Palmer. Though he assessed clearly what damage Walton had done ("Walton's fascinating portraiture has taken so firm a hold on the popular imagination that it may truly be said to constitute at present the most serious obstacle to a cool assessment of Herbert"),[4] in his effort to correct Walton's perspective, Palmer also placed undue emphasis on the years at Bemerton, favoring the poet above the priest.

Hyde, though he added little to our knowledge of Herbert, should be remembered for one perceptive remark: the notes on Valdesso, he said, "raise the question, suggested by his letter to his mother in her sickness, not when he became a completely furnished divine, but whether he was ever anything else."[5] Hyde's is the last of the attempts at full-length biography that began with Duyckinck. Between his day and ours the important biographical accounts have been the two noted for their economy and balanced views: the first by Canon Hutchinson in his edition of the *Works* (1941); the second by Joseph H. Summers in *George Herbert: His Religion and Art* (1954). Hutchinson undertook an orderly presentation of what was known about Herbert. It is hard to remember now that when Hutchinson was writing, the Palmer edition and biography were the ones scholars knew best and that Hutchinson therefore had to bring some sort of balance to the views fostered by Palmer as well as by Walton. The 1945 and subsequent reissues include a brief notice of Herbert's having been Member of Parliament for Montgomery.

Hutchinson's account, admirable for its conciseness, tone, and perspective, has become the basis for all subsequent study of Herbert's biography. Summers, in his short essay, brought forth the information about Herbert's parliamentary service and began to question some of Walton's assertions about Herbert's "Court-hopes" and other interpretations, mainly in an ef-

[4] *The English Works of George Herbert* (Boston: Houghton Mifflin, 1905), I, 46.

[5] *George Herbert and His Times* (New York: Putnam's; London: Methuen, 1906), p. 307.

fort to allow the poems their own integrity rather than let them continue to be read "like glosses on a suspect biography."[6]

A final work to which students of Herbert owe much is David Novarr's *The Making of Walton's "Lives"* (1958), a valuable corrective that puts the reader forever on his guard against some of the artful old biographer's practices.

But the man Herbert is more than the record, is beyond even the best presentation of fact. All too often biographers caught up in the spell of Walton have merely acquiesced in the portrayal of Herbert as a forerunner of the type of "gentle Jesus, meek and mild," despite the clear indications in his poems of his "sudden soul" and her "youth and fiercenesse" and despite his elder brother's comments on the Herbert "passion and choler." At the end of the reading of these many books of biography, accurately or inaccurately presented, the reader must return to the Herbert he first came to know through his writing. A verse is *not* a crown; yet what the facts may obscure, the verse conveys. Heminge and Condell gave the readers of the First Folio the best advice in the world for those who would know an author, any author: "Reade him, therefore, and againe, and againe."

[6] *George Herbert: His Religion and Art* (London: Chatto and Windus, 1954), p. 28.

APPENDIX B

Herbert's Handwriting

The handwriting of an author makes little difference to the general reader who looks at a manuscript of Dickens or of *Sir Gawain* with the uncritical glance of a captive tourist; and even among students in the field it is usually only the editors of texts who are forced to make a professional study of an author's handwriting. Today, a good fifty years after M. St. Clare Byrne first set forth the elements of the study of older handwriting, probably not one master's candidate among fifty in English literature can read two lines of the secretary hand unaided; indeed, it would not be too much to say one in five hundred. Students of history are much more likely to develop a working knowledge of the handwriting of the past, but usually through the same necessity that drives the occasional English major to the manuals of secretary and italic hands.

It is not surprising therefore that no systematic study of George Herbert's handwriting has been undertaken. My intention here is to describe the materials for such a study and to suggest some points I have gleaned from my own work that may be of help to others who want to pursue the matter.

Three documents survive that we may use as samples of Herbert's italic hand: in English, his letter to Sir Robert Harley of 26 December 1618 and the "Reasons" handed to Arthur Woodnoth in October 1631, both written in haste; in Latin, a carefully penned letter to Lancelot Andrewes, with a few lines of English superscription, probably written in the autumn of 1619. (The letter to Harley bears an English superscription in a hand different from Herbert's italic.) From these three documents we may verify the italic hand used for the Latin poems in *W* and for the precious final stanza of "The Elixir" and may assure ourselves that, aside from *W*, we have no poem, English or Latin, in any known hand of Herbert.

Like many of his contemporaries, Herbert had learned more than one hand—certainly some form of secretary in his earlier days that was later almost entirely supplanted by the italic hand used in the schools and the universities, particularly for writing Latin. As Latin became more and more his official language, italic became his usual hand. But vestiges of the secretary hand continue in his later writing.

Although Herbert's use of the italic hand in English is limited to the documents already mentioned, it is possible to trace in his signatures over many years several characteristics basic to any study of his handwriting. These signatures occur in the documents listed below:

1. 3 October 1614	Trinity College Admissions (minor fellow)
2. 15 March 1615/16	Trinity College Admissions (major fellow)
3. 2 October 1617	Trinity College Admissions (sublector quartae classis)
4. 26 December 1618	Letter to Sir Robert Harley, Loan MS. 29/202, B.L.
5. Autumn 1619	Letter to Bishop Lancelot Andrewes, Sloane MS. 118, fols. 34–35, B.L.
6. January 1619/20	Orator's Book, II, 532, Cambridge University Archives
7. February 1628/29	Marriage bond, Salisbury Diocesan Registry
8. 26 April 1630	Subscription at installation, Salisbury Diocesan Registry
9. 19 September 1630	Subscription at ordination to priesthood, Salisbury Diocesan Registry
10. End of 1631	Transcript of Bemerton parish register, Salisbury Diocesan Registry
11. August 1632	Will of Dorothy Vaughan, P.R.O. PROB 11/162, fol. 101

12. 25 February 1632/33 Will of George Herbert, P.R.O. PROB 11/163, fol. 25

When Herbert wrote his name, he always wrote it in full, and he always spelled his surname as we spell it today: Herbert. Any purported signature that abbreviates his Christian name as "Geor." therefore (as the Pickering and other nineteenth-century editions do) may be rejected. If the surname is spelled "Harbert," it was not written by George Herbert.

An important feature of Herbert's signatures is the style of *e* used: secretary *e* appears along with italic *e* and (later) Greek *e*. The twelve signatures in the documents listed above employ the letter *e* as represented in the following chart by G (Greek), I (italic), and S (secretary).

Language	First *e*	Second *e*	Third *e*	Fourth *e*
1. Latin	I	–	I	I
2. Latin	S	–	S	S
3. Latin	I	–	I	S
4. English	I	S	I	S
5. Latin	S	–	I	I
6. Latin	I	–	I	I
7. English	S	S	S	S
8. Latin	G	–	G	G
9. Latin	G	–	G	G
10. English	G	S	G	G
11. English	G	S	G	G
12. English	S	S	S	S

The first point to be made is that the secretary *e* was used over a period of seventeen years. Twice, under conditions of stress (in signing the marriage bond and the will), Herbert used the secretary *e* only. In the letter to Harley he used it at the end of his Christian name; indeed, the terminal secretary *e* was habitual in all samples of his English signature, in his writing in English and Latin correspondence, and in the Latin poems.

The terminal use of secretary *e* in conjunction with italic *e* changes to its use in conjunction with Greek *e* when Herbert adopts that letter for medial use. Unfortunately there is no sample of Herbert's signature for a period of nine years, from January 1619/20 to February 1628/29, which happens to include the time when Herbert began to use the Greek *e*. He uses it for all three *e*'s in the Latin subscriptions at Salisbury in 1630, and its use is continued in the English signatures of 1631 and 1632.

When we examine the three letters, we find no use of the Greek *e* in the English letter to Harley in 1618. The Latin letter to Andrewes, some months later, employs the Greek *e* in the Greek quotation only and limits the use of italic *e* to *ae* combinations, with two exceptions; otherwise, the secretary *e* is used exclusively. But the Greek *e* is used frequently (once terminally) in the "Reasons" given to Arthur Woodnoth in 1631. In the two earlier documents, both italic *e* and secretary *e* are used; in the later one, all three *e*'s appear.

In the Latin poems in *W* the italic *e* is little used; the Greek *e* is used often; and the secretary *e* to a surprising extent, consistently for the small number of words ending in *e*. (One interesting combination in "Roma," line 3, is *deerat,* in which the first *e* is Greek, the second italic.) If these poems were composed in 1622 and 1623, and copied into *W* soon after, it would be clear that Herbert had begun using the Greek *e* early in the decade. The practice was so well established that, although the Greek *e* by no means displaced the secretary *e,* the italic *e* had been almost totally banished. The use of the Greek *e* medially in his signature (when he was not under stress and apparently reverting to a practice learned in childhood) and its frequent use in the "Reasons" argue that it came close to replacing the italic *e* in his later years.

The persistence of the secretary *e* in Herbert's handwriting supports the conclusion that secretary was the hand he learned first and turned to, probably without realizing it, under stress or in haste. The same statement could not be made about his use of any other vowel or consonant in English; but even in Latin, where terminal *e*'s occur less often, Herbert constantly uses the secretary form. For further study the student must develop an alphabet of the forms used in Herbert's acknowledged hand in the letters or the poems. He may then address himself to the question whether the English poems in *W* are in Herbert's secretary hand or that of a copyist.

The comments on the preparation of *W* in Chapter 3, above, and in the introduction to the facsimile edition of *W* set forth in greater detail some of the similarities between Herbert's italic hand and the handwriting in the English poems in *W*. After my own early examination of these English poems, I was not satisfied that they were the work of a scribe and therefore continued to consult students experienced in close study of handwriting of this period, to return periodically for a fresh look, and to correspond with authorities who deal with what are generally called questioned documents. As a result, I suggest that the matter is open to further close examination.

Given the unquestioned samples of Herbert's hand—in the letters and the Latin poems and the various signatures—we find that Herbert's hand has for a century been assumed to be a regular italic, exemplified in the English superscription of the letter to Andrewes that Greg published in 1932 in *English Literary Autographs.* Grosart's dictum about the amanuensis for *W* has thus far precluded serious consideration of the possibility that Herbert used any hand other than italic.

On first examination the secretary hand in *W* appears utterly unlike the acknowledged samples of Herbert's hand—all italic, or predominantly italic; but on closer examination—beginning, say, with the running heads and the corrections in Herbert's acknowledged hand—one finds numerous deviations from the practice of the round secretary hand, not only in the use of italic for certain "distinguished" passages (those set off from the rest; intended to be printed in italic type), but in similarities between letter formations here and in unquestioned samples of Herbert's writing.

One of the difficulties in making comparisons is that there are only the two letters in English and the English superscription of the Latin letter to Andrewes to provide samples of Herbert's practice in writing English words and letter joinings that occur in English but not in Latin. Another problem is that both English letters were written hastily (in what one examiner of questioned documents terms "natural writing"), whereas the poems in *W* were copied with painstaking care. The hand is therefore not really cursive, but artificial; in fact, some letters and words seem to be drawn rather than written, to assure that each line would fit its allotted space in this small bound volume.

The superscription of the letter to Harley should be examined with special care: "To my Noble ffreind/ Sr Robert Harley Knight/ of the Bath at/ Brompton Casle." Most of the handwriting is a round secretary similar to that of the English poems in *W*, with Harley's name and that of the castle distinguished in italic. The superscription is too small a sample on which to predicate analysis about Herbert's secretary hand; but it is another indication that he had learned such a hand and perhaps had used it extensively at one time.

Why did this secretary hand appear here? The letter to Harley was written at Sir John Danvers' behest, probably with Sir John sitting at leisure or pacing back and forth dictating; and anyone who has ever taken this kind of dictation without the blessing of shorthand knows the pressure on the one who does the actual writing. I suggest that Danvers was still talking to Herbert as Herbert prepared to write the address and that Herbert, catching the word "Castle," wrote a large *C* instead of the *T* he intended (in "To"). There was no way to make the *C* look like the *T* he would normally use in italic—either a simple letter much like the printed form, or one that joined a following letter; but by adding a flourish he could make it look more like a secretary *T* (like that used in running heads of "The Church" and "The Church Militant"). The lower segment remains disproportionate, however; the letter is larger than any other in the address. He then completed the address in secretary, save for the proper names. If this address is indeed in Herbert's secretary hand—and it is rather hard to see how anyone else would have written the address on a dictated letter—the sample is too small to settle the question I have raised.

Assumptions about the dating of *W* have never been very specific. When I was trying some years back to establish a date for the manuscript, I found that it was thought to have been compiled, at the latest, just before Herbert accepted the living at Bemerton, whatever crisis of "imploiment" it involved being interpreted to mean ordination as priest. My inclination after nearly ten years of intermittent work with this manuscript is to place its composition and its preparation well within the years at Cambridge. I suggest that we consider whether Herbert himself, having composed "The Church Militant" about 1613, developed a plan for the three-part volume of his English poems that would lead from introduction ("The Church-porch") through poems about Christian experience ("The Church") to an unanticipated but witty ending—not as one might expect, "The Church Triumphant" in the next world, but back to "The Church Militant" in this. If this third section, the ultimate goal, was completed first and copied into the bound volume in a hand that the young Herbert had learned early, the secretary hand, it is at least possible that as he completed the other sections of this volume, he employed the same secretary hand for them. Certainly the running heads suggest such a procedure.

I would add only that it is not likely that Herbert, who apparently did not circulate his poems among his friends, would entrust a copyist to compile this book of poems both highly personal and precisely ordered. His brothers Edward and Henry, better able to afford scribes, themselves made fair copies of some of their works. Whether or not he did the actual copying of the English poems in *W*, however, George Herbert planned the little volume and later read it through with great care, corrected it, and for a time used it as the basis for revising some of the poems. Since no major textual or critical question hinges on this matter, perhaps it is best merely to leave it an open question.

Readers interested in examining the matter further now have available a facsimile edition.[1] Some material from my introduction has been presented in shorter form in Chapter 3.

[1] *The Williams Manuscript of George Herbert's Poems*, introd. by Amy M. Charles (Delmar, N.Y.: Scholars' Facsimiles & Reprints, 1977).

APPENDIX C

Herbert's Ring and His Picture

This on my ring,
This by my picture, in my book I write:

Lesse then the least
Of all Gods mercies, is my posie still.

It would be too great a coincidence if today we could see and read Herbert's motto on a ring he wore or on a picture he had by him. If the ring and the picture he mentions in "The Posie" actually existed, they have never been known among the students of Herbert. Nonetheless, there is a ring, and there are pictures, though none bears such a motto.

The ring is of particular interest because its main feature is John Donne's seal of Christ crucified on an anchor, the symbol Donne, at the time of his ordination, had adopted to replace a family seal of a sheaf of snakes. In his life of Donne, Walton gives the impression that Donne had a number of seal rings made as gifts not long before his death, "ingraven very small in *Heliotropian* Stones, and set in gold, and of these he sent to many of his dearest friends to be used as *Seals,* or *Rings,* and kept as memorials of him, and of his affection to them."[1] Anyone who has seen Bishop Ken's seal in the Salisbury Cathedral Library would recognize it at once from Walton's description.

But not every seal of Christ on an anchor was made at Donne's own behest; and among several that are known, variations exist. Dame Helen Gardner, who has discussed at some length the seal and its use in Herbert's poems, speaks of a pendent seal cut in chalcedony, with the added motto "Sit fides sic fixa Deo."[2]

[1] Walton, p. 63.

[2] *The Divine Poems of John Donne,* ed. Helen Gardner (Oxford: Clarendon Press, 1952), pp. 138–147.

The ring reputed to be Herbert's is different still, a massive gold ring with oval seal and the motto "Sit fides mea sic fixa Deo." It has been much enlarged to fit the hand of some subsequent owner, and it appears to have been much worn. (I can wear it on a thumb, and my hand is not small.) If the handprints in *W* are Herbert's, his fingers were long and slender, as one would expect.[3]

The great interest that J. J. Daniell took in any matter related to Herbert is responsible for the rediscovery of this ring. Somehow he located it in the possession of one W. Agerst of Cambridge.[4] In the first edition of Daniell's biography (1893) the name appears in slightly different form: "This ring is religiously preserved in the hands of the Rev. W. Ayerst, Ayerst Hall, Cambridge."[5] Ultimately the ring came into the hands of a Miss Annie Bannister of Warminster, who left it to the vicars of Warminster for the use of succeeding vicars.[6] It is now kept in a bank vault, along with the church plate.

This ring, both for itself and for its association with Donne, is a particularly intimate token. We have too few objects that we know Herbert handled; but among them, we may be sure, are the Elizabethan chalice still used at St. Andrew's, the door and the alphabet bell in the belfry of that little church, the manuscript of *W*, three letters, the Orator's Book at Cambridge, and possibly one book in the chained library that was at Chirbury.

As for Herbert's picture, it is accurate to speak of only one, despite its several manifestations. Several portraits of Donne and of Milton have come down to us; we have at least three portraits and a portrait bust of Edward Herbert; Henry Herbert's likeness is known in one portrait and a copy of it. But the only evidence that there was any portrait at all of George Herbert exists wholly in a fine pencil drawing made from it by Robert White (1645–1703), an artist of great skill, evidently in

[3] The handprints show more clearly on some film copies than on others, depending on the contrast. Apparently they resulted from pressure applied when the pages of the bound volume were to be laid open flat for writing. They are less obvious in the original.

[4] *Wiltshire Notes and Queries*, I (1893–1895), 479–480.

[5] *The Life of George Herbert of Bemerton* (London: S. P. Cok., 1893), p. 222n.

[6] *Wiltshire Archaeological and Natural History Magazine*, XXIX (1917), 126–127.

preparation of an engraving for the first edition of Walton's *Life* (1670). Since Herbert had died twelve years before White was born, it is obvious that White worked from an original not now known.

Van Dyke is the painter usually suggested, although Cornelius Janssen (or Johnson), who painted Nicholas Ferrar and his mother, is another possibility. (Such attributions are generally subjective and generic, like the automatic attribution to Zuccaro of any late-sixteenth-century painting of a beruffed lady, though Zuccaro spent only six months in England, in 1575.) There is no contemporary documentary evidence about the original of the likeness from which White worked; actually the only evidence we have is that of the names of successive engravers and the dates of the works in which they sought to represent Herbert as in life he was. (Paintings based on White's drawing will be discussed below.)

The source of all known likenesses of Herbert is the drawing by Robert White, now in the Houghton Library at Harvard University. Ironically, while successive engravings conveyed less and less of the quality of this fine original, the drawing itself was not published until George Herbert Palmer photographed it and included it as his frontispiece in 1905, finally making available to readers an accurate representation of the original they had seen imitated many times earlier.

The drawing had come down to George Young, a clerk in the Bishop's Registry, Salisbury, from Izaak Walton. J. J. Daniell[7] and a note among Bishop John Wordsworth's papers in the Salisbury Diocesan Record Office provide the following provenance: Robert White based his engravings of 1670 (in the *Life*) and 1674 (tenth edition) on this drawing, which then remained in Walton's possession, eventually passing from his daughter Ann Hawkins to her son William, thence to his eldest daughter, who married the Reverend Henry Hawes, rector of Bemerton. In time Hawes gave it to George Young's aunt. Palmer did not mention the drawing as part of his collection in the bibliography he completed in December 1910; but evidently he was later able to buy it, because it is now in the Herbert collection that Palmer gave to the Houghton Library.

[7] Daniell, p. 245.

Palmer's remark that it is "drawn with a delicacy of line impossible to reproduce"[8] is no exaggeration: after one has examined the whole series of other likenesses, this drawing stands apart, sensitive and subtle beyond description.

The deterioration of the image began in White's own engravings and became marked by the time his pupil John Sturt (1658–1730) made a new engraving for the twelfth edition (1703). Later engravings include those by John Baldrey (*Lives,* ed. Zouch, 1796), J. Chapman (second Richard Edwards edition, 1806), Augustus Fox (1835; used in Pickering editions of 1838 and 1846), an unsigned engraving (Charles Daly edition, 1849), another unsigned engraving (Willmott edition, 1861), W. J. Alais (based on White's engraving of 1674; Grosart edition, 1876), Robert White (1674 engraving, in *Lives,* Chiswick Press edition, 1904), C. Sigrist (a new engraving based on the White drawing, Nonesuch Press edition, 1927), and G. Clint (a new engraving based on a White engraving, probably of 1674, in Margaret Bottrall's *George Herbert,* 1954 [the prefatory note misprints in naming "E. White" and in stating that the White engraving served as frontispiece to the 1640 edition of *The Temple*]).

This list, though not complete (largely because of the regrettable habits of print dealers), provides some impression of the importance of White's drawing and engravings as sources for all subsequent representations of Herbert's likeness. Even the best engraving, however, falls far short of conveying the spirit of White's drawing.

One copy of the White drawing exists, a relatively late one by Walter Francis Tiffin, of Milford Street, Salisbury, made about the middle of the nineteenth century. Since Tiffin also copied White's signature (as it appears, for example, in the frontispiece of this biography), some understandable confusion about which was the original and which the copy has resulted. Tiffin's copy came into the possession of the Reverend F. O. White, who, apparently believing it to be the original drawing by Robert White, offered it for sale to Bishop Wordsworth in

[8] *The English Works of George Herbert,* ed. George Herbert Palmer (Boston: Houghton Mifflin, 1905), I, 51.

1891. (He described it as "an inestimable relic" that he could bring himself to part with only because he had a poor parish.) From the extant records it is not clear when Wordsworth bought this copy, which is now in the South Canonry in Salisbury Close. Bishop Wordsworth had a hundred collotype prints made by the Oxford University Press for his own distribution; and *The Festival Book of Salisbury* (1914) included a reproduction of Tiffin's copy.

Although Tiffin lost something of the sense of authority in White's original, particularly in the more limpid expression of the eyes, his work is important as the probable source of three oil portraits successively descended from it. The first of these was the painting bought in Bishop Wordsworth's behalf by R. G. Bartlett, at a sale in Amesbury in 1893 of possessions of the family of the water-colorist Kemm (who had themselves bought it in London about thirty years earlier). The Tiffin drawing, its probable source, must therefore have been made before 1863. Bishop Wordsworth described both the original White drawing and the painting in a letter to the editor of the *Salisbury and Winchester Journal* of 26 December 1893. This painting (10½ by 13¾ inches) was unfortunately destroyed in a fire in the South Canonry in the spring of 1964.

Lacking this painting, we cannot say with certainty that it was based on the Tiffin copy of White's drawing; but from the deterioration of the image between White's rendering and Tiffin's it appears likely that the Tiffin copy was the source of the portrait the bishop purchased, from which the two paintings at Bemerton derive.

The earlier of these is an oil painting in the rector's study, much more general in detail and in expression than the White drawing, with the note "GEORGE HERBERT/ COPY OF AN OLD PAINTING/ BY ERNEST CARLOS." A copy of this painting, in the room west of the vestry, includes this longer note: "The Rev^{d}. G. Herbert/ (1641)/ Copy of a picture./ By Ernest S. Carlos/ copied from his copy/ by A. T. Fisher. 1923/ The original said to be in the Palace Salisbury. The copy by Mr Carlos belongs to the Rectory. Bemerton."

In the latter part of the nineteenth century a supposed portrait of Herbert attracted minor attention after an inquiry that was answered by G. P. Maricote in *Notes and Queries.*[9] J. J. Daniell tried to locate it, and perhaps in this search came across the painting that Bishop Wordsworth bought in 1891. Though Daniell failed to find the picture Maricote had described, he included a notice of it in his biography: "There is a portrait somewhere, floating on society, (which has been lately seen,) beautifully painted, with arched nose, full grey eye, dark hair and dress, collar and tassel tie, on panel, with the name, 'Mr. Herbert,' on the back. This may be the Vandyke, which is supposed to have been sold at Wilton; or it may be the Bemerton painting (also a Vandyke), saved (if any treasure could be saved) by loving hands, at the demolition of Highnam."[10]

Although Daniell did not locate this picture, his remarks sent me to the National Portrait Gallery, where some of the notes on file pointed to Lancing College, Sussex, as the probable location of the portrait late in the 1920's. Through Mr. Baird W. J. Handford, a retired master, I learned that the portrait is now in the possession of Professor Peter Self of London; John Kerslake, of the National Portrait Gallery, inspected the portrait and concluded that this portrait bears no relationship to any known picture of George Herbert. The painting is not by either William Dobson or Cornelius Janssen (or Johnson), artists to whom it has been attributed, but is probably the work of a fairly primitive hand during the 1650's or (if the sitter is wearing a wig) the 1660's. The portrait is an oil on canvas, approximately 30 inches by 25 inches, with a good deal of the original craquelure remaining. The subject has brown eyes (the pupils are retouched), long nose, long face, and long chestnut hair, and he wears a gray steely-blue gown with ivory-white bands and tassel. The painting is mounted on an early-nineteenth-century stretcher, relined, with Christie's stencil on the top bar ("171 ES") and, in chalk on the bottom stretcher, "June 29 28." A manuscript label, bottom left, reads: "Portrait of George Herbert/ painted by William Dobson/ (1610–1646)/ given to Nathaniel Woodward by the Senior Fellows of/ St. Nicolas March 21/ 1868." In another hand, another label reads: "G. A. Ward, Art Dealer of Cheltenham, thinks the por-

[9] XVI (4 July 1857), 16. [10] Daniell, p. 244.

trait may be by Cornelius Janssens (1590 to 1662/64)." There is no need to be concerned over this attribution—not when one considers how many cheap new violins have been labeled Stradivarius.

What is known of the provenance of this portrait begins with its being given to Nathaniel Woodward, founder of Lancing College and other schools, by the fellows in 1868. The picture apparently passed from him to his son William Blackford (unmarried) and on his death to William's sister Elizabeth Audrey, who married Sir John Otter. Christie's sales records of 29 June 1928 show Lot 52, the portrait (with an accompanying letter), as having been sold anonymously by Sir John Otter; but according to Mr. Handford's account, the portrait was passed on in the family, first to Martin Otter, whose sister Rosalind married Henry Self, and finally to their son, Professor Peter Self. The photographic negative of this portrait is filed under reference number 750 at the National Portrait Gallery. Although it has no discernible connection with other likenesses of George Herbert, it may be helpful to know that there is no need to pursue it further.

It is beyond hope that any portrait or drawing of Herbert's time will ever come to light; yet, since we have Robert White's sensitive pencil portrait, even without knowing its source, we are nonetheless well supplied.

APPENDIX D

George Herbert at Venice, 1618

The title of this appendix is only as misleading as the records of the time. Were we to accept the records as they stand, George Herbert would appear as a mutinous young ensign under Sir Henry Peyton's command who had barely escaped hanging.

There is no question of the name of this young man: in the *Calendar of State Papers, Venetian,* in the original Italian letters among the State Papers in Venice, and in both the published and manuscript letters of Sir Henry Wotton (then the English ambassador at Venice), the name is unquestionably that of one Mr. George Herbert.[1]

Yet during the summer of 1618 George Herbert the poet was fully occupied in Cambridge, "setting foot into Divinity" and preparing for his new office as university lecturer in rhetoric. Probably he had rather recently completed his first poem called "Affliction," in which he remarked bitterly that his life was removed from "The way y^{t} takes the Towne"; but the Herbert who was in Venice was having all too active a life. Though the poet Herbert may have protested about the limitations of the academic life, there is no reason to suppose that the fellow of Trinity College and the unfortunate young ensign are the same man.

Two passages in the *Letters and Dispatches* of Sir Henry Wot-

[1] *CSPV,* 1617–1619, pp. 291–311, 332–333; Henry Wotton, *Letters and Dispatches . . ., 1617–1620* (Roxburghe Club, 1850), pp. 28–81, 121–122; Archivio di Stato—Venezia: Collegio Secreta, Esposizioni Principi, Reg. 29 da c. 78^{v} a c. 84^{v}, da c. 87^{v} a c. 89^{r}; Lettere Principi, Inghilterra, c. 132; Senato, Secreta, Delib., Reg. 112 da c. 269^{v} a c. 270^{v}, da c. 264^{v} a c. 266^{r}; Reg. 113 da c. 55^{r} a c. 56^{r}; Senato, Secreta, Dispacci, Capitano Generale da Mar, Filza 1080, dispaccio n. 79.

ton attest the character of this young naval officer. Sir Henry refers to him as "one Mr Harbert who was Ensigne to Captaine Billingsley, and a Gentleman of much discretion, though by mischaunce wrapped in this late vnhappy thing"; and Will Leete calls him "a goodly gentleman his name is Auntient Herbert, he is banished frō ye Armada, & is wth vs at Venice, and with him an other very proper gentleman, Mr George."[2]

The mutiny that led to Ensign Herbert's narrow escape from execution took place early in the summer of 1618. Wotton first mentions it in a letter to Sir Robert Naunton dated 26 July 1618.[3] A letter from Wotton to Naunton earlier the same day reported that it was "certaine mutinous persons of the Holland troupes" who had been summarily executed; in the second letter Wotton says he has learned that the mutiny "on the shore of Dalmatia" against the Venetian Captain General Piero Barbarigo was raised by English "Mutiners . . . of the late arriued vnder Sr Henry Peytons conduct . . . who demaunded the same paie that the foresaid Hollanders had, and made that the subiect of theire diuision." The difference apparently resulted from something Wotton had commented on earlier, Peyton's lack of foresight in not allowing for fluctuation in the rate of exchange when he made a contract for the sailors to be paid "*di moneta corrente.*"[4]

It is possible to piece the story together from the scattered references in the *CSPV* in the months that follow, to learn the names of most of the English ships and their masters, even to read Barbarigo's summary and learn of the eventual reinstatement of Ensign Herbert. In the Venetian papers, however, Herbert's claim "to deserve public thanks for what he did upon that unhappy day"[5] is not substantiated, though Wotton's protest before the Cabinet in Venice is reported in detail.[6]

In Wotton's letters the chain of events becomes much clearer. Wotton sets forth the details of the episode in a letter of 26 July to Sir Robert Naunton;[7] further information develops in subsequent letters by Wotton and by William Leete;[8] but the comprehensive account comes in a report by the Reverend Mr.

[2] Wotton, pp. 44, 46–47. [3] Ibid., p. 41.
[4] Ibid., p. 33. [5] *CSPV*, p. 292.
[6] Ibid., pp. 291–293. [7] Wotton, p. 41. [8] Ibid., pp. 43–48, 55–56.

Southake, the chaplain to the Englishmen, which Wotton included in a letter of 16 October to Naunton. (Southake himself, Wotton mentions at least twice, had returned to England about the middle of August and probably had made firsthand reports when he arrived there, in spite of the efforts at persuasion by certain Venetians in England.)[9]

When the various accounts are combined, it appears that a relatively minor incident was enlarged beyond proportion by Barbarigo's arbitrary handling. The trouble was confined to the crew commanded by Captain Billingsley, a company of 150 or so who, when they went ashore on 4 July, learned from some of Sir John Vere's men of the difference in pay and forthwith refused to return to their ship until they were assured of being paid at the same rate as the other hired Englishmen and the Dutch. After complaining to Barbarigo, Billingsley was told to try to persuade his men to return to their ship, but neither he nor Sir Henry Peyton himself could influence them. Barbarigo apparently decided to make examples of the recalcitrant crew.

But in the meantime two of Billingsley's officers, Lieutenant Horwell and Ensign Herbert, with others, persuaded the men to lay down their arms and return to their ship. It was for this act, probably, that Herbert considered that he deserved thanks, not condemnation.

Barbarigo, however, refused to let these men return, but had two groups of ten sent to galleys where they were questioned through "a Dutche Pirate who could speake some :20: words of English."[10] The next day notice was given for their execution, says Southake. He adds that Barbarigo scorned their request for spiritual consolation by their own chaplain, "asking yf they would haue their preacher hanged w^t^h them for company?"[11]

There are discrepancies in the account, of course; but given Wotton's characterization of Barbarigo[12] and the omission of

[9] Ibid., pp. 78–81. On 17 August Wotton tells Naunton that he has sent letters by "Mr Southack" (p. 49).

[10] Ibid., p. 79. [11] Ibid.

[12] Ibid., p. 56: "But hauing spent his youth most infamously in the highest degree, and being by nature weake and base, he seeketh to redeeme himselfe from contempt, by these austerities standing not by anie vertue of his owne, but by his fathers meritt, who died in the battayle of Lepanto, being then a Commaunder of note. This is the Character of his manners and of his fortune, to

information about other accused Englishmen who were not executed, the rest rings true enough. Those who were hanged were Lieutenant Harwell, Captain Stroude (so titled by courtesy), Sergeant French, Corporals Fuller and Watchorne, and Percival Lumley, Marmaduke Morgan, and John Clotworthy. Herbert, though he was condemned, was not hanged.[13]

By whatever stroke of luck he escaped hanging, it was because of the insistence of Sir Henry Wotton that Ensign Herbert was reinstated by Barbarigo. From what we know of the career of Thomas Herbert, who became captain of the *Marmaduke* in 1620 and fought the Algerian pirates and later (1625) became captain of the *Dreadnought,*[14] there can be little doubt that he was the young Ensign Herbert at Venice.

How then did the name of George Herbert, fellow of Trinity College, Cambridge, emerge in the records of this altercation under the Venetian command in the summer of 1618? The most likely explanation is that Sir Henry Wotton confused the names of these two younger brothers of Sir Edward Herbert; and the presence of "a sonne of Sr Ferdinando George"[15] at the same time may have reinforced subconsciously the name *George.* The Venetians in turn took this name from Sir Henry's documents; and on paper, at least, the young Cambridge scholar replaced his younger brother in the sort of adventure denied him in his "lingering book" and Cambridge gown.

And the young ensign? "Mr Herbert of whome I wrote vnto you receiued satisfaction not onely by a pardon sent frō ye Generall & free liberty granted him but also aduanced to the place of Leiutenant: who was but Auntient before."[16]

---

wch I must adde, that there is not a more superstitious man in the whole state. So as we may not vnreasonably suspect him in this Action, vnder the countenance of iustice to haue spent some of his spight against our Religion."

[13] Ibid., p. 44. Wotton twice uses the spelling "Horwell" and once the spelling "Harwell." Barbarigo's account of 9 September 1618 is given succinctly in *CSPV,* pp. 309–310.

[14] Thomas Lediard, *The Naval History of England in All Its Branches* (London: John Wilcox, 1735), II, 459; *CSPD,* 1625–1626, p. 111.

[15] Wotton, p. 44: "Lastly heere is a sonne of Sr Ferdinando George of verie hopeful abilities, who as a volontarie hath disposed of himselfe, disliking the irregularities of this warre."

[16] Ibid., p. 64.

APPENDIX E

Thomas Laurence, Herbert's Successor at Bemerton

In *The Festival Book of Salisbury* (1914) Canon Douglas Macleane, rector of Codford St. Peter, cited some passages from the sequestration records for Wiltshire in an effort to determine what some of Herbert's liturgical practices at Bemerton may have been. I suggest that the charges against Thomas Laurence contained in this book be read in the context of similar charges preferred against other Wiltshire clergymen in 1646.

The records cited by Canon Macleane are found in B.L. Add. MS. 22084 (not Harl. 22084, as Macleane's note on page 110 reads). The entries about "Docto^{r} Lawrance, Late Recto^{r} of Bem[er]ton" appear on folios 8, 8^{v}, 9, and 11 of this volume (foliated back to front). Canon Macleane cited only the first five charges against Laurence (and parts of two others); since *The Festival Book* is not readily come by today, and Canon Macleane omits some charges, I quote the record in full:

LAWRANCE	A charge of dellinquency taken against Docto^{r}
1° July 1646	Lawrance, Late Recto^{r} of Bem[er]ton (as followeth)

1 That he hath bin a great Inovato^{r} in his church at Bem[er]ton in [par]ticular hee caused the Comunion Table (callinge itt the blessed bord to be turned Aulter wise) and raised the ground vnder itt, and Rayl'd itt,[1]

2 That hee would haue the Pulpitt remoued from where itt stood, because itt was (as hee said) the most convenient place to build a Rood loft—/[2]

[1] [Douglas] Macleane, in *The Festival Book of Salisbury,* ed. Frank Stevens (Salisbury, 1914), p. 109.

[2] Ibid. There is no evidence that Laurence actually *had* his rood loft.

3 That the blessed bord (as hee call'd itt) beinge turned and rayl'd, hee then Read halfe prayer, turninge him selfe wth his face towards the people, and the other p^{te} of prayer hee read turninge his face from the people; often turninge himselfe to the blessed bord. And alsoe hee forbid the people to singe psalmes at the receivinge the Sacrament, and afterwards, forbid them to singe psalmes att all.[3]

That hee gave his Curate A shorte sett forme of prayer & charg'd him wth a stricte Iniunction not to vary from itt nor to vse any other word[es]. And also not to preach aboue once in a fortnight.[4]

That hee caused A May Pole to bee sett upp at his dore and also in the same place a bowleinge Greene: & kitleinge Alley. It beinge Adioyninge to the church yard, wherein euery Saboth day here was dauncinge bowlinge & kitleinge and himselfe to Countenance itt. Hee vsually gaue the fidlers six pence & his dynner, on y Saboth date.[5]

That hee sent a Curate from Oxford who told the people that the Docto^{r} made choise of him on purpose because hee was a greate drinker.[6]

That his owne man did reporte that the Docto^{r} made him to worke on the Saboth day in his Garden at the time of Sermon.[7]

That hee hath bin a nonResident a Longe tyme in his [par]ishe, and since the warres hee hath lived in the Garrison of Oxford and haue refused to Come inn notwthstandinge the Com^{ttee} haue often giuen notice to his wife to send to him, for at least a yeare since.[8]

That hee hath refused to take the Nationall Covennt beinge tendered vnto him—at his appearance before this Comittee after the surrender of the Garison of Oxford./[9]

Thomas Coopper of Winterborne examened touchinge Docto^{r} Lawrance saith That before these troubles in ye tyme the sd Docto^{r} liued at Bemerton, hee tollerated & allowed Kitleinge bowleinge & dauncinge on the Saboth daye after eveninge prayer. ye bowleinge & kitleinge was neere ye Church & ye dauncynge vsed in his owne howse, wch hee Countenanced, wh the p^{r}sence of him selfe and famyly & maynteined it to bee very fitt for Recreation.[10]

Wm Bowlton of Quidhampton exam^{d} touchinge the delinquency of Docto^{r} Lawrance (saith) That the Docto^{r} did Invite him to come to take his dinner att his howse euery fortnight Sunday, and saith that after evening prayer hee did [per]mit his Ex$^{t.}$ to play vpon his Instrum$^{t.}$ (beinge a Treble)[11] at his the sd Doct^{r} howse, & did [per]mit

[3] Ibid. [4] Ibid. [5] Ibid. [6] Omitted by Macleane.
[7] Omitted by Macleane. [8] Omitted by Macleane.
[9] Omitted by Macleane. [10] Omitted by Macleane.
[11] Macleane, p. 109.

daunceinge vpon the Saboth day in his [par]ish, & hee did not forbid itt or speake any thinge against itt.[12]

That hee did also [per]mit his [par]ishoners on the Saboth daies usually to play at Bowles & Kitles & dide neuer forbid them or speake any thinge ag^{t} itt.[13]

That the sd Do^{r} did vsually ducke, & make obaysance to the Communion Table, at his Comeinge in to the Church & at his goeinge forth, and did allwayes bowe at the name of Jesus.[14]

That the sd Do^{r} went awaye from his [par]ishe at the begininge of these troubles, and lived in the Kings Garrison at Oxford (and as hee hath heard, hee Continued there tell that Garrison was Surrendered to the [Par]liam^{t}.[15]

Wittnesses ex. on the behalfe of Doctor Lawrence — Examinacon of Wittnesses taken on the p^{te} and behalfe of Doctor Thomas Lawrance late Rector of Bemerton the 13th of ffebr 1646

Cxofor Gray of Wilton
gent. saith That the said Docto^{r} was absent from his Cure at Bem^{r}ton a good space of tyme, but hee knoweth not how longe it was, but conceiueth it was a boue halfe a yeare. And that hee hath heard hee was at Oxford beinge then ye Kings Garrison./

Edw. Poore of Bem[er]ton
yeoman (saith) That there hath bin daunceinge, bowleinge, and Kittleinge vsed on the Saboth day at Bem]er]ton, but not very often, and that the said Docto^{r} hath bin absent from his Cure at Bem[er]ton dureinge most of the tyme of the troubles, and hath bin Resident at Oxford a good space but before the surrender, hee went to Worcester another of the Kings Garrisons.

Jo. Strngnell of Bem[er]ton
Yeoman (saith) That the said Docto^{r} was fayre in his Carriadge towards his [par]ishioners and did preach well, and hee did never heare him vse any expression in his preacheinge or prayer against the [Par]liam^{t}, but saith that the Comunion Table was turned Altar wise. And that the said Docto^{r} did bowe towards it. And further saith That there was fidleinge some tymes on the Saboth daies, in the Docto^{rs} howse, but it was for recreation for his Children and that there was vsed also in the [par]ishe, bowlinge and Kittleinge on the Saboth daies./

[12] Omitted by Macleane. [13] Omitted by Macleane.

[14] Macleane, p. 109.

[15] Omitted by Macleane, who says only (p. 110), "There were other complaints."

Tho. Warde of Bem[er]ton
yeoman (saith) That there was bowlinge and Kittleinge vsed on the Saboth daies att Bemerton, the Doctor Liueinge there, and that there did vsually come a poore fellow that was a fidler, to the Doctors howse on the Saboth daies, and play to his Children, to whome to [sic] Doctor vsually gaue six pence & his dynner./

Robt. Warde of Bem[er]ton
yeoman (saith) That there was a poore man A fidler, did vse to come to the Doctors howse, the Saboth daies, and did play to his Children, & had his dynner & some money of the Doctor, but hee saith it was for recreacon, And saith, that there was bowlinge & Kitleinge on the Saboth daye, but the Doctor tooke noe notice of itt.[16]

To assess the seriousness of these charges against Laurence, we must first look beyond them to other passages in the records of the committee: although Canon Macleane's citation of some of the charges of delinquency against Herbert's successor at Bemerton calls attention to the general state of affairs in Wiltshire when the Committee for Sequestrations was sitting, the records of the committee show more about their prejudices than they do about George Herbert's practices during his incumbency. Almost without exception their charges do not necessarily mean that Laurence had introduced or had not introduced practices or changes when he came to the parish, but merely that conditions of which the committee did not approve existed (here as elsewhere) at the time Laurence was ejected from his living. The depositions show rather clearly what line the questioners took.

The committee objected particularly when clergymen had declared their loyalty to the king or had followed practices that the Puritans abhorred, practices one may readily enumerate by examining at random charges made by the committee against other Wiltshire parsons. Mr. Aylesbury, for example, took the king's oath and kept Friday fasts (folio 8). Mr. Bower followed suit, but offended further in not taking the national covenant and not preaching more than twice a year (folio 9). Mr. Walker used the sign of the cross in baptism (folio 9). Mr. Reyley of

[16] Robert Ward was one of Herbert's churchwardens who signed transcripts of the Bemerton Parish Registers.

Newton Toney commited the double (and equally reprehensible?) offense of frequenting ale houses and extolling the Prayer Book (folio 4^{v}). Mr. Rede, regrettably, was said to be a common drunkard (folio 7). Most of the charges against Laurence were made against other priests in the diocese as well.

Can these charges against Laurence, then, be used to determine Herbert's practices during his tenure at Bemerton—specifically whether he was Puritan or Laudian? (The terms are used by Canon Macleane, who states that "Herbert's position is not that of a developed Laudianism" and argues that there was "a pre-Laudian use in some matters" in Herbert's churches.)[17] I think not.

Even as a young man Herbert was not doctrinaire, as we may see from his attitude toward transubstantiation and the Real Presence in the rejected *W* poem "The H. Communion":

> ffirst I am sure, whether bread stay
> Or whether Bread doe fly away
>   Concerneth bread not mee.

If we consider the three elements of the Laudian reform—"the altar at the east end, the rails, the communicants kneeling at the rail to receive the Sacrament"[18]—we find that Herbert was not inclined to argue specifically for any one of them, but that even in his Cambridge days and in the midst of rather strong Puritan influences, he considered the Communion table to be an altar and therefore to be placed against the east wall. In two chapters of *The Country Parson* he makes comments that place him rather with the anti-Puritans, though not in any doctrinaire way. Regarding the use of the sign of the cross in baptism (a point frequently raised but not of course appropriate in the discussion by Addleshaw and Etchells of Laudianism in Anglican architecture), Herbert says succinctly "he willingly and cheerfully crosseth the child, and thinketh the

[17] Macleane, pp. 108–109.

[18] G. W. O. Addleshaw and Frederick Etchells, *The Architectural Setting of Anglican Worship* (London: Faber and Faber, 1948), p. 128.

Ceremony not onely innocent, but reverend."[19] *Hony soyt qui mal pence.*

About the arrangement of the church and the practices within it, Herbert's comments in both "The Parson's Church" and "The Parson in Sacraments" are important. As one would expect of a priest with Herbert's sense of order and fitness, his country parson is to take care "especially that the Pulpit, and Desk, and Communion Table, and Font be as they ought, for those great duties that are performed in them."[20] But since he is not doctrinaire, Herbert does not set forth the arrangements in detail. In his discussion of the sacraments, however, he is more specific, though far from argumentative (let alone belligerent), in gently urging the most important of the Laudian practices, that of drawing near the altar and kneeling for Communion rather than remaining seated in the nave, or even coming into the chancel but declining to kneel: "For the manner of receiving, as the Parson useth all reverence himself, so he administers to none but to the reverent. The Feast indeed requires sitting, because it is a Feast; but man's unpreparedness asks kneeling. Hee that comes to the Sacrament, hath the confidence of a Guest, and hee that kneels, confesseth himself an unworthy one, and therefore differs from other Feasters: but hee that sits, or lies, puts up to an Apostle: Contentiousnesse in a feast of Charity is more scandall than any posture."[21] And there, however quietly and skillfully he puts it, is an end on't: for Herbert, despite the figure of sitting at the board of Love in "Love" (III), in Christian charity there was no place for such partisan argument or boorish refusal.

Yet, though Herbert does not offer specific arguments for the Laudian reforms (first instituted when he was still a divinity student at Cambridge), it is clear that he had caught the spirit of them; and in the "Come ye hither" of "The Invitation" we understand that he expected the parishioners to "draw near" to the altar to share "the churches mysticall repast."

[19] *Works,* p. 258. [20] Ibid., p. 246. [21] Ibid., p. 259.

Index

A Life of George Herbert

Designed by R. E. Rosenbaum.
Composed by Vail-Ballou Press, Inc.
in 10 point VIP Baskerville, 2 points leaded,
with display lines in Baskerville.
Printed offset by Vail-Ballou Press on
Warren's No. 66 text, 50 pound basis.
Bound by Vail-Ballou Press
in Joanna book cloth
and stamped in All Purpose foil.

Library of Congress Cataloging in Publication Data
(For library cataloging purposes only)

Charles, Amy M.
A life of George Herbert.

Includes index.
1. Herbert, George, 1593–1633—Biography.
2. Poets, English—Early modern, 1500–1700—
Biography. I. Title.
PR3508.C48 821'.3 [B] 77-3116
ISBN 0-8014-1014-2